SECURING AMERICA'S FUTURE

SECURING AMERICA'S FUTURE

NATIONAL STRATEGY IN THE INFORMATION AGE

Daniel M. Gerstein

Foreword by General Wesley K. Clark

PRAEGER SECURITY INTERNATIONAL
Westport, Connecticut • London

Library of Congress Cataloging-in-Publication Data

Gerstein, Daniel M., 1958–
  Securing America's future : national strategy in the information age / Daniel
  M. Gerstein.
    p. cm.
  Includes bibliographical references and index.
  ISBN 0-275-98877-5 (alk. paper)
  1. National security—United States.   2. Information systems—Protection—
  United States.   3. Cyberterrorism—United States—Prevention.   I. Title.
  UA23.G553 2005
  355'.033073—dc22   2005017477

British Library Cataloguing in Publication Data is available.

Library of Congress Catalog Card Number: 2005017477
ISBN: 0-275-98877-5

First published in 2005

Praeger Security International, 88 Post Road West, Westport, CT 06881
An imprint of Greenwood Publishing Group, Inc.
www.praeger.com

Printed in the United States of America

The paper used in this book complies with the
Permanent Paper Standard issued by the National
Information Standards Organization (Z39.48–1984).

10 9 8 7 6 5 4 3 2 1

For Sarah and Rachel...

...And the future generations of Americans who will reap the benefits of a new national security strategy

CONTENTS

FIGURES AND TABLES

Figures

Tables

FOREWORD

FOR MORE THAN A decade U.S. foreign policy has seemed to be adrift. The well-understood guidelines of the Cold War gave way to nothing so distinctive. Instead our nation seemed to slip from foreign policy challenge to challenge and national security crisis to crisis, with little impact on domestic opinion.

From the fall of the Berlin Wall through the terrorist strikes of 9/11, America was caught up in a powerful web of economic and political forces—the end of the Iron Curtain and division of Europe, burgeoning trade fostered by the North American Free Trade Agreement, vastly improved communications driven by cell phones and the explosion of the Internet, and extraordinary economic growth in East Asia as China and India became major economic powers. Together these forces created a vast global opening for American business, travel, international finance, and trade.

But despite America's adeptness at capturing the economic and social benefits of these new opportunities—creating 22 million jobs in eight years—no sensible public understanding emerged of the risks attendant to the new era. No slogans provided the guidelines for foreign policy, and public dialogue on security matters seemed overshadowed by almost every other issue.

Shortly after retiring from the Army, I was conversing with the publisher of a major East Coast newspaper. Times have changed so much, he said, as he recollected how generals and admirals used to be frequent houseguests and foreign policy the stuff of nightly conversations around his family's dinner table.

The events of 9/11 turned America's public dialogue upside down. Distant lands, leaders with unpronounceable names, and little understood faiths and cultures became the talk of everyday life. Foreign affairs moved from the back pages to the front pages of newspapers across the nation. And national security was resurrected as a major issue.

For much of America this dialogue was not only unfamiliar but new and alien. They had come to accept America's security and safety as their birthright. For others, there was an I-told-you-so undertone of the ensuing dialogue, with the opportunity to correct old mistakes in how we used force, dealt with Allies, responded to challenge, or treated domestic political criticism.

What emerged was a nation grappling to understand the new realities, looking to its elected leadership and its Armed Forces, while bitterly divided by partisan political rivalries.

The United States acted, in the days immediately after 9/11, to strike Afghanistan and displace the Taliban regime, and some eighteen months later to invade Iraq. It was called by some the Global War on Terror. Or the Preemptive Strategy.

As many Americans said, we had to strike back and we would strike again whenever we were threatened. And for some, this was reason and answer enough. They could see the big historical analogies to Pearl Harbor or to the Cold War. We were attacked, threatened.

But others wanted to plunge deeper into the hows and whys of national security, to seek understanding of the means and ways by which America might be made more safe, and to begin to craft more effective policies and institutions to meet the new challenges facing the country.

Dan Gerstein's book provides precisely the basis for this deeper, more refined understanding of the background, requirements, and alternatives for American national security in the twenty-first century.

Here in one volume are all the basics: the definitions of national strategy, the backgrounds and summaries of American experiences, the analysis of the Cold War, and the national security institutions that have evolved in consequence, along with the current threats and difficulties we face.

Importantly, Gerstein tackles the key military questions, including the American experience with the use of force, but he also recognizes the complexities and interdependencies that make excessive reliance on military power alone prone to failure.

Particularly useful are Gerstein's recommendations for how to bring together not just joint military power but also interagency power to provide assistance in creating jobs, rebuilding infrastructure, reorganizing agriculture, building the rule of law, creating effective and corruption-free governmental institutions, and so on.

The truth is, for all the discussion about military transformation, the evidence from Iraq suggests a different perspective.

Military transformation has tended to seek the replacement of manpower with technology, to replace shorter-range weapons with longer-range weapons, and to replace brute force power with "precision strike" effectiveness. The world saw it all in the invasion of Iraq in March 2003.

But even as the discussion about transformation was being initiated, the transformation embodying those characteristics had already been largely affected.

The real need for transformation is demonstrated by the continuing difficulties faced by the armed forces in Iraq and in Afghanistan in 2003 and later. For the transformation actually required now is in the management of operations after the war is over: how to establish public security; how to build the rule of law; how to encourage social, political, and economic development.

This process is very much face-to-face and not amenable to remotely directed operations. One measure is "boots on the ground" and not just U.S. military boots but also allied forces, and not just military forces but also the whole array of international and U.S. agencies to assist in political modernization and economic development. How this is to be done, and how the military must interface with it, is at the heart of the real debate America should be having about "transformation."

In this respect, Gerstein's book is a very important contribution to the public dialogue, for it provides perspective, analysis, insight, and recommendations in this crucial area. But equally, the information of this book is the stuff for informed dialogue and discussion across a range of U.S. national security issues.

General Wesley K. Clark
Former Supreme Allied Commander, Europe

ACKNOWLEDGMENTS

YEARS AGO I HAD a boss who liked to say that the "intellectual must lead the physical." Perhaps at no time did this become more apparent to me than during the writing of this book. The act of putting thoughts down on paper can be measured in months; however, the research and development of concepts and ideas has taken some twenty-eight years over the course of a military career.

I feel fortunate to have had the advantage of the best teachers and mentors during this period, both in and out of uniform. These great leaders provided me opportunities to learn, grow, and think strategically very early in my journey in the profession of arms. I am indebted to great soldiers like General Wesley K. Clark, U.S. Army (Retired); General Barry R. McCaffrey, U.S. Army (Retired); General Gordon R. Sullivan, U.S. Army (Retired); and Colonel Ralph "Sandy" Hallenbeck, U.S. Army (Retired); who allowed and encouraged me to work on the key national security issues of the day. Service with some of the key civilian leaders in the Department of Defense (DoD) and Department of State have been equally invaluable to the development of the book.

Worthy of particular mention are the DoD schools including the Command and General Staff College at Fort Leavenworth, Kansas, and the National War College in Washington, DC. The value of these experiences is difficult to convey, but they have provided immeasurable contributions to my understanding of national strategy, security, and defense. I mention this as some today question the importance of these institutions due to operational commitments around the globe. I would make the contrary point that today, more than ever, these institutions of higher learning in the military are a crucial investment in the future.

I would be remiss if I did not acknowledge the Council on Foreign Relations for their significant contribution to this project. First among equals in this regard is my Research Assistant, Christine Quinn, who provided important insights and contributions throughout the development of the book. Several Fellows, including Helima Croft, Intelligence Fellow; Colonel Chris Haave and Colonel Ronald Bailey—the other senior Military Fellows; James Lindsay; and Max Boot, also provided key insights. David Kellogg and Trish Dorff saw the book in its initial draft and made significant recommendations, which were gladly accepted and have made the book stronger. Mary Anne Weaver, the Press Fellow, also played a vital role in the understanding of the publishing process.

This book is dedicated to my family, my wife Kathy and daughters Sarah and Rachel. We are a military family involved in the business of protecting and defending the Constitution of the United States. It may seem strange to think of defense in these terms, but I can remember many times coming home from deployments or training exercises with my unit and being greeted, individually and as a unit, by the families, including mine, in welcome home ceremonies—or on other occasions, hearing how the families pulled together in times of need to care for or comfort a fellow spouse or family.

Last, for the soldiers who must execute the great policies and strategies that our nation's leaders develop. We owe these great Americans the best training, education, equipment, and plans that our nation can deliver.

INTRODUCTION

OVER THE COURSE OF the last fifteen years, the United States has moved at an ever-increasing pace into a new era, the Information Age. The ability to acquire, sort, and distribute data has increased several orders of magnitude over this relatively short period of time. This increased capacity is both extraordinary and overwhelming. We are driven by a law, not of nature but of man's creation, Moore's Law, in which Gordon Moore of Intel Corporation observed an exponential growth in the number of transistors per integrated circuit and thus computing power, and further predicted that this trend would continue. His observations and predictions have been and remain on target, with no reason to believe that current trends will not continue for the foreseeable future.

In many respects, we are largely unprepared to reap the full benefits of this new era, as our methods, procedures, and indeed our thoughts remain anchored to the Industrial Age that we are rapidly leaving behind. Perhaps nowhere is this more true than in the highly bureaucratized world of national security.

In thinking broadly about the issues of U.S. national security and defense, one can essentially consider two broad categories of action: foreign and domestic actions for security and defense to protect U.S. territory, interests, property, or people; and "hard" or "soft" power. While the range of tools is as varied as the elements of national power, a logical grouping of hard power and soft power provides articulation of the manner in which the United States has executed strategy throughout our history. Using this construct forms a diagram with four quadrants referring to the use of either hard or soft power in a foreign or domestic setting (figure 1). For example, deploying the military to enforce a

FIGURE 1. Relationship of Use of Power to Achieving Security
and Defense

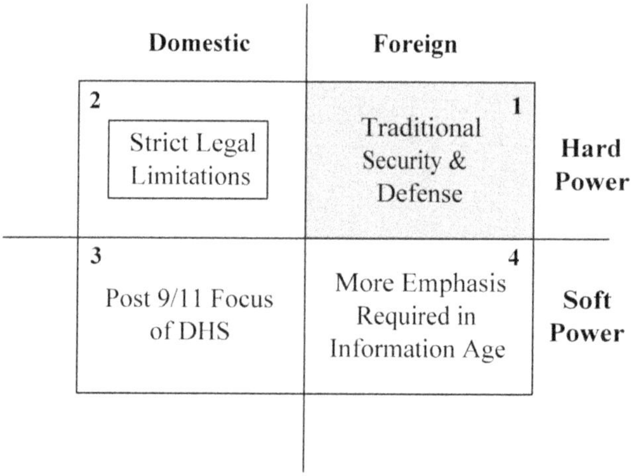

	Domestic	**Foreign**	
2 Strict Legal Limitations		**1** Traditional Security & Defense	**Hard Power**
3 Post 9/11 Focus of DHS		**4** More Emphasis Required in Information Age	**Soft Power**

peace settlement or using the media as in the case of Voice of America illustrate
the application of hard and soft power respectively as applied to foreign nations
and peoples. Likewise, protection of domestic water supplies from terrorists
attacks or using the military to quell the Los Angeles riots in 1986 illustrate the
domestic use of soft and hard power, respectively.

The point is this. Most of the security and defense initiatives have historically been directed toward using hard power externally to achieve national
goals and objectives. These efforts have been led primarily by the Department of
State, the Department of Defense, and the Intelligence Community. Over the
course of our history, the United States has developed the most formidable set
of capabilities ever seen by humanity, with seemingly limitless power and reach.
These initiatives are contained within the first quadrant of figure 1.

Since the attacks of 9/11, the United States has begun a concerted effort
to focus domestically using all the elements of power as well as to coordinate,
synchronize, and integrate the efforts of numerous federal, state, and local
government agencies and organizations. The Department of Homeland Security
has been charged with these efforts. Of particular note is that there are strict limits
on the use of hard power within the borders of the continental United States or on
our citizens, either here or abroad. The post-9/11 domestic focus is captured in
the second and third quadrants, of course subject to legal limitations. As a result
in this analysis, three of the four quadrants have been considered leaving only the
case of the use of soft power in a foreign setting. This is an area where comparatively modest programs exist, but which will become more important in this
new globalized Information Age. It is also an area ripe for additional emphasis.

In examining this construct, some may reach the conclusion that U.S. National Security Strategy, the National Strategy for Homeland Security, and Intelligence Community reforms will be sufficient for ensuring America's security in the twenty-first century. I believe the opposite is true. These strategies each address security from different vantage points and begin from different starting points. So to expect that they will reach the same goal, or do so without exposing seams along the way, looks to be a "mission impossible." Rather, the recommendation is for a new National Security Act of 20XX that will take a comprehensive view of the Information Age environment, national goals and objectives, and the ways and means available to satisfy these goals and objectives.

Therefore this book focuses on establishing a framework for development of a new U.S. national security strategy in the Information Age. Inherent in this discussion is an examination of the implications of the transition from the Industrial Age to the Information Age. What makes the Information Age so different? What do these differences mean for the formulation of a national or grand strategy of our nation? To embark on such an undertaking implies a basic understanding of the state of the current national security strategy of the United States and the conditions under which this strategy evolved. A guiding premise is that the transition to the Information Age mandates a complementary shift in national security strategy. To date, no such shift has occurred.

Thus my thesis is as follows: As we move further into the Information Age and the resultant globalization, the ability to harness all of the elements of national power in an integrated, coordinated, and synchronized manner will be even more critical to the successful defense of the United States, our people, and our ideals and values. Unfortunately, when one examines the execution of U.S. national security strategy, it is evident that today our efforts are more heavily weighted to the use of hard power for achieving our strategic goals and objectives.

The most recent formal National Security Strategy (NSS) of the United States, published in 2002 by the Bush administration, does, in fact, provide more in-depth discussion of the complete set of the elements of power than its predecessors. However, the traditional elements (political, military, and intelligence) remain the tools of choice, with only a cursory treatment of the other elements, including economic, social, cultural, and informational. As a result, we are defending our nation and our people using an incomplete and, in some cases, wrong mix of capabilities.

Even where the appropriate sentiments have been expressed, the resources and processes to achieve the goals stated within the NSS have not been made available; the result is an unachievable and infeasible national strategy. Therefore, the conclusions of this book are as follows:

1. The world is moving into the Information Age at an alarming rate, and this trend will have a significant impact on the formulation and execution of U.S.

national security strategy and policy. The Information Age and the accompanying globalization will dramatically increase the number and severity of threats facing the United States and our allies. We must understand and account for these changes in our new formulation of grand strategy.

2. The current definition and application of strategy, and national strategy in particular, are inadequate. They must be revised to more fully account for the move into the Information Age. Strategy has been defined as the linking of *ways* and *means* to achieve *ends* while mitigating *risk*. In the future, we must factor *environment* into any reasonable discussion of strategy.

3. The United States must rebalance our national strategy by rebalancing our ways and means. It is nearly impossible to discuss national strategy without defaulting to military relationships, rather than a more effective means of addressing all major elements of national power in a balanced manner. In the preconflict relationships between nations, states, and world actors, the nonmilitary ways and means can and should be preeminent. However, our current national security strategy remains heavily weighted to the political-military, with little direct focus on the other elements of power. In the Information Age, the nonmilitary elements of power will dominate, with particular emphasis on information.

4. The U.S. government must be reorganized to more appropriately respond to the challenges of the Information Age. Inherent in this discussion is the harmonization of efforts between the Departments of Defense and Homeland Security. In addition, the Department of Defense must undergo a holistic review and restructuring to develop the capabilities that will be required. This will mean divesting itself of those capabilities that no longer fit into the strategy, operations, and tactics. The difficulty will be eliminating systems, procedures, and platforms that may have great capability, but are no longer effective within the defense system of the future.

This book is divided into two parts. The first part is titled "Setting the Stage" and provides a description of the Information Age, making use of a set of principles to assist in defining this new age, and in particular contrasting it with the Industrial Age that we are rapidly leaving behind. Strategy as a concept is discussed to ensure a common baseline from which to begin discussions of development of a new strategy for the Information Age. Also included in Part I is a brief history of U.S. national security strategy with particular emphasis on the one hundred-plus-year period from 1898 to the present. At the end of this section, the 9/11 Commission, Commission on National Security/21st Century, the most recent U.S. NSS, and the National Strategy for Homeland Security are presented for the reader. Some time is devoted to our national security history, as it is my belief that this is instructive in developing an understanding of the events that have shaped this nation and also imperative for gaining an appreciation for how the United States arrived at the point in time and space where we find ourselves today.

Part II is titled "Thinking Differently about National Security." The main chapter in this part, "Developing a U.S. National Security Strategy for the Information Age," is subdivided into four sections, each dedicated to developing the supporting rationale for the conclusions presented in the book. The first section, "A New Way of Thinking about National Security Strategy," makes the case for broadening the manner in which we think about and deal with strategy. The next section, "Organizing for Combat," develops recommendations for changes required in an Information Age world. The third and fourth sections, "The Need for a New National Security Act of 20XX . . ." and "Rebalancing National Capabilities," recommend changes to the U.S. government organization, with an emphasis on the Department of Defense.

In putting together this book, I have had the opportunity to conduct a great deal of research and to think both broadly and in detail about the topic of national security strategy. In these personal deliberations, a strong conclusion has emerged that U.S. national security strategy has been based largely on ideas and concepts, with little hard analysis or facts to back up decisions and actions that we undertake as a nation. Sometimes the decisions and actions have resulted in favorable outcomes, while in other cases ideology has led us astray. As this nation transitions to the Information Age, a thorough analysis must be conducted of all aspects of national strategy or grand strategy development to include the adequacies and inadequacies of our current strategy and how the new age will impact on the world and the U.S. role in global affairs. This in turn will allow for development of a comprehensive national security strategy for the Information Age.

Given my background, including both undergraduate studies at the U.S. Military Academy at West Point, which provides a heavy dose of math and science in the curriculum, and graduate work at Georgia Tech in Operations Research and Systems Analysis (ORSA), an area of study heavily weighted to using problem-solving techniques on real-world and seemingly intractable problems, it should come as no surprise that a consistent theme throughout the book is the use of more rigorous techniques in policy formulation and the execution of national security strategy.

To the national security strategy and policy practitioner, these sorts of techniques may not resonate well and could lead to immediate dismissal of the recommendations contained within. It is my hope that the opposite outcome is achieved and the new techniques and way of looking at the world may add to the body of national security thought and knowledge.

On the other end of the spectrum, some may expect an in-depth treatment of the application of force in the Information Age and expect equally in-depth treatment of information operations, or what many now call IO. However, this is not a book about manipulating bits and bytes for military purposes, nor is it a book about cyberwarfare and cyber dominance. Clearly, these are important issues that will certainly be discussed on the periphery as they pertain to the development of national strategy. Therefore, a reader expecting an in-depth study of these issues will likely be disappointed. My clear intent is to conduct a high-level examination of the implications of the Information Age for national security strategy matters.

As a nation, the United States is perhaps in the most precarious position in our history. Only on three other occasions has our nation been so vulnerable: (1) at the founding of our nation and our break from the English Crown, (2) during the U.S. Civil War, and (3) during and in the aftermath of World War II. It is my belief that the response must be bold and audacious, with the result a new national security strategy for the Information Age.

Part I

SETTING THE STAGE

1

TOWARD A NEW NATIONAL SECURITY STRATEGY FOR THE INFORMATION AGE

Discussions of national security strategy invariably turn to issues such as national interests, deterrence, the military balance of power between the United States and potential adversaries, or the ability to project forces. After 9/11, one could argue that this list was expanded to include, as the first among equals, homeland security and defense. While all of these remain relevant measures of national security, they are no longer sufficient for a complete discussion of national security strategy in this postindustrial, globalized Information Age world.

Simply stated, elements of power other than the traditional or hard power political-military-intelligence components of the equation must become coequal partners in the national security process; furthermore, this applies to both foreign and domestic initiatives. For too long, we as a nation have been relying on these traditional elements of power to ensure our security—that is, hard power focused outwardly.

Events of 9/11 coupled with current globalization trends signal a need for a new and more inclusive formulation of national strategy. As a nation, we must employ all of the tools of the state in an integrated, coordinated, and synchronized manner both within and outside our borders. We must develop the structures, organizations, policies, and procedures with appropriate resourcing to ensure America's security. It is not that hard power will no longer be relevant, but rather that in a globalized world, the full range of resources and capabilities must be employed to ensure success.

Given the evolution of U.S. grand strategy over the last 230 years, certain fundamental truths have emerged which signal that the United States has become and will continue to be a world leader with global responsibilities and capabilities unique to our nation. As the dynamics of global interactions change and the demands placed on the U.S. government for national security increase, we must rethink our national security strategy in some fundamental ways, including how resources are allocated. While it would be possible to continue to increase hard power spending, it is not clear that this would fundamentally provide a higher degree of security. The real question is how to increase security and best allocate the nation's scarce resources to achieve the maximum security for America.

NATIONAL SECURITY THREAT SCENARIOS

The following three scenarios serve to illustrate the national security dilemma we are facing in the emerging Information Age. They have been selected deliberately to cut across a broad range of security and defense issues. Additionally, they are complex scenarios that require the integration, coordination, and synchronization of a variety of U.S. government departments and agencies.

> Scenario 1. An illegal immigrant arrives in the United States and begins
> to live and work in the country.

Which agency or organization should be concerned about this breach? Initially, this seems like a straightforward legal or immigration issue. But what if the scenario is expanded such that the illegal immigrant was involved in some illicit activity or had been exposed to some environmental contamination?

Obviously, the U.S. Border Patrol has responsibility for the initial incursion. As the individual moves away from the border area, the problem also moves inland. Local authorities would be concerned if they were aware, but would really only act if this individual was involved in an illegal activity or was turned in to the authorities.

If the immigrant has spent time in a foreign military, trained in a terrorist camp, has recently spent time in one of several foreign countries, or is on the watch list, then the FBI and the Intelligence Community (IC) will certainly have an interest, as perhaps would the Department of Defense (DOD) in terms of counter-terrorist operations and support to civilian authorities. If the illegal immigrant has worked on a farm during the seven days prior to entry, the Department of Agriculture could be concerned as well, and certainly if the illegal immigrant has been exposed to an infectious disease, the Department of Health and Human Services would have great interest.

This single issue crosses into numerous areas including the Departments of Homeland Security, Justice, Defense, Transportation, and Agriculture, to name a few. But these are just the obvious ones. The scenario could be expanded almost indefinitely to demonstrate the potential impact on nearly the entire list of departments and agencies in the U.S. government. And this does not even begin to address the cooperation required between local, state, and national governments and agencies.

Unfortunately, once the individual breaches the single-barrier system at the border, he is virtually free to move about the country. Only an illegal or suspicious activity will trigger a response or query from a government agency. Perhaps what is of more concern is that even if a single indicator was identified by one agency, the ability to collect, collate, analyze, and disseminate information across the U.S. government currently does not exist at the level necessary to ensure a response, much less a coordinated response.

So is this a simple matter of illegal immigration or a matter of national security?

> Scenario 2. A madrassa (Islamic school) in the border area between Afghanistan and Pakistan is teaching local children.

A local Islamic school is providing instruction to school-age children. The primary educational text is the Koran, and instruction is presented by clerics or a mualanah, the head of each madrassa. Most of the education is oriented toward religious interpretation of the Koran and in particular the relationship between the Koran and events of the day. For example, the students are taught that the Palestinian-Israeli issue has its roots in the scriptures and that the Israelis are encroaching on sovereign Arab lands. The children and young adults are taught of the jihad or struggle—as part of this education, they are instructed that it is their duty as Muslims to engage in this movement. Some are infected with the virulent form of jihad and filled with ideas of suicide bombing and attacks against the infidels to drive them out of the region. Equally troubling is that in several instances, the local madrassa is virtually collocated with a terrorist training camp, indicating a close relationship between the two.

Clearly the State Department, IC, and DOD have great interest in the products of this narrowly focused, theologically based education system. Students with no formal training graduate with notions of half-truths and anti-Western propaganda that they have been indoctrinated with during their educational experience. They have not been afforded an education that would translate into earning power or economic development, much less prosperity.

What about other elements of the U.S. government? For example, what could or should the Department of Education do to assist in promoting the type of broad-based educational system that leads to democratic reforms and, by association, economic development? In an agriculturally based society, can the Department of Agriculture or the Department of Commerce assist to improve yields and provide ready markets for these goods, respectively?

Today, these sorts of developmental assistance programs are outside the purview of these departments. Their focus is within the United States.

However, could or should their missions be expanded in the interest of national security?

> Scenario 3. The United States is leading a coalition under United Nations (UN) sponsorship to conduct peace enforcement operations under Chapter 7 of the UN mandate—in other words, engaging in combat operations to enforce a peace.

The deliberations concerning the UN mandate involve the U.S. Mission to the UN, the State Department, the IC, and the DOD as the conditions including the authorities and responsibilities for the combat force are established. While the State Department and the U.S. Mission are in the lead, the IC and DOD are working closely to develop the situation, begin to alert the forces and pre-position personnel and material, and plan for the missions that are envisioned as deriving from the UN mandate.

Based on the deliberations, other elements of the USG are highly likely to be involved. For example, given that a peace enforcement operation is to be conducted, in all likelihood, the rule of law and legal authorities will need to be developed or restored. The Department of Justice has significant responsibilities in this area, as examples from the missions to the Balkans with the deployment of "police monitors" have demonstrated. Perhaps years of conflict or simply lack of development has left the area with limited infrastructure, particularly readily available energy resources, but still the potential for development. Could the Department of Energy support in this role? In failed states, the human needs invariably are nearly overwhelming. What can the Department of Health and Human Services do to assist?

Again, there is a requirement for various organizations, departments, and agencies within the U.S. government to have adequate capability to respond to this sort of security and humanitarian crisis. The application of traditional or hard power elements including the DOD, IC, and State Department are imperative for the initial phases of the operation. However, they are highly unlikely in isolation to result in a long-term solution or address the roots of the conflict in any meaningful way.

While each of these hypothetical scenarios comes at the issue of national security from a different perspective, they all clearly have significant implications for security and defense. By way of a disclaimer, the scenarios could easily have been expanded to include a more traditional national security issue such as the defense of the Korean Peninsula, in what the military calls a Major Theater of War (MTW). However, the point will be made later and frequently throughout the book that preparations for traditional defense issues have largely been adequately addressed—it is really the nontraditional or complex operations (i.e., those requiring a broad range of cooperation rather than just military intervention) that require more attention.

In the first scenario, the focus is on protection of U.S. sovereign territory directly, while in the second, the scenario looks at how to indirectly influence populations to become more democratic. Last, in the third scenario, the clear requirement is to employ hard power followed by a longer-term addressing of the roots of the conflict using nontraditional or soft power elements. Each scenario also demonstrates the potential for greater contributions from the nontraditional elements of power that could made available by a change in U.S. policy allowing a broader cross section of the government to support the security and defense of our nation.

The scenarios have some other common threads as well. They are complex issues requiring a variety of responses across a broad range of agencies, organizations, and departments. In none of the scenarios will the hard power elements (i.e., political, military, intelligence, legal) be sufficient to completely alleviate the problem. Information sharing, public diplomacy, and situational awareness all figure prominently into any successful outcomes.

THE INADEQUACY OF EXISTING STRATEGY

The focus of this book is to delve into these concepts and establish a set of principles for developing a new national security strategy or grand strategy for the United States in the Information Age. A guiding premise is that the transition to the Information Age mandates a complementary shift in national security strategy. To date, no such shift has occurred.

Therefore, the thesis is as follows: As we move further into the Information Age and the resultant globalization, the ability to harness all of the elements of national power in an integrated, coordinated, and synchronized manner will be even more critical to the successful defense of the United States, our people, and our ideals and values.

Throughout the period in which the United States has published a National Security Strategy (NSS), beginning in 1988 as mandated in the Goldwater-Nichols Defense Reform Act, the document has consistently been heavily weighted to the political-military elements of power, with only a cursory treatment of the other elements including economic, social, cultural, and informational. While the most recent NSS, published in 2002, reflects a more even treatment, it still tends toward a lopsided formulation of national security policy. As a result, we are defending our nation and our people using an incomplete and, in some cases, wrong mix of capabilities. Even where the appropriate sentiments have been expressed, the resources and processes to achieve the stated goals have not been allocated.

For example, while the 2002 strategy discusses the need to use all of the elements of national power in an integrated, coordinated, and synchronized manner, there is little ability within our government to bring these elements together. Consider the introductory section in which President Bush states,

Defending our Nation against its enemies is the first and fundamental commitment of the Federal Government. Today, that task has changed dramatically. Enemies in the past needed great armies and great industrial capabilities to endanger America. Now, shadowy networks of individuals can bring great chaos and suffering to our shores for less than it costs to purchase a single tank. Terrorists are organized to penetrate open societies and to turn the power of modern technologies against us.

To defeat this threat we must make use of every tool in our arsenal—military power, better homeland defenses, law enforcement, intelligence, and vigorous efforts to cut off terrorist financing. The war against terrorists of global reach is a global enterprise of uncertain duration. America will help nations that need our assistance in combating terror. And America will hold to account nations that are compromised by terror, including those who harbor terrorists—because the allies of terror are the enemies of civilization. The United States and countries cooperating with us must not allow the terrorists to develop new home bases. Together, we will seek to deny them sanctuary at every turn.[1]

Clearly the words are right, but what changes in the structure, systems, or processes of the government have been made to facilitate this coordinated response? Have the necessary resources been provided to ensure the successful accomplishment of the stated goals? The short answer is no, certainly not to the level appropriate for the new threat environment created by the Information Age and the development of networked, adaptive, and dangerous threats.

In reality, few changes have been made to more fully expand the resources and therefore the capabilities for implementing national security beyond the traditional view of the strategy as being oriented to the political-military elements of power. President Clinton did make a move toward more fully integrating the economic piece by adding his economic advisor as a permanent member of the National Security Council. However, this change to the national security apparatus is narrowly focused on a single element rather than being a complete and holistic incorporation of all the elements of national power into a coherent grand strategy document.

More recently, the U.S. government has been expanded to include a Department of Homeland Security. This was an important step; however it also complicates the issues by drawing a distinction between foreign and domestic security strategies. Another complicating factor concerns the process of transition to a new Information Age strategy. Real change is inherently difficult and is not always greeted warmly by those invested in the old ways. Consider the recent findings of the National Commission on Terrorist Attacks upon the United States, *The 9/11 Commission Report*:

The current position of Director of Central Intelligence should be replaced by a National Intelligence Director with two main areas of responsibility: (1) to oversee national intelligence centers on specific subjects of interest across the U.S.

government and (2) to manage the national intelligence program and oversee the agencies that contribute to it.[2]

The initial White House response was to announce the establishment of a position that would report directly to the President as part of his staff and have no directive authority and, perhaps more important, no budgetary authority over the IC. This would likely have resulted in little or no real change and would have done even less to eliminate the seams that exist in the intelligence structure today and that certainly contributed to the failures prior to 9/11. Since this initial announcement by the White House, the administration's position has changed to a more forceful implementation of the 9/11 recommendation; however, the debate between Congress and the White House on this issue continues. Despite legislation in late November 2004 that gives this new position unprecedented oversight, direction, and even budgetary authority, seams remain which must be addressed through a broad reexamination of the roles and missions of the U.S. government.

Overall, the 9/11 Commission report takes a significant step toward broad-based recommendations for policy and structure reform for the U.S. government. The forty-one recommendations cut across the traditional elements of national power in a holistic way, providing a comprehensive look at our national security apparatus. But by itself, the report is not sufficient. It does little by way of recommendations for soft power issues. More appropriately, the complete set of recommendations must be analyzed individually and collectively to determine how the government and our processes must be reorganized in response to the challenges and opportunities that will continue to confront the United States in this new era.

ELEMENTS OF STRATEGY

Before it is possible to begin this discussion in earnest, a working definition of strategy must be established. An exhaustive examination of the topic will not be conducted, but rather a presentation of a common baseline from which to proceed.

The seasoned strategist is likely to be offended by the introduction of strategy in such an elemental fashion. Certainly my intent is not to offend. However, many books dealing with U.S. national security strategy operate on an implicit assumption that the reader understands what strategy is along with its critical components. This may not always be the case. Therefore, given the stated purpose of this book to examine principles and recommendations for a new national security strategy for the Information Age, it seems prudent to briefly present this topic.

So what is strategy? Who is responsible for developing it? Is there a way to measure a strategy against the outcomes achieved to determine if stated objectives are being met? These are all very appropriate and insightful questions. They appear clear in formulation, yet the answers are not as straightforward.

Strategy is a word that is used frequently and appears to have a nearly infinite number of meanings. There are strategies for winning at cards and strategies for improving sales. Commentators are always asking athletes and coaches what the strategy was for winning the game. There are grand strategies, national strategies, and military strategies. A corporation may have a vision that would contain a strategy for improving the efficiency and effectiveness of its operation. What do all these mean? Are the meanings similar? Are they the same? The definitions of strategy and the subordinate elements add some clarity to the issue.

Early definitions of strategy tended to relate most directly to the concept of military strategy and thus to military strategists. However, over time, the definition has broadened to incorporate more general meanings. The *American Heritage Dictionary of the English Language*, Fourth Edition, defines *strategy* as:

1. a. The science and art of using all the forces of a nation to execute approved plans as effectively as possible during peace or war.
   b. The science and art of military command as applied to the overall planning and conduct of large-scale combat operations.
2. A plan of action resulting from strategy or intended to accomplish a specific goal.
3. The art or skill of using stratagems in endeavors such as politics and business.

While this definition provides some insights into strategy, it falls short on providing insights into the elements of strategy or the strategist. However, given this definition, it seems prudent to consult an authoritative military resource to see what is said about strategy and strategic thought. The military publishes an official list of terms within the Joint Staff that reports to the Chairman of the Joint Chiefs of Staff (JCS).[3] The definitions of strategy, national strategy, and military strategy are as follows:

> *Strategy.* The art and science of developing and employing *instruments of national power in a synchronized and integrated fashion* to achieve theater, national, and/or multinational objectives.
> *National strategy.* The art and science of developing and using the *diplomatic, economic, and informational powers of a nation, together with its armed forces, during peace and war* to secure national objectives.
> *Military strategy.* The art and science of employing the *armed forces of a nation to secure the objectives of national policy by the application of force or the threat of force.*[4]

Some common themes exist in these definitions. First, each includes references to the art and science involved in the employment of capabilities. This implies that no single cookie-cutter approach can be developed for strategic thought or employing national capabilities. There is a body of knowledge and thought that can assist in guiding the strategists, which is reflected in the science; however, strategy also has a component that is subject to the interpretation of the strategists, which is the art of developing a strategy. Second, each of the definitions includes the desire, in fact the requirement, to achieve objectives. The final common thread deals with the use of resources and capabilities in certain (artful and scientific) ways to achieve the stated objectives.

Given the definitions above, it should come as no surprise that early strategists had their roots in strategic thought as it relates to the execution of military matters. The list of these strategists spans the period from antiquity to the present and, as one would expect, is quite lengthy. Included in this list are figures such as Sun Tzu, who wrote *The Art of War* which has guided strategic and military thought for over 2,400 years; and Thucydides, who wrote the *History of the Peloponnesian War* describing the war between Athens and Sparta from 431 to 404 BC. In the 1700 and 1800s, a number of theorists wrote about the link between strategy and tactics, and about the relationship between national strategy and military strategy. Examples of strategists from this period include Maurice de Saxe, Fredrick the Great, Napoleon, and Clausewitz and Jomini, who wrote with an eye to describing and analyzing Napoleonic warfare.

More recently, a number of strategists have endeavored to describe warfare and relations between nations. This list of distinguished strategists is indeed long and includes such notables as B. H. Liddell Hart, J. F. C. Fuller, Michael Howard, Alfred Thayer Mahan, General Dwight D. Eisenhower, Winston Churchill, General Billy Mitchell, Martin Van Crevald, John Lewis Gaddis, Bernard Brodie, and Alvin and Heidi Toffler. The list could go on and include hundreds, if not thousands, of authors. The topics vary widely as well. In this short representative list, the topics include World War II, airpower, sea power, warfare in the nuclear age, the strategy of containment, and future warfare.

Another trend is the proliferation of books on strategy that focus most heavily on relations between nations and peoples rather than on military strategy. The list of authors here is considerably longer. Examples include *The Rise and Fall of Great Powers* by Paul Kennedy, *The Clash of Civilizations* by Samuel P. Huntington, *The Lexus and the Olive Tree* by Thomas Friedman, and *Soft Power* by Joseph S. Nye Jr. Some books, such as *Balkan Ghosts* by Robert Kaplan, describe strategic thought about more narrowly defined regions, in this case the Balkans. Whether the authors choose to take on the concept of strategy directly in these types of writings or more subtly address the issue is irrelevant, as they are clearly focused on strategic thought and strategic issues.

Although strategists may debate the definitions with a word here or there, common ground does exist with respect to the definition of strategy. In U.S. military schools (and the definition we will adopt for the baseline from which to precede), strategy is defined as the linking of *ways* and *means* to achieve *ends*.

In this formulation, *risk* is the fourth aspect of the definition that is factored into the strategic calculations to account for inherent friction (or the fog of war). Essentially, risk allows for the introduction of uncertainty into the strategic calculation and must be considered as a way to address the possible range of outcomes that could result from the application of ways and means. Of course, this is the currently accepted formulation of strategy. Later it will be argued that a new formulation is required to more fully account for strategy in the Information Age.

The aim of the strategist, therefore, is to bring into balance the various elements of a strategy. The ways and means must be sufficient to achieve the desired end. If not, the strategy is infeasible. Likewise, if the ends (objectives) that are established exceed the ability of the ways and means, then the strategist must either reduce the desired objective or increase the resources (means) or alter their use (ways). The relationship between ends, ways, and means is often likened to a three-legged stool. If one of the legs is shorter than the others, then the strategy is out of balance.

For the United States, the NSS has been the single authoritative document that described our national goals and objectives, and most closely resembles what would be referred to as a grand strategy or national strategy.[5] As an introduction to the NSS, consider that in the latter half of the twentieth century, our strategy was to protect the homeland and U.S. interests by engaging with other nations and staging forces away from our shores. But in 2001, 9/11 demonstrated that this strategy is no longer feasible for protecting U.S. citizens and interests, either here or abroad. It follows, then, that our national security strategy must change in some very fundamental ways. One of the first significant responses was the establishment of the Department of Homeland Security. Others will be needed in this new Information Age.

Thus, as we look at the security and defense challenges facing us today, the same key questions naturally surface. What are the implications for national security of the Information Age? What lessons has 9/11 taught us, and are we any safer today as a result of actions taken since the attacks? Are the steps that we have taken adequate? If "forward defense" is no longer sufficient, then what should the new strategy be? To begin to address these questions, we must examine the implications of this new Information Age and the circumstances under which the United States has come to the point in space and time that we find ourselves today.

2

THE EMERGING INFORMATION AGE

The world is moving into the Information Age at an alarming rate, and this trend will have a significant impact on the formulation and execution of U.S. national security strategy and policy. The Information Age and the accompanying globalization will dramatically increase the number and severity of threats facing the United States and our allies.

THE EMERGING INFORMATION AGE is a highly uncertain, confusing, and complex period in human history that presents both challenges and opportunities. Nations, societies, and individuals that can adapt the fastest will survive, while the others will likely be roadkill on the information superhighway. It almost goes without saying, but there will be clear winners and losers, as well as haves and have-nots. Furthermore, this culling process will most certainly fuel instability and insecurity in this new era.

The emerging Information Age is also an unprecedented time in human history. The growth in capabilities for sharing knowledge will far exceed man's ability to acquire, process, and synthesize all of the various inputs into usable information. New techniques are essential to dealing with the complexities of the Information Age. Many Industrial Age ways that we have grown to accept as truth need to be reexamined and if necessary transformed to account for these significant changes.

For a historical perspective on the rapid transition to the Information Age, the growth of the Internet provides an excellent example. In *Information Rules* by Carl Shapiro and Hal R. Varian, the authors describe this growth as follows:

> The first email was sent in 1969, but up until the mid-1980s email was only used by techies. Internet technology was developed in the 1970s but didn't really take off until the late 1980s. But when internet traffic did finally start growing, it doubled every year from 1989 to 1995. After the internet was privatized in April 1995, it started growing even faster.[1]

These statistics dealing with Internet usage are now woefully outdated, as the book was published in 1999; growth has continued during the ensuing period at even greater pace. Today the Internet has become even more pervasive. It is possible to conduct virtually all aspects of one's life from behind a computer screen. One can order books, cars, and even groceries online. Virtual offices have emerged where employees are able to interact more effectively, yet have little or no human contact. One can have access to virtual libraries and classes. Today, few areas exist where Industrial Age processes are more effective and are not being overwhelmed by the Internet.

These examples illustrate the impact of only one aspect of the transition to the Information Age, the Internet; others, such as advances in communications and information sharing, provide additional evidence of the significant change that is underway and insights into prospects for the future.

As we are in the early stages of transformation to the Information Age, the initial advances are likely to be considered to be extremely rapid, but in retrospect, say fifteen or twenty years from now, they may seem plodding and even elementary. Consider that in the Industrial Age, new techniques for manufacturing or harvesting cotton were considered to be revolutionary, but really only scratched the surface in terms of potential.

In the Industrial Age, production mattered. The ability to mass-produce material was the measure of effectiveness. One could walk into a warehouse and count the stock to determine if production quotas had been met. During World War II, the ability to mass-produce all types of war material was largely seen as a key to the United States' success in the war and our emergence on the world scene as a global power. In short, in the Industrial Age, power was a function of mass, and the use (or threatened use) of force was the driver for achieving national security objectives.

In the Information Age, power will be a function of knowledge, and ideas will be the glue that binds together or repels peoples, societies, nations, and alliances. So how do we measure success in the Information Age? We certainly cannot count pieces of data and assume that more is better. This sort of raw data is only part of the equation; to be useful, data must be converted into knowledge. Is it possible to develop measures of effectiveness for the Information Age? How do we deal with the fact that it is extremely costly to produce the initial information, but there is virtually no cost to reproduce and disseminate it? What about protection of vital information? If we begin to depend on these information capabilities, what happens if there is a catastrophic crash or attack? These are some of the essential questions that must be addressed or at least considered.

The Information Age will also result in a natural amalgamation of peoples across the globe, and with this mixing of societies will come the potential for a fracturing of nations and societies. The first phenomenon is called globalization, defined as "the emergence of a global society in which economic, political, environmental, and cultural events in one part of the world quickly come to have significance for people in other parts of the world. Globalization is the result of advances in communication, transportation, and information technologies."[2] The second force is called irredentism and will likely be an equally powerful force driving nations, societies, and peoples apart by fueling the frictions and tensions of peoples brought closer together through the use of information technologies.

We must also learn to deal with issues such as the role of the nation-state in this new age. As societies have developed, the peoples of the world have gone from being nomadic hunter-gathers to being tied to the land as farmers, landowners, entrepreneurs, and businesspeople. Cities and villages and indeed societies have developed, first as collections of peoples living in close proximity under the protection of feudal lords, then as part of city-states and finally as part of nation-states. It is this nation-state system that has led to the creation of the international system that is in place today, including the United Nations, International Monetary Fund, and World Bank. The Information Age will have a significant impact on this state system as we know it today. Some may even question whether this system will survive.

DESCRIBING THE ENVIRONMENT

It is within this framework that the Information Age must be considered. The end result in this book will not be a region-by-region or nation-by-nation articulation of the projected future environment, but rather a broad examination of the key factors that will drive the Information Age.

The intent of this book is to assist in the formulation of a new national security strategy. Therefore, the relationship between the environment and implications for national security policy formulation are highlighted. Twelve principles have been identified as key to the development of a new national security strategy for the United States in the Information Age. However, before diving into the twelve principles, a concern worthy of consideration that cuts across each of the principles and illustrates the competition for ideas and the changing environment. This concern is the execution of the current global war on terror or GWOT.

The global war on terror focuses primarily on organizations that perpetrate terrorism or terrorist acts and, by extension, on those organizations and individuals that support terrorist groups and ideology, clearly an important part of securing America in the future. However, an unintended consequence of this effort has been to treat al-Qaeda and other terrorist groups as standard organizations with hierarchical chains of command and processes that drive toward their objectives, rather than the ideologically based, networked, "popular" movements that they are. Therefore, the United States and our allies have chosen methods and means that are largely oriented toward compelling nations or organizations, yet little has been done to attack the roots of the problem. We are attacking the terrorists' organizations leaders and members—in fact, estimates (as of the presidential debate in 2004) are that two-thirds of the al-Qaeda leadership as it existed on 9/11 have been killed. However, in an ideologically based global insurgency, perhaps this is not the best measure of effectiveness.

Indeed, al-Qaeda, in combination with other Islamic terrorist cells, has demonstrated an ability to morph, adapt, and transform. In a true network sense, these terrorist elements are cooperating when it is in their interest and acting independently in other situations. They are competing with ideas and beliefs as their foundations and limited military power (or precision terror strikes) as their catalyst for generating support in their fight against their enemies, particularly the West. Just as the worm that is cut in half is able to regenerate and continue to live, so too have the terrorists demonstrated this capability.

Thus the concern is really this: killing the leadership may not necessarily halt this global insurgency or ensure America's security. Using force to defeat ideas may be a strategy-task mismatch that needs to be reevaluated and adjusted. The changing nature of this threat is documented by Michael Scheuer, the former chief of the CIA's bin Laden unit and now best-selling author of the book *Imperial Hubris*, criticizing the Bush administration's handling of the war on terrorism.

Another, lesser concern remains the identification of a "global war on terror," which implies a monolithic threat. This very act tends to obfuscate the true roots of the conflict and minimize the perceived plight of the peoples of the world that these terrorists claim to represent. This statement in no way implies a legitimacy in the terrorists' actions, but rather does allow for a recognition that there is passive (as well as a much smaller active) support within the global Islamic nation.

Given this caution as an introduction, the twelve principles of a new national security strategy are described in the following sections.

PRINCIPLE 1: GLOBALIZATION IS A REAL FORCE

Globalization, fueled by information technology, will be the dominant force in the Information Age. The bringing together of peoples with common ideas will be extraordinarily powerful. Information sharing and the potential for cooperation will be unlike anything ever experienced during the whole of the history of humankind. All aspects of human interaction will be affected, with great potential for increases in human knowledge and prosperity.

Unfortunately, globalization will also be an extremely divisive force, contributing to instability, insecurity, and outright conflict. Information technology will increase the disparity between the rich and poor peoples of the world, and between successful nations and failed states. What is more important is that those not able to capitalize on the information revolution will now have the means to understand that the development gap is widening as they are falling farther behind. Today, many people around the world have established personal Web sites to share information and promote their personal causes. Terms such as *blog* (short for Web log) have been created to describe information posted on these sites. People maintaining these sites have essentially become writers and publishers with no editorial staff to check the validity of the information that is being posted.

Undoubtedly, globalization will also change the way we think about common structures such as organizations, societies, nations, states, and nation-states. A new lexicon will need to be developed to deal with and describe capabilities and entities in the Information Age. We will measure capacity in terms of gigabytes and data throughput speeds, but we must also find a way to measure the growth of knowledge and, even more important, useful knowledge.

Globalization is not something that can be turned off and on like a light switch. Now that the genie is out of the bottle, there will be no way to return to the status quo before globalization. Information technologies that drive globalization will continue to mature and expand. Minute by minute, the force of globalization is gaining a greater degree of irreversible momentum. Even if one wanted to halt or slow this process, our desire for greater economic prosperity and thirst for information would overcome any efforts to do so.

In *The Lexus and the Olive Tree*, Thomas Friedman provides a simple yet highly effective analogy describing globalization. Friedman argues that people desire the worldly possessions indicative of success and progress. This is represented by the pursuit of the Lexus, a high-quality automobile. At this same time, people are conflicted because they want to maintain the deep roots or family ties represented by the olive tree. The ensuing dilemma is that the two desires are in conflict since, to amass the wealth necessary to buy the Lexus, people must break from the comfortable surroundings where they have lived in order to acquire the means to purchase the car. The discussion really serves to illustrate the difficulties for societies and peoples in making the transition to a globalized Information Age world.

The Industrial Age was perhaps the high-water point for the nation-state in many regards. Power developed along these lines; standing in the world community was based on state affiliation. In fact, the United Nations was established to facilitate constructive relations among nation-states, not individuals. In a sense, an individual has little or no standing within the UN. Certainly, individuals do not have seats on the Security Council or in any official forums; only states can obtain this power or position. But as we have moved into the Information Age, new transnational issues are beginning to dominate.

So what is becoming of the nation-state? In some cases, globalization will lead to fracturing of states as Cold War institutions breathe their last gasp or peoples search for new identities, while in other cases states will come together to better compete as a bloc of nations, rather than as a single voice crying to be heard.

Nations are generally considered to be a group of people organized under a single, independent government within a country. When considering this definition, discussions invariably turn to issues such as sovereignty, borders, and rule of law. But there is another definition of nation that is becoming more relevant: "a nation is also defined as a people who share common customs, origins, history, and frequently language, or a nationality."[3] Here traditional concepts such as sovereignty, borders, and rule of law may or may not apply.

Consider that in 1945, the UN had 51 members but that by 2002, membership had grown to include 191 nations. But this growth only reflects nations in the classical sense. It does not include the newer concept of a nation such as the Kurds, who live within the national borders of Turkey, Syria, Iran, and Iraq. What about the Palestinians? They have no nation in the sense of a country, yet clearly they have claims as a nation based on common customs, history, and language. What about the nation of Islam, those people of the world that practice the Muslim religion which now number 1.2 billion worldwide? Are they a nation? The answer to that question most likely depends on who you are asking.

The UN lists 191 members, but the world may actually have two or three times that many nations, peoples linked not by geography but by ideas and common threads. The Information Age is both fueling and facilitating this growth. Global communications, particularly the Internet, have provided the means to share common ideas, coordinate activities, and collaborate in ways that previously could be accomplished only in person.

The concept of nations based on borders and ideas has already been discussed, but what about a nation based on economics? Transnational economics will tend to further blur the lines between states and even individual allegiances to states. Will a person be more likely to support the policies of an employer or of the state in which he or she lives?

Microsoft Corporation had revenues of $36.8 billion per year in 2004.[4] In a comparison of its revenue to the gross domestic product (GDP) of the nations of the world, Microsoft ranks 80th out of 230.[5] But is it a nation? What is its legal standing? Does it, or any other multinational corporation, have any special rights or privileges in the international community based on size and revenues? What if an employee of Microsoft working in a third world country wants to apply for a passport from Microsoft? In the future, would the employee be permitted to hold dual citizenship from Microsoft and his or her home country? Or could the employee petition to become a citizen of Microsoft's parent country, the United States?

The question really becomes, can a nation or state be virtual or must it have borders or the other traditional structures that commonly define a state? The more that information technologies proliferate, the greater the potential for sharing ideas and coming together in formal and informal ways that are likely to challenge the traditional concepts of nations and states.

Another important outcome related to the state system (both formal and informal) is the increasing number of failed or failing states. The 2002 National Security Strategy states, "America is now threatened less by conquering states than we are by failing ones."[6] According to a Brookings Institution source, a failed state is a country in which the central government does not exert effective control over, nor is able to deliver vital services to, significant parts of its own territory due to conflict, ineffective government, or state collapse.[7]

Why should the United States care about these failing states? Inevitably, the strife and instability from failing states spill over into adjacent states, within regions or even globally. The results are often transnational threats and crises such as terrorism, drug and human trafficking, disease, environmental issues, international crime, refugee flows, or illegal immigration. Humanitarian disasters are also frequently associated with failing states, and respect for democracy and human rights, core values of the United States, are normally absent in these failing countries.

The Information Age will both encourage and accelerate the demise of nations as well as allowing failures to be played out across the global stage. In a sense, transnational interactions made possible through information technology will weaken and perhaps, in some cases, eliminate the primacy of the nation-state. With seemingly unlimited media coverage and dissemination, citizens in failing states will have access to information that will highlight their plight. For example, a person living in a failing state who may have a relative dying of HIV/AIDS may gain awareness of treatments available in developed or developing nations. This awareness could begin to fuel a feeling that his or her government is not doing enough in this area. The same could be true if citizens of a country that does not permit peaceful demonstrations see a demonstration in another country played out on television. The Information Age will give people awareness outside of their immediate vantage point and make individuals and societies more cognizant of relative deprivation. The next logical step is that these newly informed people could potentially act on these feelings.

Taken to its logical conclusion, the perceived or real deprivation will inevitably lead to a balkanization similar to what has occurred in several regions, including the former Yugoslavia, the Soviet Union (and now in Chechnya within Russia), and throughout Africa in places such as Rwanda and Burundi. The case of Bosnia-Herzegovina is a classic example of how this fracturing can occur. Bosnia had a long history of migration patterns and of being conquered and occupied. This left the country with three distinct cultures, religions, and societies living virtually on top of each other—ostensibly three nations under one geopolitical boundary. The situation had been kept in check by a strongman, Josip Broz Tito, but following his death Yugoslavia fractured into seven provinces, including Bosnia-Herzegovina. Based on economic issues, a demographic profile that would have seen the Muslim portion of society gain a disproportionate amount of power over time, and religious differences, the country erupted in conflict. Estimates of the number of killed and displaced vary widely, but the magnitude of the humanitarian crisis was clear. The spark that ignited the hostilities was a series of news reports and subsequent political activism.

At the same time, scenes of humanitarian crisis on television have the potential to generate calls for a coalition of the willing to take action to alleviate the suffering. This has played out several times since the end of the Cold War in nations such as Somalia, Haiti, Bosnia, Kosovo, Liberia, Cote d'Ivoire, and the Sudan.

This discussion of nations and states is not meant in any way to imply that the United States or even mature developed nations will become irrelevant. However, for nations that are developing or for which the future is uncertain, the tensions will be significant and their survival as nation-states is not at all assured.

One additional issue under the heading of globalization concerns the development of superpowers made up of a collection of sovereign nations such as the European Union (EU). Since its inception, the EU has been both a political entity and a forum for economic cooperation. In 2002, the EU took the next step toward true integration and went to a common currency—only Sweden, Denmark, and the UK opted to retain their own currency. Over time, the EU has continued to systemically add nations as member states. The combined effect is that the collective GDP of the fifteen EU member nations was $9.6 trillion in 2002, as compared to $10.1 trillion for the United States. However, with the addition of ten new member nations in May 2004, the effect was to increase the EU's GDP to $10.4 trillion in 2002 dollars.[8] Couple this with the political structures for developing coordinated foreign policy positions and a military capability that provides collective security andprotects EU interests, and the Europeans have a counterweight to U.S. influence. Individually, the nations may have a collective power of x if a sum of power could be generated, but together perhaps their power is $2x$ or maybe even x^2. Clearly the EU is an example of the whole being greater than the sum of its parts.

With globalization comes an inevitable change in the ways conflict is likely to occur and be waged. In *The Clash of Civilizations,* Samuel Huntington writes of this emerging age and impending change,

> The great divisions among humankind and the dominating source of conflict will be cultural. Nation states will remain the most powerful actors in world affairs, but the principal conflicts of global politics will occur between nations and groups of different civilizations. The clash of civilizations will dominate global politics. The fault lines between civilizations will be the battle lines of the future.
>
> Civilization identity will be increasingly important in the future, and the world will be shaped in large measure by the interactions among seven or eight major civilizations. These include Western, Confucian, Japanese, Islamic, Hindu, Slavic-Orthodox, Latin American, and possibly African civilization. The most

important conflicts of the future will occur along the cultural fault lines separating these civilizations from one another.[9]

Huntington's work reflects his belief that the principle fault lines will fall along cultural boundaries. The use of Huntington's concept is not meant to imply that all of his conclusions have been accepted a priori; rather, his treatment of globalization provides an interesting perspective and proposes a theory that has gained some traction, at least in describing the future environment. The interesting point is that our international systems have really been established to deal in a state-to-state manner, yet in this globalization, conflicts are just as likely to be culture-to-state, business-to-state, or even Non-Governmental Organization (NGO)-to-state. How does this affect the current international system?

Irredentist forces based on culture and culturally related issues such as religion, ethnicity, and language will be a strong force for turmoil and instability. Until the emergence of the Internet or the spread of other information technologies, it is hard to imagine how a culturally based movement could rapidly come together from across the world into a cohesive and perhaps even threatening manner.

The issue is not that people identify culturally, but rather that problems emerge if the primary identification of a society is cultural rather than state. An even worse case would be if an individual's loyalty went first to the cultural identification, then to the economic affiliation, and last to the state. The United States will not be immune from these implications should our citizens choose to place another priority ahead of the state and choose to act on these nonstate loyalties.

All of this is not to say that the emergence of the Information Age and the resultant globalization do not have great potential. In fact, there are numerous examples of corporations increasing productivity through information technology enhancements. Consider the case of a software development corporation that is literally able to work around the clock using three eight-hour shifts in three distinct locations around the world. At the end of each shift, the work is forwarded from one set of employees to the next. By having three shifts, the twenty-four-hour cycle can be maintained, as can productivity. In this example, Java software applications were being written in multiple locations. At the end of each duty day, the coders send their work to the next location. The cycle continues at the third location and ends with the return of the updated software back to the original location for the next duty day. The employees call this concept "Java around the world."

In other cases, services in many sectors or industries are being outsourced to locations where labor is cheaper. Industries from computer software servicing and troubleshooting to banking are making use of assured voice and data communications to gain a competitive advantage in the marketplace. The issues that result are significant, as many of the countries involved lack laws dealing with intellectual property rights and have less transparent banking and accounting practices. One possibility could be to close up the holes through harmonizing and rationalization of laws and policies; however, we must be aware that this potentially will impact on issues of state sovereignty. Another obvious impact of this outsourcing is that jobs and thus revenue are leaving the United States. While on the surface this appears to be beneficial for corporate bottom lines, what happens if a natural disaster impacts on one of these foreign locations or internal strife occurs? How is the business—or for that matter the employees—impacted?

In considering the interrelationships between peoples, states, politics, and economics, it is instructive to examine the effect on the global economy of four major hurricanes hitting Florida in the summer and fall of 2004, or the destruction of the World Trade Center on 9/11. These events had significant impact on peoples, societies, and states far beyond the area that was physically changed by these events. The direct and indirect losses from the 9/11 attacks were estimated to cost well into the tens of billions of dollars and were felt well beyond New York state or U.S. national borders.

If one overlays the economic template described above on the state borders and cultural map that Huntington discusses, it is clear that conditions fueling instability and conflict are already in place and growing daily. The more information technologies proliferate, the greater this tension will become, and the more that traditional boundaries will become less relevant.

However, this is not to imply that globalization will only have the negative effect of sowing the seeds of instability and conflict. Economic prosperity, enhanced understanding of the world, and the spread of democracy will all benefit dramatically through the increased interactions brought about by globalization, fueled by the spread of information technologies.

PRINCIPLE 2: THE WORLD IS GETTING SMALLER

Related to the topic of globalization, but worth a separate discussion, is the concept of the resizing of the world. Of course, the term *resizing* does not imply a physical change in size, but rather a changing of the spatial, temporal, and intellectual basis of our understanding of the world and thus our interactions within the global community, whether between states or cultures.

In an abstract sense, one could demonstrate the concept in a sort of mathematical notation, such as the equation below. To allow for the possibility that other factors are contributing to this resizing, the equation has been left open-ended. However, the three primary considerations are distance, time, and knowledge.

$$\textit{Size of the world} = f(\textit{distance, time, knowledge} ...)$$

Distance

Actual distances remain virtually unchanged, although the ability to negotiate distances and thus to impact on faraway lands or even places once thought to be inaccessible has changed. Of course, natural or manmade change can occur, potentially altering the actual measured distances. Examples might include natural changes resulting from earthquakes or floods such as the devastating tsunami in South Asia in December 2004, which killed over 300,000 people and displaced several million more in twelve countries of the region; as a result of this disaster, large areas of land were forever altered. In the same manner, manmade changes can also affect distances, for example strip mining, which has literally reduced some mountaintops to plateaus. But even these changes are insignificant compared to the total size of the world.

Consider that when Christopher Columbus set out on his expedition, it took from August to October 1492 to make the journey from Spain to an island in the Caribbean thought most likely to be San Salvador or the Bahamas. The round-trip journey back to Spain (after some additional exploration) took until January of the following year. This illustration demonstrates that a journey of this magnitude and risk was measured in months and only undertaken by the heartiest of seafarers after considerable provisioning. Today, the same journey can be made in a matter of hours for the price of an airplane ticket. Even within our borders, the way in which we think of distances has changed. Trips that once took months to complete are now routinely made in hours as well. In some cases, the ability to transmit, receive, and share data has eliminated the requirement for travel altogether.

Other areas have also been affected. In military terms, a force was said to have interior lines if the distance between headquarters or resupply depots and the front lines was less than the enemy's distances. The advent of railroads essentially changed the time-distance relationships such that geometry was less important than the time expended to get to the front with reinforcements, supplies, or messages. If a force only has ten miles between its staging area and the front line and can travel at two miles per hour, and another force has its stocks forty miles away but has access to transportation that travels at forty miles per hour, then the second force makes the trip in one hour, while the first force takes five hours to complete the trip. Therefore the second force would have achieved interior lines, albeit not in a purely physical sense.

Thus the notion of distance becomes important as it relates to time: time to move from location A to location B, or time to get information from location C to location D. If the distance between two locations, A and B, is one hundred miles, but a video teleconferencing link is established between the two locations, the physical distance becomes irrelevant. The sites could be next to each other or halfway around the world; the time required to pass information is infinitesimal. Whereas previously, messengers were utilized to traverse physical space, today information is literally available at the touch of a keyboard. Instantaneous, real-time communications are expected, even demanded.

Examining conflict and combat operations provides insight into what factors are relevant with regard to the battle space. Considerations such as the lethality

and ranges of the weapon systems are more important than simply a calculation of distance in terms of being able to mass the effects of capabilities (and
forces). As an example, consider that the average number of soldiers deployed
per square kilometer of front declined from 100,000 in ancient times to 3,883
during the U.S. Civil War, 404 in World War I, and just 36 in World War II. It
declined further to 25 in the 1973 Yom Kippur War and has kept falling since,
down to 2 in the 1991 Gulf War.[10]

However, even density of forces, lethality, and ranges will take a backseat to
the ability to gain knowledge and prevent the adversary from acquiring knowledge. This, coupled with the ability to effectively communicate with populations
and control or manage information, will be essential. This collective ability to
gain and maintain information dominance will be of far greater importance to the
outcome of future conflict than distance.

The information explosion has also significantly affected both politics and
economics. Today, communities that are thousands of miles apart on the map can
potentially be virtual neighbors capable of sharing the same ideas or cooperating
economically. News, both good and bad, can be shared instantly across the globe,
with the establishment of virtual communities as a result. The possibilities for
economic growth and societal development are incredible. Large flows of capital
have been made possible through the application of information technologies.
The result has been a revolution in financial transactions, trade, and economic
development. Consider that before the expansion of information technologies,
traders were forced to send runners to the airport to meet airplanes coming from
Europe to pick up the latest copies of the *Financial Times* to get a few hours'
jump on the market, while today the information is readily available at the touch
of a keyboard without leaving the office.

The proliferation of information is also having a significant impact on the
spread of democracy. The same forces that are required for economic development and prosperity are fueling the growth of democracies and democratic institutions. David Gompert of the Institute for National and Strategic Studies
(INSS) at the National Defense University writes, "Democracy and power are
also linked insofar as political freedom is inseparable from economic freedom
and the latter is indispensable for success in the creation and use of information
technology."[11]

This is bad news for dictatorships and other forms of authoritarian government. As societies strive to compete economically, they will be forced to
adopt information technologies and other liberal reforms that will in turn lead to
political freedoms and, over time, to more democratic forms of government, if
not full-fledged democracies. Failure to make these political and societal reforms will disadvantage the economies of nations that refuse or are unable to
move to more democratic forms of government. What business would be interested in investing in countries where there are no legal protections, where
corruption runs rampant, or where the economy is state controlled?

Time

The discussion of distance leads to a corresponding analysis of how time has been impacted by technological and informational advances. Changes in transportation and communications have compressed the time needed to traverse distances, move information, and maintain contact. While these changes are significant, perhaps even more so is the compression of time available to make decisions.

The more rapidly information can be passed, processed, and analyzed, the greater the demand for immediate decisions. The decision maker is forced into the dilemma of having to make immediate decisions because, in some cases, failure to do so constitutes a decision not to act. For this reason, both policy analysts and military commanders work to master the decision cycle to allow them to make decisions faster than the adversary.

The next major advances in the Information Age are likely to be related more to the development of decision support tools than to the continuing application of Moore's Law. Given current processor speeds, the limiting factor is the ability of humans to process the various inputs. Even if transistor speeds were to increase by several orders of magnitude, the ability to synthesize data, which is related to the absorption capacity of the individual, has not increased as dramatically, so further enhancements would not be particularly useful. With order-of-magnitude enhancements to decision support tools will come complementary improvements in the acquisition of knowledge and the ability of the decision maker to act more rapidly.

Knowledge

While time and distance changes are significant, perhaps the most important changes are in the development of knowledge or information-processing capabilities. It is not enough to acquire data or information; one must process the inputs into usable knowledge to have any benefit. Consequently, as the world is getting smaller, the body of knowledge is growing rapidly.

The difference between what is known and what is unknown is changing greatly in favor of the known. The Information Age is the driver. The body of all knowledge can be divided into three categories: "known knowns," "known unknowns," and "unknown unknowns." The body of knowledge that is now in the category of known knowns has increased dramatically. Advances in the sciences, exploration both around the world and within our galaxy, and the information explosion wherein news cycles once measured in days are now measured in hours and minutes are just a few examples of how the growth in known knowns has accelerated. Things considered to be absolutes or facts fall into this first bin. Additionally, the information that falls into the second category, known unknowns, has also grown. Certainly there are things that we do not know to be truth or may even understand to be unpredictable, such as the weather. But through investigation and understanding, we have learned that these are known unknowns, many of which, through advances in the first category, can be reduced to a probabilistic outcome. Consider that we cannot know with absolute assurance where a hurricane will hit, but forecasters can use models to predict a zone of impact and reduce the uncertainty of this known unknown. So it follows that if the body of all knowledge is finite, and the first two categories have increased, then it stands to reason that the third category, unknown unknowns, or the body of knowledge that we are essentially unaware of, has decreased.

The manner in which people acquire information has dramatically changed as the information revolution has progressed. Visual means of communicating and information gathering are becoming the dominant forms of acquiring knowledge. While it does not replace the printed media or radio, the ability to pass digital images, both with and without the benefit of sound, is powerful.

The images from the Abu Ghraib prisoner abuse scandal in Iraq, where U.S. forces are alleged to have committed war crimes against civilians and captured enemy combatants, are extraordinarily powerful. It was not until the images began to be released that the depth of the issue was understood. Ten years ago, it would not have been possible to capture, mass-produce, and disseminate these images, let alone to have had the live coverage of coalition operations in Iraq.

However, with advances in digital technology, routing of information, and communications, it has become not only possible but expected to combine the capabilities of a digital camera (with full-motion video or still pictures), computers, routers, and satellite communications to provide live feed of combat operations, bringing U.S. national security policy directly to the living rooms of Americans or to coffee shops in Amman, Jordan. The digital revolution works to provide knowledge across the globe, regardless of political or ideological affiliation.

It has become virtually impossible, and would certainly not be desirable, to control the proliferation of these information technologies, as they are key factors in the increase in economic prosperity, global productivity, enhancements of quality of life, and democratization, to name a few benefits. However, one of the downfalls of the information revolution is that information is processed based not just on what is shown or provided but also on the lenses through which the information is filtered. Consider that the combat images beamed to the United States showing the deaths of enemy combatants in Iraq will be viewed as heroic, while the same images flashed throughout the Arab world are likely to be seen as unjust and murderous. Another filter is the voice-overs that accompany the images. The coverage on a network such as CNN, ABC, CBS, or NBC is likely to be considerably different from that on Al-Jazeera, the Arab-based network, or even

Interfax or Itar Tass, the Russian news networks. The bottom line is that culture, religion, society, and other filters matter in the processing of information and development of knowledge.

The information revolution is also impacting how we process knowledge. In the Industrial Age, information flowed vertically up and down chains of command, whether in business or in the military. The flow went from the top of the organization, where direction and guidance were given, down to the lowest levels, where policies were implemented. In the same way, information from the lowest levels was passed up the chain of command, voicing concerns or perhaps even making suggestions on process improvements or providing feedback. In the Information Age, the vertical structure has been violated. A new flattened architecture or horizontal structure allows even the people at the lowest levels of the organization to communicate directly with the most senior levels. An e-mail sent from an assembly line worker to the CEO of the company can be read immediately. There are no filters on the information as it is passed in this direct manner.

Compression of traditional hierarchies does not apply only to the flow of information; actions are affected as well. In much the same way, soldiers at the lowest level of the military unit can make decisions, take actions, or implement policies in ways that have strategic impact. More to the point, a tactical action undertaken by a soldier can have operational or strategic consequences. The very nature of an operation can be changed by a seemingly insignificant action. The implications of this will be discussed further under principle 3.

So what does the concept of the world getting smaller mean to national security policy formulation? The implications are significant. Physical proximity is no longer the sole or even most relevant indicator of threat. The computer networks of the United States can be threatened from 3,000 miles away using destructive electronic intrusions or from 30 yards away using conventional weapons. The result can be the same—the destruction of the capability to process information.

The ability to acquire, process, and analyze information is critical in this resizing of the world. With complementary increases in knowledge development, the world is becoming even more interrelated and in a very real sense smaller. Therefore, the manner in which the United States will conduct foreign policy and national security strategy in the Information Age will be significantly influenced by this phenomenon.

PRINCIPLE 3: THE NATURE, CHARACTER, AND CONDUCT OF CONFLICT ARE CHANGING

An ongoing debate among strategists, and in particular military strategists, is whether the nature, character, and conduct of warfare or conflict are changing. The issue is important, as the outcome of the discussion cuts directly to the question of how to enhance the national security strategy of the United States. If one concludes that these attributes of conflict are not changing as a result of the transition to the Information Age, then perhaps the current national security apparatus can be assessed to be adequate. However, if one concludes the opposite, then it follows that new strategies will be required to account for the changes in the nature, character, and conduct of conflict in this new age.

In examining the issue, the National War College within the National Defense University in Washington, DC, uses the definitions in the box for beginning the dialogue with its military, foreign military and government civilian students undergoing its year-long course of study.

Prevailing thought has been that the nature of conflict has remained and will remain fixed and largely as it has been described for centuries by military theorists. As Clausewitz wrote in *On War* over 200 years ago, "War is a continuation of politics by other means."[12] In his voluminous writings, Clausewitz frequently discussed the close relationship between conflict and states. In his formulations, the key components were: (1) war is a human endeavor and (2) it is the manner by which states advance their political objectives and interests. If one buys into this concept, then the logical conclusion is that Information Age conflict (and warfare) is likely to be largely similar to Industrial Age conflict.

However, my argument is that indeed the nature, character, and conduct of conflict are changing dramatically and being effective in this new environment requires a new way of thinking about and acting on national security issues. Even the way we think of conflict is evolving in the Information Age. Information technologies are enhancing the capabilities to probe, threaten, or attack an adversary or competitor, either directly or indirectly. These threats are certainly not limited to military endeavors. Even economies, information networks, and the media, to name a few sectors, are potential targets and must establish protective shields to guard against these threats.

The combination of the various elements of power used in waging and deciding the outcome of modern conflict signals a significant change in the nature of conflict. Looking back at the Napoleonic era, when large massed

---

▶ *Nature* of war: What enduring feaures make war a unique human endeavor?
  •What makes war distinct?

▶ *Character* of war: Who fights and to what end?
  •Who/what is the enemy?

▶ *Conduct* of war: How warfare is carried out?
  •What are specific modalities of the fight?

formations met on the fields of battle in a sort of winner-take-all contest, it is clear that the military was the primary means of decision. If political solutions could not be agreed upon, forces came together over a narrowly defined area and engaged in conflict to determine the outcome. Following the battle, the winner would leave outposts to ensure that the battlefield decision was enforced. Political settlements were concluded and policed through the use of these outposts.

Today, competition, which in many cases serves as the precursor to outright conflict, is being conducted between nations or blocs of nations on a daily basis. This could take the form of economic competition or coercion, computer attacks on networks and infrastructure, industrial espionage, demographic warfare (through the use of forced migrations, for example), deliberate cultural encroachment, ideological warfare, or even the use of information to influence the policymakers or societies of nations.

Another major shift has been the "dehumanizing" of conflict. Pushing war and conflict away from the uniquely human endeavor it once was through the use of advanced systems and capabilities has created a tendency toward this dehumanization. In early conflict, the strength of the individual soldier was the key component of warfare and therefore played a significant role in the outcome. In recruiting an army, physical prowess was regarded above all else. The ability of soldiers to handle individual pre–Industrial Age weapons such as the spear and sword were based on personal attributes such as speed, stamina, and strength.

In the Industrial Age, these characteristics remained important, although their relative importance diminished. The ability to operate machinery such as the machine gun, tank, or airplane demanded a different mix of skills. It is not that speed, stamina, and strength were no longer important; they were just not as critical. A soldier proficient at another aspect of warfare such as aiming a weapon could overcome deficiencies in other individual skills. This dehumanization of warfare will continue at rapid pace. Soldiers proficient at the use of electronics and computers can now direct the destructive force of Information Age weapons systems with alarming accuracy. With further enhancements in information technologies, these trends will undoubtedly continue to increase and expand. While some soldiers will continue to experience the direct combat role, this number as a proportion of the force is diminishing rapidly. The first blows of the next major conflict are considerably more likely to be probes of computer networks rather than destruction of the enemy's radar systems or force-on-force engagements.

Warfare and conflict waged by nonstate and transnational actors is changing both the nature and character of conflict as well. The works of previous strategists such as Clausewitz, Sun Tzu, or T. E. Lawrence allowed for insurgency as a manner of conflict and thus addressed both conventional wars between nations and internal insurgencies. However, there was no recognition of the special type of warfare made possible by the advent of the Information Age, transnational conflict (and war) like that being conducted by al-Qaeda today. This type of war cuts across national borders, looks to alter the policies, and even purports to threaten the existence of "enemy states" such as Israel, the UK, and the United States. Terrorists today often have no national identity and move around largely unfettered, spreading conflict and instability. Consider Osama bin Laden, who was born a Saudi but has moved to Sudan, then to Afghanistan, and now perhaps to Pakistan to perpetuate his terror network.

The changing objectives of conflict represent another extremely troubling development in the waging of modern war. The deliberate targeting of civilians and infrastructure with no link to the conflict other than their affiliation as citizens of a particular nation clearly demonstrates a dramatic change in warfare. While collateral damage to infrastructure and civilian casualties have always been an unfortunate part of conflict, today terrorists are making these peripherals part of the planned target set. Despite the significant violations of the Laws of Armed Conflict that are part of the Geneva Conventions that these actions represent, terrorists have targeted and likely will continue to target nonmilitary elements of societies. The implications for national security and defense are extraordinary. In the case of 9/11, attacks on these types of objectives led to over 3,000 innocents killed, billions of dollars in damage, and additional billions in economic losses resulting from the strikes.

Some might argue that the targeting of civilians during World War II, by the Germans using V-2 rockets or by the Allies against German factories, which resulted in heavy civilian casualties, is similar to the targeting of civilians and infrastructure discussed above. However, a major difference is that the target set in World War II was largely military, with civilians and infrastructure either secondary initiatives or collateral damage, whereas today, there is a migration to targeting civilians and infrastructure first, with little or secondary targeting against hard military targets.

The case of targeting infrastructure is particularly troubling for another reason. Approximately 85 percent of our nation's infrastructure is controlled by the private sector, which suggests that developing strategies and tactics to defend critical infrastructure will be a complex issue with compromises required by the U.S. government and private industries. It will not simply be a case of the government developing policies and resourcing them; the private sector will have a key role to play in the process.

As yet another example of the change in objectives, for many terrorists or fundamentalists involved in conflicts today, the enemy is not a single nation or even a collection of nations, but rather progress and the proliferation of ideas. A thought worthy of consideration is that we are using Industrial Age systems and methods produced for large-scale warfare to wage war against what is essentially an ideological conflict. It is entirely possible and even likely that our means of waging the conflict will not be sufficient to change the behavior of the idealistic and determined enemies we are likely to face.

The rationale for the combatants' actions represents yet another change to the character of conflict. In many respects, the reasons for previous conflicts have tended to be related to trying to change national policies or economic reasons. In fact, nations continue to have large standing armies, navies, and air forces to be able to address these conventional threats and ensure protection of their citizens, national property, and borders. However, today groups of disenfranchised individuals are coming together to wage warfare as anarchists. Their rationale for war is irrational, at least by traditional standards. It is not, as Clausewitz stated, "the continuation of politics by other means." Seemingly, no politics and certainly no "negotiated settlements" are possible.

The Information Age also has dramatically changed the conduct of conflict. While managing the flow of information has always been a recognized imperative in conflict, the Information Age is expanding the ability to proliferate ideas, organize the masses, and provide direction.

Consider the example of an internal insurgency fueled not by mass gatherings, but rather through virtual meetings and connections. The case of the autocratic Government of Iran (GOI) demonstrates the impact of information technology on governments and societies. The GOI in late 2004 began shutting down Web sites and Internet cafes that had become popular, giving the explanation that students at universities were browsing indecent sites. As a measure of the impact that information technology is having on Iranian society, consider that the number of Internet users has risen from 250,000 to 4.8 million during the last four years, with over 100,000 Web logs, many of which are politically based.[13] The problem for the GOI is its own survival. The theologians running the government want information provided to the people to be based on their pronouncements or the Koran rather than on free-flowing dialog and the invasion of external themes and messages that could "corrupt" the people and allow independent thought. In short, the Internet is a pervasive and perhaps uncontrollable threat to the current regime's survival. While in this case this is good news for the spread of democratic ideals and institutions, it will not always be true; a by-product of this free flow of information will sometimes be instability and perhaps even conflict.

Perhaps the clearest examples of the change in conflict are seen in the conduct of war. The proliferation of all types of means, technologies, and manner of prosecuting conflict provide the most profound indication of the changes that have occurred. The next two sections on *increased complexity* and *greater availability of means* will discuss these changes in detail.

PRINCIPLE 4: THE WORLD IS BECOMING INCREASINGLY COMPLEX

Advances in information technology and the coming of the Information Age signal a corresponding increase in the complexity of world. With each step further into the Information Age, the challenges presented by increasing complexity will expand significantly, perhaps even by orders of magnitude over relatively short periods of time. Both the magnitude and pace of change will result in greater complexity. Inherent in this equation will be the greater variety of threats and responses that we will have to master to be successful in this new age.

The discussion under principle 2 really serves as the lead-in to this discussion of complexity. As the temporal and spatial dimensions are transformed, there will be more interactions and inevitably clashes between nations, societies and peoples. Many of the traditional structures and ways of dealing with conflict will not be sufficient. Transnational issues today, including immigration, environmental degradation, and illegal trafficking across state and national boundaries, coupled with seams caused by differences in national laws, policies, and customs will undoubtedly increase the complexity of these interactions.

These types of interactions between nations and by peoples across national boundaries will also have profound implications for waging conflict in the Information Age. For example, consider how the complexities have increased based on the emergence of multinational corporations and integrated economies. If the United States uses its economic power in a coercive manner against a country where U.S. corporations are operating, invariably these companies will be impacted, most likely in a negative manner.

Furthermore, Information Age adversaries will also likely have a broader range of response capabilities available in their arsenal. Adding to the complexity is the requirement to respond to a full range of threats to U.S. national security from Preindustrial and Industrial Age threats to Information Age adversaries. In other words, the number of threats is growing, and the result is that our security strategy must change accordingly.

Therefore, the United States must have the capability to conduct full-spectrum operations. This refers to the ability to conduct operations ranging from the low end of the spectrum, which includes nation building and disaster relief, to the middle of the spectrum, which includes peace operations, to the high end, including conventional combat operations and nuclear war. Mastering high-intensity combat operations in anticipation of waging war against the Soviet Union and Warsaw Pact required a considerably more narrow set of skills than the requirements imposed on a full-spectrum force.

Many will see this as a purely military requirement; however, this is no longer the case. The notion of full-spectrum operations must include the respective contributions of capabilities from across the elements of national power. The reasoning is this. For each of the operations along this spectrum, a number of tools and response capabilities must be used, including, but not limited to, the military. The most relevant example is the case of nation building where requirements for infrastructure development and reconstruction, training of police and security forces, establishing a functioning legal system, and educational reform will all likely be required.

Furthermore, being able to conduct these operations sequentially or individually will not be adequate; we must have the capability of fighting a "three-block war." This phrase was first used by the commandant of the Marine Corps, General Krulak, in the aftermath of operations in Somalia. The idea was that forces—and by extension the other government agencies participating with the military—needed to have the capability to operate in multiple types of operations in a nearly simultaneous manner. For example, in one block, humanitarian operations might be ongoing. In the next block over, operations might entail the separation of forces or peacekeeping. In the third block, forces might be participating in combat operations to defeat an adversary. If this concept is not complex enough, the forces on the ground also need to have the ability to transition rapidly between operations, so the force involved in combat could very rapidly be expected to transition to a humanitarian operation immediately following termination of hostilities. While the term *forces* has been used, we will need to think more broadly about what constitutes these units. It is likely that in the first block of this three-block war, soldiers, contractors, State Department officials, and city planners, as an example, will all be working in a coordinated manner to conduct nation-building operations. Finally, adding to the complexity is that in the Information Age, we must be able to conduct these operations and make these transitions with cameras rolling and live footage being beamed around the world, as in the case of operations in Iraq in March 2003 during Operation Iraqi Freedom.

The Information Age has essentially accelerated and brought to the forefront a new category of operation or threat: information operations or IO. Consider that in the 1980s before the vast proliferation of the Internet, there was little need to protect computer networks as we must do today. Few had access; the technology was not broadly understood; and those that did have access tended to be in trusted positions such as in the military or in government. Today the network is available virtually around the world. For the cost of a computer and an Internet Service Provider (ISP) a nearly unlimited flow of data and information becomes available. Even in remote regions, the Internet is accessible using satellite telephones to link back into the network. Today, there are large operational facilities that specialize in protecting civilian and military networks. These facilities constantly monitor the written transmissions flowing across the network in real time. Anomalies are flagged for further investigation and suspect Internet Protocol (IP) addresses are flagged or blocked to be put on a watch list or prevented from accessing certain sites.

As additional evidence of the increase in complexity, consider the threats defined in 2003 by the Transformation Office within the Office of the Secretary of Defense, which include four future challenges the United States is expected to face:

1. *Traditional*—Those seeking to challenge American power by instigating traditional military operations with legacy and advanced military capabilities. Examples include conventional air, land, and sea forces and nuclear forces of established nuclear powers.

2. *Irregular*—Those seeking to erode American influence and power by employing unconventional or irregular methods. Examples include terrorism, insurgency, civil war, and emerging concepts such as "unrestricted war."

3. *Disruptive*—Those seeking to usurp American power and influence by acquiring breakthrough capabilities. Examples include sensors, information, biotechnology, miniaturization on the molecular level, cyber operations, space, directed energy, and other emerging technologies.

4. *Catastrophic*—Those seeking to paralyze American leadership and power by employing weapons of mass destruction (WMD) or WMD-like effects in unwarned attacks on symbolic, critical, or other high-value targets. Examples include 9/11, terrorist use of WMD, or rogue missile attack.

Each of these threats has an Information Age component and certainly a nonmilitary component as well. For example, a traditional threat would invariably rely on the use of the media as part of its campaign. A more sophisticated traditional threat would more probably attempt to disrupt operations using attacks on our unsecured information networks as well.

We have seen that the terrorists who perpetrated the 9/11 attacks (which are considered to be both irregular and catastrophic threats) made extensive use of the Internet in coordinating their pre-attack plans. The threat of disruption in many regards has its roots in the Information Age. A number of the methods and technologies are only made possible through the use of advanced information technology capabilities. The damage from 9/11 alone demonstrates the close relationship between this "military strike" and political, legal, intelligence, economic, cultural, societal, and information components of power.

At the height of the Cold War, the major focus of national security efforts was on the traditional threat, although irregular threats received some attention as well, mostly as they related to the strategy of containment and the standoff with the Soviet Union. However, over the course of the last decade, with the end of the Cold War and based on increases in technology, a wide variety of disruptive and catastrophic threats have emerged. The temptation will be to change focus from the traditional to the other threats. This will be especially true as the perceived threat of a traditional confrontation diminishes or remains constant, while the potential for irregular, disruptive, and catastrophic threats will continue to increase. However, for a global power, retaining the capability to respond across the full spectrum will be essential.

Close examination of these threats clearly indicates the requirement for more than a simple military response capability. Said another way, multiple elements of national power will be required to respond appropriately to the complex threats articulated above. Political forces are key to ensuring access to possible battlegrounds, including some nontraditional media such as cyberspace. The political element is also essential for defusing conflicts prior to their initiation or resolution in the aftermath of a conflict. The rule of law and legal authorities are key to ensuring that perpetrators of crimes, even against humanity, are prosecuted and that forces have the full authority to act. Economics will invariably be required as coercive means as well as to provide "carrots" in the post-conflict period. Throughout operations, information will be an important driver. Prior to conflict, the enemy's networks can be probed or even attacked, and intelligence will be essential during all phases of the conflict.

In fact, a strong case can be made that prior to the initiation of conflict, the other elements of power will be more important than the military. Consider a catastrophic threat using WMD. The work done through political, intelligence, and law enforcement means will be key to stopping a WMD event from occurring.

PRINCIPLE 5: THERE IS A GREATER AVAILABILITY OF MEANS

Just as information technologies have proliferated, so too have the means available to engage in conflict and conduct war. These means vary from weapons specifically designed to kill and maim to systems for probing the desired adversary. Some of the conflict is "soft," which more strongly reflects competition between nations. Other conflict will be at the higher end of the spectrum using conventional or even unconventional policies, weapons, and tactics.

The increased complexity described above leads naturally into a discussion of the greater availability and use of a wider variety of means. A case in point is the employment of the media and other informational outlets by adversaries against which we are waging the global war on terror. One could certainly argue that bin Laden's statement on October 29, 2004, just prior to the U.S. election, that "we are continuing this policy of bleeding America to the point of bankruptcy," demonstrates that he is waging a war of both ideas and economics. His plan for perpetrating the events of 9/11, costing approximately $500,000, which resulted in billions in damages and lost wages, and now billions more for the prosecution of the global war on terror, was more an assault on political, economic, cultural, and informational elements of our society than a pure military strike.

We must remain mindful that as we have moved toward the Information Age, the previous threats to our nation's security have not evaporated. The traditional threats remain and in some cases have been increased through the application of information technologies to Industrial Age weapons or capabilities. Consider the progress of the U.S. military in upgrading weapons systems with new technology. An example is dumb bombs (with no guidance system) used by the U.S. Air Force in the mid-1980s that have been retrofitted with precision munitions kits, enabling the once-dumb bombs to have global positioning system (GPS) guidance.

The proliferation of conventional weapons has been and will continue to be extensive.[14] Virtually all nations of the world have standing armies and air forces, and most nations with access to major waterways have naval forces as well. The largest component of national defense for these nations tends to be the army, and most of these forces have some modern weaponry. Air forces tend to be small and in many countries limited to cargo aircraft or older fighters designed to provide a limited air defense capability, primarily against other nations within their region. Navies for nations that have them tend to be "brown water" forces, meaning they are capable of operating only in littoral areas. Few have the ability to venture far from their own national coasts.

The United States and our chief competitors for arms sales, Russia and China, sell a wide variety of weapons including helicopters, tanks, infantry fighting vehicles, aircraft, small arms, and ships. The United States is by far the largest vendor, with sales around the globe including NATO nations and Japan as well as the developing nations in Europe, the Middle East, and East Asia.[15] Once these weapons systems are sold, they can make their way across the globe and into the hands of various state and nonstate actors.

WMD are another class of weapons that have received much publicity, particularly in the aftermath of the demise of the Soviet Union and Warsaw Pact. Whole programs such as established by the Nunn-Lugar Amendment are designed to collect and dispose of nuclear weapons from the states of the former Soviet territories so that they do not fall into the hands of rogue nations or terrorists. Unfortunately, limiting the proliferation of weapons and especially these technologies is proving extremely difficult, as many of these weapons are based on dual-use technologies. For example, the same basic technology for developing a nuclear power plant is used in the production of weapons-grade uranium or plutonium, the key ingredient in nuclear weapons. Another challenge has been the control of fissile material. This is also proving problematic, as the total amount produced remains largely unknown due to lack of appropriate control measures at production sites coupled with the ease of concealing the material. The same is true for biological weapons, which have a close relationship with the development of vaccines or other health-related therapies. In the development of chemical weapons, the issue is even more acute, as the precursors for many chemical weapons are readily available, and the process of manufacturing a crude chemical weapon is easily learned.

Imagine a world in which a terrorist has a nuclear, chemical, or biological weapon. What price would the United States be willing to pay to recover the device? Would that price be measured in dollars, lives, or values? Now added to the mix are Information Age threats that can be used to alter perceptions, incite populations, interfere with electronic communications, and even cause conflict. Having the capability to employ information as a tool of policy or a weapon is becoming more important in the Information Age; in addition, the means to do so are becoming more readily available.

The use of information in conflicts is certainly not new. Sun Tzu wrote of the importance of the use of deception and situational awareness over 5,000 years ago. Concerning deception, he wrote, "All warfare is based on deception," and "When able to attack, we must seem unable; when using our forces, we must seem inactive; when we are near, we must make the enemy believe we are far away; when far away, we must make him believe we are near." The ability to use deceptive information to cause the enemy to act or not act continues to be an essential part of warfare. Sun Tzu wrote what has become perhaps his most famous maxim concerning the critical nature of information: "If you know the enemy and know yourself, you need not fear the result of a hundred battles. If you know yourself but not the enemy, for every victory gained you will also suffer a defeat. If you know neither the enemy nor yourself, you will succumb in every battle."[16]

Today it is not just the ability to gain intelligence about the adversary that is key but also the ability to control the flow of information to actors including states, nonstate entities, and individuals, so that they are persuaded to act or not act in certain ways. The genocide in Rwanda in 1994 had its roots, in large measure, in the use of mass communications. Using the local radio stations to enrage and direct the population, the Hutu leaders announced a call to arms, in which estimates are that over 500,000 Tutsis were hacked to death over a three-week period. The messages broadcast by local radio stations were the catalyst for these atrocities.

As another example of the central role of information in modern military operations, consider that in Bosnia-Herzegovina in 1997, a major task of the NATO force participating in peace operations was to halt the broadcasting of anticoalition propaganda. On the Serb side of the country, negative messages about the NATO forces, the Muslim-Croat portion of the country, and the upcoming elections threatened to destabilize the nation and perhaps even incite an outbreak of renewed fighting. Based on these concerns, NATO forces took the Serb radio and television stations off the air during this critical period just prior to the elections. The stations were allowed to come back on the air only after they agreed to broadcast more moderate, pluralistic messages.

The control of information is becoming more challenging with the proliferation of information technologies. Today, every person with access to the Internet is a writer and publisher. Web sites that discuss everything from cooking to the politics of the Islamic fundamentalists in Indonesia can be found online. But how much of the information on the Web is true? Certainly there is no editorial review board considering the information prior to its posting.

Technical threats such as computer worms and viruses can be employed to disrupt or even destroy networks and computers. An enemy, or for that matter a hacker on an electronic joyride, can pose a threat from thousands of miles away simply using a commercially available computer and access to the Internet. In this Information Age, whole industries have been created to deal specifically with electronic threats to individuals, business, societies, and governments. The disproportionately small cost of means (i.e., under $500 for an entry-level computer) for the potentially large impact on global networks, perhaps billions of dollars of losses, is extraordinary.

Advanced techniques for combining multiple technologies into a system have great potential, but also potentially devastating consequences if misused. Consider nanotechnology, which combines biotechnology and computers. The potential of developing systems that directly threaten the United States and global society are at least as great as the potential for using this technology for positive purposes. Consider a scenario in which an advanced system based on nanotechnology spins out of control and begins to attack people, perhaps causing an inadvertent biological disaster. The implications for national security strategy and the health of the world in general are extraordinary.

The use of robotics in the development of unmanned aerial and ground vehicles will change society and national security strategy in some fairly significant ways. As society begins to incorporate more robotic capabilities, migration into areas impacting national security strategy will undoubtedly occur. What are the consequences of an unmanned aerial vehicle that is deployed as part of an advanced missile defense shield that is tampered with by an enemy trying to probe for vulnerabilities, and this tampering changes the computer code to the point that the system engages a civilian airliner from an innocent third country? Who is responsible for this disaster? Does this probing of the defensive shield constitute the initial phases of war, or merely, as in the Industrial Age, the daily interactions of competitors and enemies?

Other means of combining revolutionary advances in physics with information technology are creating new categories of weapons. An article that appeared in 2004 in the *San Francisco Chronicle* reported,

> The U.S. Air Force is quietly spending millions of dollars investigating ways to use a radical power source—antimatter, the eerie "mirror" of ordinary matter—in future weapons. The most powerful potential energy source presently thought to be available to humanity, antimatter is a term normally heard in science-fiction films and TV shows, whose heroes fly "antimatter-powered spaceships" and do battle with "antimatter guns."[17]

What are the implications of a system such as this in the hands of a determined adversary?

The linkages between national security threats and nontraditional means will become more pronounced in this emerging age. A company specializing in development of advanced farming techniques could develop biotechnology-based methods capable of destroying whole industries. Concerns over these dual-use technologies, those technologies with potential for use in civilian or military applications, will become even more pronounced.

A class of threats related to the inadequacies in border security remains a great concern, as the borders of nations around the world have been and remain porous, with little or no policing. In *America the Vulnerable*, Stephen Flynn of the Council on Foreign Relations makes the case that the United States remains vulnerable to a variety of low-tech threats:

> Despite increased awareness, we still offer our enemies a vast menu of soft targets: water and food supplies; chemical plants; energy grids and pipelines; bridges, tunnels and ports; and the millions of cargo containers that carry most of the goods we depend upon in our everyday lives. The measures we have cobbled together to protect these vital systems are hardly fit to deter amateur thieves, vandals and smugglers. Worse still, small improvements are often oversold as giant steps forward, lowering the guard of the average citizen and building an unwarranted sense of confidence.[18]

To support this assertion, consider that we are screening passengers prior to boarding flights to Baltimore-Washington Airport and in some cases confiscating nail clippers and pocket knives, while at the same time, less than twenty miles away hundreds of thousands of containers pass through the port of Baltimore in a week. Granted that airport checks are primarily focused on screening passengers to thwart in-flight threats, but the order of magnitude of the threats being guarded against is absurd. In the case of the aircraft, the concern is mainly for the passengers, crew, and plane, while for the containers, the concern could be for a whole city if a nuclear device was being smuggled into the country through the ports.

This is a very bleak assessment, even more so when one considers that the threats addressed above require minimal technological know-how, are highly available, and are largely unguarded against. Consider the implications of other high-tech threats. Technology will undoubtedly allow larger threats to be placed in smaller packages, thus complicating detection. The smaller packaging of threats means more intrusive inspections to detect threats. Perhaps advanced screening methods can minimize the use of overly intrusive screening methods, but it is doubtful that they can be eliminated altogether.

Information technologies will also allow the environment to be altered through electronic manipulation. Examples include something as simple as altering photos by either adding or deleting information. More sophisticated capabilities include the use of stealth technologies to alter the electromagnetic signature associated with an object. In the case of stealth aircraft, special external shapes, electronic emissions control, and coatings act to reduce radar return and thus the probability of detection of the object. Through the use of technology, it is possible to make objects virtually disappear, by blending into the background through the alteration of the visual spectrum. Sounds can be replicated to convince the intended target that planes are overhead or, conversely, that there are no planes in the vicinity.

Information fusion will also be a threat in this new Information Age. Capabilities will exist and be proliferated that will allow information technology to be fused with other means to enhance the effectiveness of institutions, eliminate uncertainty, and attack adversaries. Other nations, nonstate actors, and even individuals have and will continue to develop these links to advance their interests.

The means available to threaten U.S. interests in the Information Age are numerous and will continue to grow. Many have been discussed in this section, but certainly not in an exhaustive manner. The intent was to provide a broad understanding of the emerging national threats (and environment) we will face in the twenty-first century.

It goes without saying that not all of the means will be directly related to the growth of information technology; some may be related to advances in other scientific disciplines as well. What will be important in this new era is how information, that is, the collection, processing, dissemination, and protection of data as usable knowledge, will be essential to dealing with these threats.

PRINCIPLE 6: FREEDOM OF ACTION WILL BE REDUCED

This concept is perhaps counterintuitive and certainly will not be pleasing to those responsible for national security strategy and policy in the United States, but in the Information Age, we will have less freedom of action.

The natural conclusion one draws in considering national security is that the more ways and means we develop to use in executing national security strategy and policy, the more secure we will be as a nation. But this will not necessarily be the case—the important factor is not the total number of ways and means, but rather the ability to employ them in combination to achieve broad national interests and more narrowly defined goals and objectives, as well as to prevent or neutralize their use by potential enemies.

Advanced technologies that enhance the senses will provide extraordinary capability to the United States as well as to potential threats. Advances in optics and acoustics will allow for acquisition of signals at longer ranges. Combining these types of capabilities with robotics or unmanned air and ground vehicles will provide a powerful oversight ability that will be relatively simple to acquire, yet will provide a significant capability to the user.

The Internet and the amassed data available electronically provides a plethora of information on which to conduct pattern analysis, review written communications, determine national policies and actions, and develop trends. The ability to generate misinformation is also greatly enhanced through the expansion in Information Age technologies. One should consider that nothing sent over e-mail is secure unless some sort of encryption system is used. However, even the commercially available encryption systems only provide a moderate level of security.

Given an IP address, it is possible to conduct a surveillance of the network or computer system that resides on the network.

Cellular telephones are another source of readily available information. Many nations have cellular capability and the complementary means to detect, track, and monitor commercial cellular systems. This technology is commercially available and not particularly difficult to operate effectively. The expectation should be that cellular conversations are not secure and that anything said over a cellular telephone is being listened to by someone.

The application of national strategy, in particular the use of force, will attract a following such that no operation will be able to be conducted outside the scrutiny of the camera. One of the first experiences with this type of scrutiny was in Somalia during intervention for humanitarian purposes in January 1993. As the first waves of Marines came ashore, they were greeted by foreign correspondents and camera crews from countries across the globe. The images of this key news event were beamed back immediately and repeatedly. This certainly was not an isolated occurrence, but rather the beginning of a trend. The concept of real-time coverage greatly expanded with the embedding of reporters during combat operations in Iraq in 2003.

While embedding of reporters has occurred in other conflicts, the real-time, nearly uncensored coverage of the operations in Iraq was unprecedented. During World War II, reporters followed units and covered the war, but filed stories were carefully screened prior to release and certainly did not appear in real time. Of course, only printed media or newsreels seen in movie theaters were available back home. Today technology has improved to the point that live feeds are available from virtually anywhere in the world. Images of conflict can be provided and interpreted in a variety of ways, both favorable and unfavorable to the United States.

Even covert actions will undoubtedly become less covert. As information technologies proliferate, the ability to detect intrusions will increase. Technologies that were once very costly, highly classified, and not easily acquired will be available commercially. Consider night vision devices, which were once the exclusive tools of intelligence organizations and the military. Today, reasonable-quality night vision goggles are available at sporting goods stores and through catalogs. The same is true for a GPS, which provides down to one-meter resolution on position.

Even access to imagery, once the exclusive purview of only a handful of nations, is commercially available to individuals at the touch of a keyboard. Using imagery updated periodically, it is possible to check for changes in the images that could signal an incursion of some sort. The more often the information is refreshed, the greater the ability to see real-time changes.

The overall trend as we have moved into the Information Age has been to diminish the ability to operate outside the scrutiny of the public eye. The psychological impact of the Information Age on the development of policy will serve to constrain and moderate behavior. Nations and public figures are likely to feel intense pressure to pass the CNN or *Washington Post* test for policy decisions, whether for foreign or domestic issues. The test is simple. How will the public react to the news of the policy? A negative answer is likely to constrain behavior, while an affirmative response is likely to cause the policy-makers to feel empowered.

PRINCIPLE 7: THERE IS A TENUOUS RELATIONSHIP BETWEEN ENGAGEMENT AND RISK

A relationship exists between engagement and risk that warrants additional reflection. Both the failure to act and taking action can be risky propositions. The key is to determine the optimum interaction to achieve stated national security strategy goals, objectives, and policies without overexposing the nation and potentially diminishing what is essentially a limited or finite national power.

A failure to engage carries a risk of not achieving national goals and objectives as a result of inactivity or indecision. Essentially it becomes a policy of paralysis in which stimulus events occur but through inaction or indecision, the decision for action is turned over to others. The pre–World War II period illustrates the point. The United States had an internationalist view of the world with respect to economic development, but an isolationist view with respect to foreign affairs. The failure to engage in the aftermath of World War I allowed a power vacuum to be created and set the stage for the rise of Nazi Germany and Imperialist Japan. Rather than remaining engaged in the interwar period, the United States allowed others to assume the global leadership role. The results were inevitable, and the United States entered the war in response to others' actions rather than in a deliberate, purposeful way carefully crafted and orchestrated by the national security structures of the day.

At the center of the discussion of engagement and risk are really two different national security strategies. The two most recent administrations provide useful examples: "enlargement and engagement," articulated by the Clinton administration in 1996; and "preemption," articulated by the Bush administration following 9/11. Enlargement and engagement took a global view, recognizing America's special role in world affairs and allowing for limited interventions for less than vital interests while ensuring that the United States remained ready to respond to major regional conflicts, particularly in Southwest Asia and Korea. The strategy was also laced with discussions of arms control treaties, working with friends and allies, peace operations, and credible overseas presence. A cornerstone of the strategy was setting the conditions for the continued demise of the vestiges of the Soviet Union and its influence as well as assisting in securing its WMDs and preventing further proliferation. It was a strategy which assumed that

America was stronger when working to achieve its interests as part of the global community of nations. The risk was that international organizations are cumbersome, slow to act and reduce issues to the lowest common denominator.

On the other end of the spectrum is the strategy of preemption as articulated by the Bush administration, largely in reaction to the horrific terrorist attacks of 9/11. This strategy affirmed "America's sovereign right to attack potential foes before they could harm the United States."[19] Clearly, what separates other preemptive strategies from the Bush strategy was the use of America's power, not for imperialist designs, but rather to spread freedom, democracy, and respect for human rights throughout the globe, while destroying threats to peace and prosperity. To state that preemption is a new concept is really to bend the facts. In fact, NATO used a preemptive strategy in dealing with the Soviet Union and Warsaw Pact from the 1970s until the fall of the Berlin Wall, based on NATO's stated policy of flexible response, which relied on threatened use of a preemptive strike including the use of nuclear weapons to thwart a Warsaw Pact conventional attack. And the United States has acted in a preemptive manner on other occasions as well, including the strike on the alleged chemical munitions factory in Sudan in 1999. However, the underlying assumptions in the Bush formulation of preemption were: (1) only America can guarantee America's security, meaning that we cannot and must not be afraid to act alone if our security is threatened; and (2) we must not turn over America's security to international bodies such as the UN.

In thinking about the balance between engagement and risk, three preeminent maxims are worthy of consideration:

1. There is a greater risk for a global power and certainly for a hyperpower in engaging and losing than in not engaging at all. In the case of not engaging, the power is shown to be indifferent, while in the case of the power losing, it is shown to be vulnerable.

2. The hyperpower's dilemma: The very power that makes the United States a hyperpower also makes the United States a target. Having a global posture and the preeminent political, military, and economic stature in the world will most certainly cause rivalries and frictions to occur.

3. It is easy to become overextended, but nearly impossible to disengage. Examples of places where we still station large numbers of troops include Europe since 1943, Korea since 1953, Southwest Asia since 1990, and the Balkans since 1995.

PRINCIPLE 8: ASYMMETRY IN CONFLICT WILL BE THE NORM, NOT THE EXCEPTION

In recent policy-level discussions about asymmetry, the implications have been that this is some new type of warfare or that we are going to have to adjust our capabilities to address asymmetrical threats. This notion seems out of sync, for in reality warfare is asymmetrical by its very nature. One side or the other is always looking to gain an advantage or match its strength against the enemy's weakness. Certainly, asymmetry is not a new concept for U.S. military planners.

At the height of the Cold War, the methods used were asymmetrical, as NATO intended to use airpower and if necessary nuclear weapons to defeat a much larger Warsaw Pact armored force. The fact is that the United States is responsible for approximately 45 percent of all defense spending in the world, so regardless of which nation or nonstate actor challenges us in the future, the result will be an asymmetrical clash.

The case of terrorism takes asymmetry to the extreme, as the resources available to these organizations, while large and impressive by individual standards (e.g., bin Laden's estimated net worth of $300 million), pale in comparison to the $500 billion the U.S. armed forces spend yearly on defense. Note that this figure for U.S. spending does not include other nondefense spending such as the Intelligence Community or Department of Homeland Security, which also have large security-related spending.

The conclusion to be drawn is that future adversaries or even hostile competitors will look to eliminate advantages in U.S. weapons, technologies, and command and control. The result will be asymmetrical conflict and warfare.

Therefore, we should not expect head-to-head confrontations. Massed formations will spell almost immediate annihilation for the enemy; this will be even more true as weapons become more precise and powerful. Decentralized and limited strikes to disrupt or demoralize will most probably be the weapon of choice for most nations that engage the United States. Insurgency and counterinsurgency techniques will be the tools used most frequently in this type of warfare. The operations in Iraq in particular are reemphasizing the difficulties of engaging in limited warfare and nation building—it is also instructive that the insurgents in Iraq have been effectively using information technologies to fuel their conflict.

One area in which the adversary could potentially have a distinct advantage is Information Operations, especially in the realm of Public Affairs or Civil Affairs, which are two of the six components of IO.[20] While it would be difficult for an adversary to have a comparative advantage in the electronic aspects of IO, such as electronic warfare or electronic countermeasures, the ability to generate messages and misinformation to the public is an area where there is at least parity, if not a balance favoring the enemy. Mass media and the ease of production of messages, whether using digital cameras linked to the Internet (as was recently done in Iraq showing beheadings of civilians), Web sites to post anti-U.S. (or coalition) propaganda, or using printed media using computers and printers are all readily available means for an adversary.

Given the assertion that the Information Age will be a competition about ideas, the information operations trends discussed above will constitute a clear deficiency that must be corrected to ensure national security in this new age.

PRINCIPLE 9: THE UNITED STATES CANNOT HAVE TOO MANY ALLIES

Consideration of the Clinton and Bush administration policies with regard to allies provides opposite extremes in describing the U.S. approach to allies. However, that is not to say that one approach is correct and the other flawed. While allies are important and will be more so in the Information Age with the need to win the public opinion war, as President Bush points out, we cannot turn our nation's security over to allies and alliances. So there must be a constructive balance.

The Clinton administration sought to incorporate allies and organizations into decisions. Consultation with allies and international organizations, including the UN, was both routine and desirable. The notion was that allies were important to provide legitimacy to operations, but also for cooperation in other areas such as economics (trade policy), the environment, or the spread of democracy and respect for human rights. The Clinton administration also invested heavily in multilateral agreements, including arms control, Partnership for Peace (PFP) which sought to expand cooperation to the East to include former Soviet Union and Warsaw Pact nations, and NATO expansion.

The approach that the Bush administration adopted after 9/11 rendered allies more of a luxury than a necessity. In the Bush formulation, the United States sought to establish the moral compass and then offer like-minded nations the opportunity to enter into a coalition of the willing. To be fair, the policies that have been pursued reflect the ideology that some key and essential allies such as the UK and Australia are in the inner circle, while others can be brought in on an ad hoc basis if security interests overlap. Clearly, there is a recognition that a coalition is desirable for operations such as Iraq, but not a necessary precondition.

Inherent in the discussion of allies is the drive to promote democracy and the spread of democratic institutions around the globe, with a key tenet that democracies do not wage war against one another. In *The Lexus and the Olive Tree*, Friedman uses the tongue-in-cheek analogy that two nations that have McDonald's restaurants have never been to war against each other. Both the Clinton and Bush NSSs, despite their differences in approach to allies, agreed on the importance of democracies to maintaining security and stability.

The 1996 Clinton NSS points out:

> Secure nations are more likely to support free trade and maintain democratic structures. Free market nations with growing economies and strong open trade ties are more likely to feel secure and to work toward freedom. And democratic states are less likely to threaten our interests and more likely to cooperate with the United States and to meet security threats and promote free trade and sustainable development.[21]

The 2002 Bush NSS echoes this sentiment:

> America will encourage the advancement of democracy and economic openness in
> both nations [Russia and China], because these are the best foundations for domestic
> stability and international order.[22]

Clearly it is within the nation's interest to promote democracies and, by infer-
ence, allies or at least nations with a like-minded set of values.

Another key to success in the Information Age will be to avoid drawing
lines at a time when borders are being "virtually" erased. With the number of
nonstate and transnational threats that are emerging, like-minded, democrati-
cally based nations that can cooperate on either a multilateral or bilateral basis
will be essential to ensuring national security. The nonstate or transnational
threats will not hesitate to exploit seams between nations and alliances, and will
indeed work to develop seams where none exist.

A system of alliances such as NATO or ASEAN can and will be useful for
developing and sustaining international cooperation on areas of mutual interest.
These should be augmented with bilateral agreements around the globe to allow
for daily as well as crisis cooperation. The agreements in all cases should be
broad and should provide the maximum amount of cooperation in a variety of
areas including the political, economic, military, social, and informational. The
United States will not be able to conduct a reasonable foreign policy or maintain
national security in a globalized world without allies.

While the United States may be able to use a go-it-alone strategy for ac-
complishing near-term goals such as the early intervention in Afghanistan, the
world will not accept a long-term go-it-alone strategy.[23] Inevitably, systems of
cooperation (both bilateral and multilateral) in areas such as politics, law, legal
cooperation and intelligence would be diminished significantly. Consider a scenario where a country is providing intelligence information to the United States
about one of its citizens but does not want to take either legal, police, or military
action immediately. The fear is likely to be that the United States may take
unilateral action within the borders of that sovereign nation to eliminate the
perceived threat. How will a scenario such as this impact on bilateral or multilateral information sharing?

Stated more bluntly, nations will not be willing as a long-term policy to
have healthy and vibrant relationships in political, economic, social, and legal
areas without serving as equal partners or at least consultants in military and
intelligence areas. Furthermore, if globalization is occurring, then it would not
be in their interests to be less than full partners in the military and intelligence
fields, as breaches will impact on these nations as well in a globalized world.

One of the major debates about future scenarios is the development of a peer
competitor and what this could portend for the future. Perhaps this is the wrong
question to ask. It is inevitable that a peer to the United States will develop.

History demonstrates time and again how national power ebbs and flows. This issue seems particularly relevant given the recent discussion of empires, which became a current topic again with the publishing of Paul Kennedy's book in the 1990s, *The Rise and Fall of Great Powers*. History demonstrates what is likely to become of these great powers. The issue really is what kind of peer will develop.

This peer might not be a single nation, but rather a group of nations acting together. An example could be the EU, with the development of its political, economic, and now military cooperation; the EU is on the way to achieving peer status. Consider that the collection of twenty-five nations—with plans to increase—currently has an approximately 2.3 million person defense force and a GDP approximately equal to that of the United States. The United States, by contrast, has a force of 2.6 million people.[24] So the EU is already a peer in many respects. Other nations such as China, India, and Russia are chasing peer status as well, and while they are likely not going to be able to match the United States item by item, they will almost certainly develop peer capabilities in some areas at some point.

Perhaps the question that we should be asking is, "How do we develop peer collaborators rather than peer competitors?" A peer collaborator would hopefully share the same basic values and interests, but not necessarily—perhaps a peer collaborator would be willing to cooperate on specific issues in a mutually beneficial way. The seeds for developing and nurturing a peer collaborator rather than competitor will need to be sown early and tended carefully. The time to begin this process is not on the eve of a major crisis or, worse yet, following a global catastrophe. Rather, the time is now.

PRINCIPLE 10: SOME COMBINATIONS OF NATIONS AND ALLIANCES MAY NATURALLY THREATEN THE UNITED STATES

It is unfortunate to have to consider that some societies and the certain nations will develop to become a natural threat to U.S. national security. Despite our best intentions, many developing nations in particular will likely look at the West and the United States in particular as an enemy. Where political instability and economic deprivation reside, it is highly likely that anti-U.S. tendencies will also be present. While this may be a natural outcome associated with developed versus developing or nondeveloped nations, the United States will need to establish a strategy for dealing with these concerns before such nations change from issue to threat.

Development of the peoples of the world will continue to proceed in a nonlinear and unequal matter. Notice that the term *state* has been omitted; this was a deliberate omission, as the Information Age will allow virtual states and groupings of people to flourish, with significant implications, as was discussed under principle 1. The point is that where development is unequal, security issues and threats will emerge.

Examples of fractured societies include several countries in Africa and many states within the Islamic community. In the case of these African nations, both internal and transnational fracturing are occurring. The internal fracturing occurs when societies implode, as with the recent killings in Darfur, a province of Sudan, where estimates are that 50,000–80,000 have been killed. In truth, even the Darfur killings could be considered to be transnational if the Zaghawa tribe being oppressed by the Sudanese government and the Janjaweed, nomadic Arab bandits, are each considered to be nations.

Looking at the Islamic community provides an example of transnational fracturing. That is, the Islamic community is spread throughout the world, and which countries members reside in determines the average GDP that segment of the community will enjoy. Obviously, Islamic community members living in the United States enjoy a different standard of living than those living in the Gaza Strip. The disparity between the two subcommunities and the interaction they may have is fueled by Information Age means and will cause tensions that inevitably lead to conflict if not addressed to the satisfaction of the entire community.

Third world ideas with Information Age capability are a dangerous combination. A perfect image of the issue appeared several years ago on the cover of a weekly news magazine, showing an African sheepherder in traditional dress tending his flock with a staff in one hand and a cellular telephone in the other. This one picture captured the coming together of the Agrarian and Information Ages. But what happened to the Industrial Age?

The progression of societies through the Industrial Age did not magically prepare them for the Information Age; rather, it forced people to confront issues and develop national policies such as containment and deterrence that are in turn useful in developing concepts for the Information Age and the challenges and opportunities that it will provide.

Certainly this concern should not be limited to African nations. The same holds for theocracies that see all issues through a religious fundamentalist lens. A theocracy that places religion above all else will naturally be threatened by the United States and, for that matter, other democratic nations. The views of a nation or society based on liberal ideology and respect for human rights will be a natural antagonist for a religion-based society that places ideology above the rights of the individual.

Another threat to the United States will be the emergence of more diverse power centers that seek to provide a counterweight to the perceived hegemonic power of the United States. While the example of the EU was already provided above, this in all likelihood will not turn into a long-term threat. However, other power centers exist that could combine, if only for a limited period, to threaten U.S. interests either at home or abroad.

PRINCIPLE 11: IT'S A MATTER OF WHEN, NOT IF

At a meeting at a foreign policy think tank in mid-2004, a speaker made the statement, "It's only a matter of time before the U.S. becomes Israel." This is a powerful statement requiring careful consideration and reflection.

The implication is that the security situation could get considerably worse in the United States. So are we to believe that the 9/11 attacks were simply a terrorist appetizer? The loss of some 3,000 innocents will likely be forever remembered in American history and has already led to two conventional conflicts in Iraq and Afghanistan as well as interventions with covert forces in literally dozens of other countries and regions, including the Horn of Africa, the Philippines, Indonesia, and Yemen.

However, despite these losses and the threats that remain, people are already talking about the long-term implications of the Patriot Act and the need to repeal the provisions that impact on civil liberties, personal rights, and freedoms. What if the United States becomes Israel and daily threats in shopping malls, movie theaters, and grocery stores increase dramatically? What about public transportation or even water supplies and other infrastructure?

Over the period from September 27, 2000, through May 1, 2004, 921 people were killed in terrorist attacks in Israel, out of a population of 6.2 million. If that same rate occurred in the United States, the number killed during that same period would have been 43,524.[25] Imagine how U.S. society would be changed or would need to change under these conditions.

Stephen Flynn in his book *America the Vulnerable* detailed the significant security implications of our largely unprotected civilian infrastructure. Imagine the personal and fiscal loss that could result from an attack on U.S. infrastructure, either our energy or water supply, or perhaps both in combination. Our enemies certainly have the ability to conduct analysis and predict the success of an operation. Let us assume that in a potential operation, the terrorist wants to have a 90 percent chance of success. Using a simple probability analogy, if one weapon is moved from the terrorist hideout through the ports and the probability of detection en route is 25 percent for the entire trip, then shipping one weapon would give the terrorist a 75 percent probability of success. By shipping two weapons with the same probability of detection, the terrorist would have a probability of 93.75 percent (calculated using the equation $1-[.25] \times [.25]$). If the terrorist ships a third weapon, the probability climbs to 98.4 percent. Of course, this discussion assumes that the weapon will detonate as planned and that the weapon is not a dud. But do we really want to place our security on the hope that terrorists are inept?

The footnote to this analogy is that a 25 percent chance of discovering a weapon is quite high given the amount of illegal contraband that flows into the United States on a daily basis. The availability of drugs on the street is evidence of the magnitude of the problem. The chance of detection can be increased using several barriers or checks in tandem. So if there is a system as described above and a second complementary system with a similar probability of detection, then the chance of success for the first weapon to get through the double barrier system is .75 × .75 or 56.25 percent. Still, by shipping three weapons, the chance of success for the terrorist climbs to over 90 percent (i.e., 1−[.4375] × [.4375] × [.4375] or approximately 92 percent), even with the double barrier system.

The bottom line is that probability and statistics are against us. Given an open society, with nearly unlimited freedoms and personal rights, it really is only a matter of time before the United States becomes Israel. Our borders are largely unmonitored and certainly unprotected. Every day, thousands of containers pour into this country—do we know what is inside them? The number of people entering through controlled access points is also significant—over 42 million per year in 2003. However, do we have an accurate way to verify their identities and ensure they are not a threat to the United States? The fact is that if enough capability is exhausted by our adversaries, the probability of success becomes quite high.

That really brings the argument to the point where we need to ask, "Is there such a thing as acceptable losses? The emotional response is that no loss of American life or property is acceptable. However, what price will we pay for an aggressive, engaging foreign policy? This discussion begs a series of questions that will be examined in greater detail in a later section, but the relevant question here is, are we as a nation prepared for the next major attack on the homeland?

PRINCIPLE 12: IT'S THE ECONOMY, STUPID

There is an important reason why democracies do not fight each other and thus why countries with greater economic capacity have less instability. To borrow a line from the Clinton-Gore campaign of 1992, "It's the economy, stupid."

A relationship exists between the formation of democratic institutions and economic prosperity. Nations that have established institutions and laws promoting individual rights and freedoms, respect for democratic institutions, and rule of law have stronger economies than nations that lack basic protections and freedoms for their people.

Generally speaking, nations with democratic institutions also have greater liberalization, better management, more transparency in financial dealings, and thus less corruption. This translates to a more equitable distribution of wealth, with more of the country's citizens afforded the opportunity to have meaningful employment, amass wealth, and attain a higher standard of living. Taken together, this translates to overall greater prosperity.

Comparing basic national statistics such as gross national product (GNP) per capita, life expectancy, population growth, median age, infant mortality, rate of HIV/AIDS infection, and literacy rate leads to the conclusion that there is a nearly direct relationship between them. Where the GNP per capita is low, it is not at all surprising to find large and growing youthful populations, high infant mortality and unemployment, and low life expectancy. It follows that nations with a low GNP per capita are also likely to have a low degree of industrialization and fairly limited Information Age capability, and thus limited means for enhancing their prospects.

TABLE 1. Correlation Between Democracy and Economic Well-Being

Top 15 from *2004* *Index of Economic Freedom*	**Government Type as Assessed in** *CIA Fact Book*	Bottom 15 from *2004* *Index of Economic Freedom*	**Government Type as Assessed in** *CIA Fact Book*
Hong Kong	Limited democracy	Vietnam	Communist
Singapore	Parliamentary republic	Nigeria	Republic transitioning from military to civilian rule
New Zealand	Parliamentary democracy	Suriname	Constitutional democracy
Luxembourg	Constitutional monarchy	Cuba	Communist
Iceland	Constitutional republic	Belarus	Republic
Estonia	Parliamentary republic	Tajikistan	Republic
UK	Constitutional monarchy	Venezuela	Federal republic
Denmark	Constitutional monarchy	Iran	Theocratic republic
Switzerland	Federal republic	Uzbekistan	Authoritarian presidential rule
United States	Constitution-based federal republic	Turkmenistan	Republic
Australia	Democratic	Myanmar	Military regime
Sweden	Constitutional monarchy	Laos	Communist
Chile	Republic	Zimbabwe	Parliamentary republic
Cyprus	Republic (only Greek side)	Libya	Military dictatorship
Finland	Republic	North Korea	Communist state, one-man dictatorship

Given these sorts of dire national indicators, it follows that nations in the situation described above would also have conditions ripe for breeding instability and conflict. For example, untrained and unemployed youth with few perceived opportunities will be a disenfranchised group that will create instability within a society. Dire economic prospects and too much time to contemplate their conditions helps foment discontent and even breed hatred among this group.

A comparison using the metrics on democracy and economic prosperity demonstrates the linkage (table 1). The economic information comes from the *2004 Index of Economic Freedom* published by the Heritage Foundation. The rankings represent an amalgamation of several factors, including corruption, nontariff barriers to trade, fiscal burden of government, rule of law, regulatory burdens, restrictions on banks, labor market regulations, and informal market activities. The information concerning type of government is provided by the *Central Intelligence Agency (CIA) Fact Book*, current as of January 1, 2004.

While the data are largely anecdotal, they do depict a relationship between economic freedom and political freedom. It is also interesting to note that several of the counties in the bottom fifteen are former satellites of the Soviet Union and thus in the early stages of liberalization and democratic reform.

Several recent conflicts also demonstrate the degree to which economic prosperity or lack thereof contributes to political instability and conflict. Consider the Balkans, where the conflict in Bosnia has roots in the demographic and economic plight of the Serbs and Croats. The Muslim community tended to be city dwellers with an increasing population while the Croats and Serbs we are agrarian based societies with declining populations. The overall prospects for the Muslims seemed to be improving while prospects for the Serbs and Croats seemed to be in decline.

The current situation in Sudan in the Darfur region is another case where economics has at least helped to ignite the conflict. Landowners, upset by migrations of a black majority population for the grazing of livestock, ignited violence against the herders.

Certainly not all conflict is a direct result of economics. However, there is a strong link. This implies that to ensure a stable and secure world, economic prosperity is a strong factor, and it follows that it is in the interest of the United States and our allies to promote economic prosperity through appropriate policies, education, and support.

3

U.S. NATIONAL SECURITY STRATEGY

RECENT ADVANCES IN INFORMATION technologies and the ability to gather, process, and disseminate information may cause some to argue that we have already arrived in the Information Age. Others may argue emphatically that we are merely at the early stages of this new era. Few still may even be willing to take the position that the world is conducting business as usual and not transforming to a new age.

Wherever one stands in this discussion, one thing is clear. New capabilities related to information and knowledge are having, and will continue to have, a profound impact on interactions between nations, societies, and peoples. Whether this signals a new age is largely an academic question; however, the very real impact that technology, primarily information technology, is having cannot and should not be ignored.

No single event signifies the end of one age and the beginning of another. Certainly, some key indicators serve to warn of impending changes to the environment, but no billboard sign flashes to alert the world of this transition. Rather, the move from one age to another happens at glacial speed, meaning that there are small movements over a long period of time. These movements will be imperceptible unless one steps back and takes a broader perspective. Only in this way will the magnitude of the change become apparent. For this reason, it would be difficult to pinpoint an exact time and place where history, nations, and peoples move from one age to another. This sort of exact determination is avoided in this discussion as it would do little more than invite criticism.

If one considers the move from the Agrarian (or Preindustrial) Age to the Industrial Age, there is certainly no agreed date at which the transition was made.

In about the mid-1750s in England, significant changes were underway that clearly indicated a major change in society. However, this change did not uniformly occur throughout the world. For example, in the United States, the move to the Industrial Age was thought to have originated in the 1790s with the development of the cotton gin by Eli Whitney. Even today, there are still societies and nations around the globe where the transition to the Industrial Age either has not occurred or is certainly debatable.

Perhaps an obvious statement but one that must be made concerns the development of nations, states, societies, and civilizations. These entities develop at different rates for a variety of reasons—the result is that if one looks around the world, Agrarian, Industrial, and Information Age societies can be identified today. While these developmental patterns and rates are interesting and certainly important to the manner in which the United States interfaces with other nations, they are somewhat beyond the scope of this book. As a result, this book focuses primarily on the United States, and therefore was written with an eye toward examining the national security implications for the United States in this new and emerging Information Age.

The examination of each period in the history of United States, even with a focus on national security strategy development, may again seem elemental. However, the discussions are intended to provide insights into how our grand strategy has evolved over time, and how each transitional point has added to the foundation. Therefore, at the end of each subsection, a short synopsis of the key contributions to our national strategy development from each period has been provided.

THE FOUNDING OF THE UNITED STATES

The current national security of the United States is in large measure a direct result of the history of our nation. The cauldron in which the United States was formed was filled with ideas and principles about what a government should do for its people and, in turn, the social contract under which the citizens of a free and open society should abide. We have largely adhered to these early pronouncements throughout our history. As well, our national security strategy and policies have also taken these legacies into account and have largely followed them.

The War of Independence was the first collective expression of our national security—that is, our fledgling nation and our citizens standing for and gaining freedom from England. With the birth of our nation in 1776 with the signing of the Declaration of Independence, our citizens signaled their desire to form an independent nation-state free from the tyranny of the English monarchy.

The Constitution and Bill of Rights reflect clear, concise statements of national purpose. They are short and succinct, yet packed with detail and implications for federal, state, and local governments. These founding documents also contain a sort of social contract that places requirements for and limitations on behavior for our citizens. Perhaps equally significant is that these foundational pronouncements have indeed stood the test of time and have remained unchanged for almost 230 years. Examination of the first lines of the Constitution clearly articulates the national security implications:

> *We the People* of the United States, in Order to form a more perfect Union, establish Justice, insure domestic Tranquility, provide for the common defense, promote the general Welfare, and secure the Blessings of Liberty to ourselves and our Posterity, do ordain and establish this Constitution for the United States of America.

The Founding Fathers could not have been clearer on the issue of securing our nation and people from any and all means of threat. These are powerful ideas, with equally weighty requirements for the public servants and citizens of our nation. In fact, it would be nearly impossible to look at any aspect of government today and not be able to trace its actions back to either the Constitution or Bill of Rights.

As our nation has grown and matured, the Constitution has been changed by way of adding amendments eleven through twenty-seven. Despite the inherent ability to make changes, the basic underpinnings of the Constitution and Bill of Rights remain intact. Key Constitutional changes such as the repeal of slavery and the right of women to vote have ensured that all of our nation's citizens are protected equally. But in the area of national security, there has been little change to the basic tenets of the original documents. It is quite remarkable that, given the changes in our society and around the world, these cornerstone documents have survived and remain relevant nearly 230 years later.

The early years of our nation's security were primarily focused on developing and exploring our own continent, with the exception of the War of 1812, in which the United States's national sovereignty was threatened for the second time since declaring freedom from England.[1] After once again settling the issue of independence from England, the United States turned toward its frontiers and the acquisition of territories on the continent that today comprise the contiguous forty-eight states. The major threats during this period were constituted by the indigenous peoples of North America, settling the untamed and largely unexplored regions beyond the Mississippi River, and from outside powers with designs on colonization of the New World. However, despite these challenges to our claims by outside powers, the national focus remained on developing relationships between the federal and state governments and exploring the West.

Also in this period, the United States developed a Regular Army both to provide for the defense of the country and to assist the westward expansion. During this early period, the defense forces of our nation were developed and became professionalized. In proportion to the amount of trade, exploration and colonization, the United States also developed a navy capable of defending America's interests abroad. In keeping with the framework of the Constitution, a key tenet of this development of the military was and continues to be civilian control.

The ability of the United States to rapidly advance in its first one hundred years was directly related to geography and natural resources. These factors combined to allow for independence and development in a way that no other nation on the globe could manage. Geography provided a relative buffer from many of the external conflicts that embroiled other nations. To attack the United States, an aggressor nation would need to organize a major and lengthy expedition that would lack the direct support of its parent nation. The expeditionary force would need to be entirely self-sufficient. The resources of our nation have likewise also contributed greatly to our development.[2] Furthermore, the values and ideals on which this nation was built provided the key foundations for balancing state and individual rights.

Certainly during the century from 1770 to 1870, there was opportunity to engage with other nations. However, the United States was able to remain free of the entangling alliances that caused blocs of nations to go to war. In Europe, the Napoleonic Wars raged for over twenty years in the late 1790s and early 1800s. Outside of sending military observers, the United States had no direct involvement. Likewise in the Franco-Prussian war in the 1870s, the United States was able to remain an observer. In this way, the United States was able to concentrate resources and focus on national growth and development. While it was a very painful time in American history, the Civil War was really a culmination of early U.S. national development.

A cornerstone of American foreign policy was delivered in President Monroe's message to Congress on December 2, 1823, the Monroe Doctrine. It became one of the most important proclamations that guided U.S. national security in this early period, establishing our intent to keep the Western Hemisphere free from colonization by outside powers.[3] The Monroe Doctrine reflects the first formal declaration of national security following the founding of the United States. Essentially, the United States informed the powers of the Old World that the American continents were no longer open to European colonization, and that any effort to extend European political influence into the New World would be considered by the United States "dangerous to our peace and safety." The United States would not interfere in European wars or internal affairs and expected Europe to stay out of American affairs.

Although it would take decades to coalesce into an identifiable policy, John Quincy Adams did raise the standard of an independent American foreign policy so strongly that future administrations could not ignore it. One should note, however, that the policy succeeded because it promoted British interests as well as American, and for the next one hundred years it was secured by the backing of the British fleet.[4]

U.S. development in terms of political, military, and economic capacity by 1865 had matured to the point where the United States was perhaps the most prosperous nation in the world. The political structures and processes that would protect our nation, interests, and citizens were in place. The economy was growing, aided by factors including our geographic location that allowed us to avoid many of the conflicts of European nations, a rich natural resource base, and a growing ability to trade with other nations. Meanwhile the military was gaining strength and capability with increased firepower, development of a navy, and the development of the railroad and telegraph systems in this country. However, the military, the national security apparatus of the United States, was largely tied to defense within the area defined by the continental borders. As a result, the Army established forts throughout the country and the Navy focused on development of coastal fortifications rather than military forces to project power around the globe. With the increases in trading, exploration, and colonization by the United States, the Navy did, however, expand its capability for projecting power. This was the state of the U.S. military on the eve of the Civil War.

The final major cataclysmic event in the forming of our nation was the Civil War. Our nation turned inward to answer the question of whether we would remain a single nation or become two separate nations. The conflict set brother against brother, states against states, and two "nations" against each other. The issue was settled on April 9, 1865, with the signing of the surrender at the Appomattox Courthouse—this act marked the final chapter of the Confederacy's history and led to the reintegration of the North and South into a single nation.

This early period from the War of Independence to the end of the Civil War was largely a time of internal national development; the United States did little in terms of interaction with other nations. Indeed, the Civil War and the period immediately thereafter even tended to stunt the growth of the United States as a global power, since during this time our national security focused on healing the nation rather than on external relations. Certainly there was little, if any, interest in becoming involved in the internal affairs of other nations or commitments to entangling alliances. It was a time of inward growth and reflection.

To more fully examine U.S. national security strategy over the course of our nation's history, the following discussion draws on a Congressional Research Service (CRS) report titled *Instances of Use of United States Armed Forces Abroad, 1798–2001*. This document (updated February 5, 2002) provides a list of the commitments of force during this period, including the location, time frame, and a brief description of each action. The subsequent analysis and generalizations are based, at least in part, on this data set.

The manner in which the United States used the military throughout our early history makes the point that early uses of force, and by extension the expression of national security strategy, had limited and narrowly focused purposes. Specifically, the one hundred-year period from 1798 to 1898 lists ninety-eight uses of U.S. armed forces abroad. Analysis indicates that each of these deployments of forces were to protect American lives and property, punish others for indiscretions against American citizens or property, ensure freedom of navigation, acquire additional lands, or protect the territorial integrity of the United States. Not a single instance is listed in which U.S. forces attempted to intervene directly in the affairs of other nations.

Of the ninety-eight instances cited, seventy were related to protecting U.S. citizens and property. Early examples of this type of action include an operation in 1801 in Tripoli to free the crew of the *SS Philadelphia*, or an 1832 action in Sumatra in which U.S. naval forces landed to storm a fort in retribution for an attack on a U.S. ship. A number of instances are also related to preventative actions taken to ensure the safety of American citizens and property during periods of turmoil in foreign nations, such as the 1833 operation in which U.S. forces landed in Argentina to protect U.S. interests during a revolution in that country.

Of the remaining actions, fourteen were conducted to ensure access to markets and freedom of navigation, a key to U.S. economic development. These instances included several operations to suppress, attack, or kill pirates who threatened U.S. free trade. These final instances included actions where U.S. forces were used in the protection or acquisition of additional territories. Examples include the deployment in 1800 of forces to Spanish territory in what is today Florida, during which U.S. forces seized Mobile Bay and defeated the Spanish garrison, or the 1818 deployment in Oregon in which U.S. forces settled the territorial dispute by annexing this area from Britain, Russia, and Spain.

Examining the regions to which U.S. forces were deployed in this one hundred-year period also demonstrates that the United States was also limiting its interventions geographically. Over half, fifty-four of the ninety-eight instances of the use of force, were in the area covered by the Monroe Doctrine. The focus of our nation's leaders was on the Western Hemisphere, with the rest of the world a distant second.

When forces were used outside the area covered by the Monroe Doctrine, the actions tended to be of a limited nature. For example, in 1856, the United States launched an expedition to China from October 22 to December 6 to "protect American interests at Canton during hostilities between the British and the Chinese, and to avenge an assault upon an unarmed boat displaying the U.S. flag."[5] Upon completion of this narrowly focused task, the force returned to the United States. This example is typical of the operations that were conducted. Most tended to be short in duration and for a specific purpose. They were not overly complex in their goals and were easily achievable. None of the operations conducted in this period had goals of intervening in the internal affairs of another sovereign nation, in contrast to recent operations undertaken by the United States and our allies in Bosnia in 1995, Afghanistan in 2001, and Iraq in 2003.

Of course, the CRS report cited above indicates only where U.S. forces were used in special circumstances and does not indicate the normal daily uses and stationing of military forces to protect U.S. interests at home or abroad. For example, the report also does not capture the establishment of forts and garrisons throughout the continental United States that were built to assist in settling the West or to protect citizens against Indian attacks, and also fails to account for the daily normal stationing of U.S. forces around the world, such as in embassies.

The normal stationing of army and naval forces to protect U.S. integrity during this early period was an integral part of U.S. national security that deserves mention. The ability to push westward was directly related to the establishment of forts and outposts. Many of today's military installations remain in areas that once served to support the development of the country. For example, Fort Leavenworth, Kansas, is on high ground directly above the Missouri River and served as a frontier outpost for travelers and settlers going west, where it provided protection to citizens and soldiers from Indian attacks and for some time acted as the border between civilization and the unsettled West.

The early foundations, including the values and ideals, emerging from the formation of U.S. national security strategy and policy continue today to play a preeminent role and will undoubtedly serve to guide policy formulation well into the Information Age.

Conclusions

- The United States is a nation founded on values and ideals and it follows that our national security strategy has been and will continue to be guided in this way.
- Special circumstances and conditions will continue to contribute to our national development and success, including natural resources and geography.
- The Monroe Doctrine has been a guiding force for the development of U.S. national security strategy.

U.S. NATIONAL SECURITY STRATEGY IN THE INDUSTRIAL AGE: THE AWAKENING

The period from the Declaration of Independence to 1898 really constitutes the early stages of the Industrial Age in this country. Capabilities and technology developed to support a modernizing nation also contributed to the development of the United States as a political, economic, and military powerhouse.

Railroads, which supported the move west and the acquisition and protection of settled territories, fueled economic development. The push west necessitated a means of communication, hence the development of a telegraph system and, by the end of the nineteenth century, the telephone. Our history as a trading nation required the establishment of a blue-water navy[6] with the ability to protect American interests around the globe—a trading nation relies as much on military power as political and economic power to ensure that interests are protected by international laws and treaties. The same steam power that propelled the fleet and the railroads ran the factories. In this way, the political, economic, and military elements of national power matured and the United States met the conditions for full emergence into the Industrial Age and eventually as a superpower.

Globally, foreign affairs and military matters changed significantly during this period, and the United States was not exempt from these influences. First and foremost, the capabilities of nations to feed their people through the use of more advanced farming equipment and techniques freed people from subsistence farming and allowed nations to field larger, more capable forces. The discovery of electricity and the development of the railroad system and more advanced ships allowed and encouraged more interactions between nations. With these interactions came the frictions and tensions that inevitably led to confrontations of a more direct and violent nature.

Colonization created competition between nations, as states vied for territories and established claims across the globe. Acquisitions provided a source of raw materials and markets for goods, as well as increasing the size of the colonizing nation's empire. For each acquisition, the colonizing nation left behind security detachments to ensure the loyalty and protection of the new colony. In this way, colonizing nations set about developing expeditionary forces with bases around the globe that needed to be protected, resupplied, and developed.

While the United States was involved in this type of activity, national desires to avoid becoming involved in the affairs of other nations limited interventions. Although the U.S. military had served as observers in actions around the globe, the first major foray outside of the United States occurred in Cuba in 1898. Russ Weigley, a military historian, writes:

> After the Battleship Maine exploded in Havana Harbor, Congress added two regiments of artillery to the Regular Army, to bring the authorized strength to 28,747 officers and men. The Spanish had about 80,000 soldiers in Cuba. The saving features as war approached were the quality of the small Regular Army, in combat proficiency if not in organization, and . . . the citizens' militia companies. Around these two poles the national strength was to rally, to begin successfully the adventure of world power.[7]

On April 19, 1898, Congress authorized the President to "employ the entire land and naval forces of the United States to secure the independence of Cuba."[8]

The Spanish-American War was notable in American military history and in foreign policy for two key reasons. First, it was successful as a military intervention during which an American force defeated the Spanish handily. Second, the conflict established the United States as a regional power willing to back up the Monroe Doctrine with force, if necessary. Previously, the United States had sent forces outside of its territorial limits for protection of its citizens or property only; however, the Spanish-American War was the first major military mission primarily on behalf of the interests of another nation.

Also noteworthy during this early period was the U.S. response to the Boxer Rebellion in China from May to September 1900. The Chinese had become resentful toward Japan and Western countries because of their economic and political exploitation and humiliating military defeats of China. In response, a secret society of Chinese called the Boxers began terrorizing Christian missionaries in 1899. Eventually, terrorizing led to outright attacks in which scores of Chinese and foreigners were killed. The Boxer Rebellion was really an attempt by the secret society to drive the Western powers out of China. The response to the rebellion by the Western powers was to put down the revolt and occupy the city. The action becomes noteworthy in that it was the first time that the United States participated in a multinational military coalition abroad.

The emergence of the United States as a global power and the changes in national security strategy can be directly traced to the development of the U.S. Navy. Secretary of War Henry L. Stimson recalled "the peculiar psychology of the Navy Department, which frequently seemed to retire from the realm of logic into a dim religious world in which Neptune was God, Mahan his prophet and the United States Navy the only true Church."[9] As the Navy grew in size and capability, the ability of the United States to operate far from our own coasts grew. Alfred Thayer Mahan, himself a naval officer and the son of the dean of faculty at the U.S. Military Academy, came to prominence primarily as a result of two historical books on sea power, *The Influence of Sea Power upon History, 1660–1793* and *The Influence of Sea Power upon the French Revolution and Empire, 1793–1812*. It was not the content so much as the visibility that these volumes generated that gave Mahan a bully pulpit from which to develop U.S. naval strategy and in turn U.S. national security strategy.

Mahan's definition of sea power, which gained believers within the highest offices of the U.S. government, highlights the direct linkage to national security that he postulated: "(1) Production; (2) Shipping; (3) Colonies and Markets—in a word, sea power."[10] Specifically, on strategy, Mahan wrote, "The stoppage of commerce compels peace. Wars are won by economic strangulation of an enemy from the sea."[11]

His writings influenced policymakers to redirect national strategy, leading to a more outwardly focused strategy. Within naval circles, his writings also had a significant impact as he led the charge to move from a brown-water navy or coastal force designed to protect America close to home to a blue-water navy with the ability to project power globally. With this shift in focus came a shift in capability that would launch the expeditionary or global focus of today.

The one hundred-plus years from 1898 to the present deserve some scrutiny, as it is during this period that the United States became first a global power, then a superpower, and now finally the world's only hyperpower. It is also during this period that the world, or at least its leading nations, moved from the early Industrial Age to the early stages of the Information Age.

This period is noteworthy for rapid and dramatic changes as well. In the thousands of years of human existence prior to 1900, humans progressed from using subsistence hunting and gathering to methodical techniques for sheltering, feeding, and protecting themselves. Societies and states formed. Progress was steady but certainly not rapid. A person living for one hundred years in the 1500s would see little change throughout a lifetime. Roughly the same can be said for a person living in the 1700s. Improvements to quality of life and the capability to sustain societies did occur, but these changes were slow and steady.

However, a person born at the turn of the twentieth century saw and experienced mind-boggling change. In 1900, there were trains, but the primary means of transportation were foot or horseback. By the end of the twentieth century, men had walked on the moon, communications had become instantaneous, and the means of transportation were numerous, rapid, and readily available. A trip across the ocean from America to Europe that took three or four weeks in 1900 can now be made in hours and is available for the price of a plane ticket. To put this industrialization into perspective with an analogy, nearly all of history has preceded on a linear scale across the ages in a plodding, methodical, and almost predictable way. Yet in the Industrial Age, change was measured not on a linear scale, but rather on a logarithmic scale where each tick on the graph was an increase of 10-, 100-, or 1,000-fold.

Just as industrialization has made logarithmic changes in the economic, social, and cultural aspects of our society and around the globe, equally dramatic changes have occurred in the United States (and throughout the world) in political and military capabilities and interactions. Stated more succinctly, national security changes in the United States as a direct result of industrialization would be as mind boggling to the person living from 1900 to 2000 as the changes in the economy, transportation, and communications.

For U.S. national security in particular, the significant change borders on the inconceivable. Beginning with the first intervention in 1898 to assist Cuba in gaining independence from Spain, the next hundred or so years of national security policy development through the end of the Industrial Age have been extraordinary. As a measure of change in U.S. national security policy from 1898 to the present, I use the CRS data set again to illustrate the point.

While the argument is made later that a national security strategy in the Information Age will need to be broader than a simple commitment of forces to achieve national security objectives, the historical precedents on the commitment of forces are instructive in understanding the evolution of America's national security strategy during the period from 1898 to the present.

It is worth stating that the data set is limited. It does not include "covert actions, disaster relief and routine alliance stationing and training exercises,"[12] which have occupied a preeminent place in modern military employment. Therefore, the data do not directly include the deployment of forces during the Cold War in Europe or Korea, and also fails to account for special operations missions or other covert operations such as the 1979 attempted rescue of hostages held in Iran. Another flaw in the data set is that a single, short-duration operation such as the deployment of three aircraft to the Congo in 1967 to provide logistical support to the government is a single-line entry, just as the Vietnam War from 1964 to 1973, as the data do not attempt to measure operations in terms of level of commitment or man-days, for example. Rather, the data focus on conventional operational deployments for specific missions. Despite these cautions, the CRS data provide relevant insight into our security policy changes during this period.

Table 2 has been developed using the original data set from the CRS report. The data originally consisted of a list of operations over time with a brief description of each. To construct the table, judgments have been made concerning the categorization of the individual instances of the use of force. Where operations had multiple purposes, an attempt has been made to identify the primary rationale for the commitment of force. As an example, the Berlin Airlift could be characterized as a humanitarian or security operation, or even as a resistance. For this analysis, it has been characterized as a humanitarian operation.

The complete data set and the definitions of each type of operations are provided in appendix A. In addition, a brief description of each listed operation

TABLE 2. Instances of the Use of Force, 1898–Present

	1898–1913	1914–40	1941–75	1976–89	1990–Present	Total
Number of years	15	26	34	23	14	112
Conventional operations	2	2	5	7	19	35
Security operations	26	22	9	3	5	65
Peacekeeping operations	2	8	2	3	37	52
Noncombatant evacuation	0	0	6	3	13	22
Humanitarian relief	0	0	1	0	5	6
Resistance and counterinsurgency	0	1	6	5	3	15
Counterdrug operations	0	0	0	2	0	2
Counterterrorism	0	0	0	2	3	5
Total	30	33	29	25	85	202
Average per year	2.0	1.3	0.9	1.1	6.1	1.8

has been provided. However, the intent is not to review each of the operations in detail, but rather to use the data to assist in drawing conclusions about the use of force in this period, and by extension the national security strategy of the United States. The time horizons were delineated as they represent transitional periods— more about these delineations is discussed in each of the sections.

SHEDDING THE MANTLE OF ISOLATIONISM, 1898–1914

Prior to 1898, the United States had established a clear isolationist national security strategy. This fact was evident in our dealings with other nations and the public pronouncements made by the U.S. government. Clearly the most aggressive pronouncement was the Monroe Doctrine, stating U.S. intentions to limit protection of our interests in the Western Hemisphere. However, beginning in 1898 with the U.S. intervention in Cuba during the Spanish-American War and followed closely by the U.S. intervention in the Philippines from 1899 to 1901, U.S. national security policy essentially began a revolution.

The initial fifteen-year period from 1898 to 1913 saw an average of two operations per year, but most, twenty-six of the thirty, were security operations to protect American citizens and property, the traditional types of operations. Only four of the operations could be classified as conventional or peacekeeping operations. Included in these totals are the first conventional operations: the 1898 intervention in Cuba against the Spanish, discussed previously, and an operation in the Philippines in which the Filipino push for independence was thwarted by U.S. forces.

The Filipino operation is particularly noteworthy as it reflects the first time that U.S. forces were deployed in a conventional operation outside an area covered within the limits of the Monroe Doctrine. The peacekeeping operations included use of force in Cuba and Panama to assist in restoring order and establishing a stable government in the former and to assist in supervising elections at the request of both political parties in the latter.

The writings of Mahan and the desire for economic growth in terms of markets and resources were certainly drivers of our national security policy during this period. In the absence of any formal national security strategy, Mahan's work served as a surrogate for a strategy to protect U.S. interests abroad and continue to expand our growing outward focus.

Conclusions

- Despite a strong desire to remain independent, the drive for economic growth and prosperity drove a complementary growth in national security capabilities and intent to use them if necessary.

- The Monroe Doctrine was a strong signal of U.S. resolve to protect our regional interests directed at nations potentially interested in operating in the Western Hemisphere.

U.S. ISOLATION AND THE SEEDS OF WORLD WAR II, 1914–40

The second period, from 1914 to 1940, includes World War I and operations leading up to World War II. As with the first period, the dominant operations were security and peacekeeping, all of which were conducted in the Western Hemisphere. Examples include the 1914 deployment of naval forces to the Dominican Republic, in which the forces stopped the bombardment of Puerto Plata and helped maintain Santo Domingo City as a neutral zone, and the 1919 deployment of forces to Honduras to maintain order in a neutral zone during an attempted revolution. Security operations were also conducted throughout the world to protect American interests, including ten separate incidents in China from 1916 to 1934, several deployments within the Western Hemisphere, and deployments to Russia and Turkey.

The degree to which the United States remained an isolationist nation, at least in principle, remains a dominant theme during this period. Aside from World War I, the only time U.S. forces engaged in a conventional operation was in 1914 against Mexico, following Mexican border incursions. The only other deployments of forces outside of the Western Hemisphere were security operations. However, it is clear that during this period, the United States not only became a dominant regional power but also established the capability for global engagement, although with less than a strong desire to do so.

U.S. participation in two key aspects of this period warrant further examination and analysis, specifically World War I and its aftermath, including the establishment and demise of the League of Nations.

World War I

World War I certainly requires more than the brief mention above. Not only was the United States a reluctant participant in the war, having entered almost three years after the war began, but it also a somewhat reluctant victor.

U.S. reluctance to enter the war reflected our desire to remain free of the entangling alliances that had consumed other nations, particularly European nations. The manner in which World War I began provides ample evidence of the concerns that U.S. leadership had with respect to alliances.

The road to war followed the assassination of the Archduke Franz Ferdinand and his wife, after Austria-Hungary presented an ultimatum to Serbia that

the assassins be brought to justice. Serbia did not respond directly to the ultimatum, but rather choose to ensure full support from her allies in the event
of escalation of the dispute. As one would expect, Austria-Hungary was not
satisfied with the Serbian response, which resulted in a declaration of war on
Serbia. Russia, bound by a treaty with Serbia, began a mobilization process that
took about six weeks to complete. Based on an alliance with Austria-Hungary,
Germany viewed the Russian actions as a declaration of war. Next France, based
on their alliance with Russia, announced war with Austria-Hungary, and by
treaty this proclamation of war was extended to Germany. Britain entered the
war based on a "moral obligation" to defend France; the two nations had, in
1904, signed the Entente Cordiale (friendly understanding) to cooperate against
Germany. With Britain in the war, all of the British colonies were de facto
drawn into the conflict. Japan, also honoring a treaty with Britain, declared war
on Germany.[13]

It is perhaps somewhat misleading to describe the list of alliances that led
to World War I in succession as done above, as it could lead the reader into
thinking that these arrangements were entered into just prior to the beginning of
World War I. In fact, nothing could be further from the truth. Most of these
alliances had been in place for many years prior to the initiation of hostilities.[14]

However, in keeping with U.S. national security strategy at the time,
President Woodrow Wilson declared a policy of absolute neutrality. This policy
remained in effect until 1917, when the United States was drawn into the conflict
based on Germany's policy of unrestricted submarine warfare. In fact, the
United States had really violated the absolute neutrality declaration long before
through its practice of providing support and equipment to the Allies and thus
taking sides against the Axis powers.

The early stages of World War I were fueled by a series of mobilization
plans that began to prepare and marshal forces for a possible war. With troops
from all nations moving toward a common point, the outcome was largely
predictable and hostilities ensued. The Germans, upon readying their forces,
implemented the Schlieffen Plan which, among other requirements, called for
the occupation of Luxembourg and an attack on Belgium.

The war began a little over two weeks after the assassination of the archduke and his wife. The early conflicts certainly provide insight into the high
casualty rate to be expected. In a two-week period from the end of July to mid-
August, the French and Germans mobilized 1,060,000 and 1,360,000 men, respectively. Within the first week of the war, August 16–23, in the Battle of
Frontiers which the Germans won, the French suffered 300,000 casualties.[15]

The early casualty rates and the stalemate that ensued were in large measure
due to outdated concepts of warfare and across-the-board failures to adjust military strategies, operations, and tactics to new weapons and capabilities. Large,
massed formations were sent to attack prepared defensive positions that were
protected with firepower unlike any previously used in warfare to date. Charging

formations of soldiers proved no match for the heavy machine guns and artillery. In one particularly bloody day at the Battle of the Somme, the British suffered 60,000 casualties out of 100,000 forces deployed, all before noon. The Somme would eventually cost the British 400,000 casualties in 140 days of fighting.

The war spread quickly to four fronts, with battles on the Western Front, the Eastern Front, in the Middle East, and on the seas. It was the last front, the war at sea, that eventually would bring the United States into the fray. In March 1917, the first U.S. merchant ship was sunk. Within a week, three more U.S. merchant ships were lost. In response, President Wilson "declared that the world needed to be made safe for democracy,"[16] and finally on April 6, 1917, Congress declared war on Germany. With entry into the war, the United States officially altered its policy of absolute neutrality.

The U.S. military's role in World War I began in a rather ominous manner and speaks to the nation's lack of preparedness to engage in a world conflict. Noted military historian Larry Addington writes,

> Despite the Allied victory over the submarine by the end of 1917, it remained to be seen whether the U.S. could make a difference in the outcome of the land war in Europe. The National Defense Act of 1916, another part of Wilson's preparedness package to keep the country out of war, defined the land forces of the U.S. as the Regular Army, the Army's Reserve, the National Guard when in federal service, and a so-called national Army to be raised by means to be prescribed by Congress in a time of war. On April 6, 1917, the Regular Army had 108,399 officers and men, the army's reserve had 16,767 officers and men, and the National Guard had 181,620 officers and men. At the same time, the national Army still existed only on paper. Neither did the U.S. have stockpiles of arms and equipment with which to prepare a large army if one could be invented.[17]

One year after the United States declared war on Germany, American troop strength in France was only 320,000, and the U.S. military-industrial complex was only beginning to turn out large amounts of equipment. By the end of the war, U.S. troop strength had grown to over 2,000,000, and it made a significant contribution to the final successful outcome of the Allies in the war.

It is no exaggeration to say that the United States was woefully unprepared for World War I in terms of national security strategy, military strategy, operations, and tactics. The policies of the United States sought to avoid committing the nation to war and thus preparations were extremely limited. The declaration of war by Congress saw the United States, from a near standing start, build a capable and credible force within a year and a half.

World War I was also noteworthy from a global military perspective for the introduction of several new classes of military capabilities including tanks, airpower, and poison gas. During the Battle of Cambrai in 1917, the first successful tank attack was waged by over 370 tanks. Initially, airpower was used for observation and reconnaissance. However, as the war continued, airpower took on the mission of bombing; both fixed-wing aircraft and zeppelins were employed for this purpose. The use of poison gas and its lethal outcome were an ominous sign and a harbinger of things to come.

Perhaps the most staggering statistics from the war deal with the cost. The direct financial costs are estimated at $180.5 billion and indirect costs at $151.6 billion. The human toll was considerably higher, with 10,000,000 dead and 20,000,000 wounded.

A fact essential to the understanding of U.S. postwar pronouncements and actions was the desire at all costs to avoid the development of another set of alliances, which had in large part led a simple incident between Austria-Hungary and Serbia to expand into a world war. Through this overarching desire, the United States certainly helped to doom the postwar period, particularly the League of Nations, and perhaps bears some responsibility for sowing the seeds of World War II.

The League of Nations and U.S. National Security Policy

Given both the human and monetary costs of the war, it should come as no surprise that world leaders sought to ensure that a catastrophe of this magnitude would not occur again. Many prominent world leaders advocated a society of nations to promote international peace and security. Advocates believed that a forum for resolving conflict and dealing with issues of the day was essential. To this end, the League of Nations was established by the treaties that effectively ended the war. President Wilson incorporated provisions for establishing the League of Nations into a proposal that became known as the Fourteen Points, with a specific charter to promote arbitration for settling international disputes; to bring about reduction of armaments; to study and remove the causes of war; and to promote world interests in all fields of human work.[18]

The Paris Peace Conference in 1919 established the League of Nations and included a covenant consisting of twenty-six articles.[19] The organization consisted of the Secretariat, headed by a secretary-general; the Council, normally fourteen members (five permanent and nine nonpermanent); and the Assembly. The Council early set up the Permanent Court of International Justice, or World Court, at The Hague in the Netherlands. Initially, the membership of the League of Nations included all of the victorious Allies of World War I and most of the neutral nations. Over time, other nations, including Bulgaria (1920), Austria (1920), Hungary (1922), Germany (1926), Mexico (1931), Turkey (1932), and the Soviet Union (1934) were granted membership.

The credibility and thus the long-term viability of the League of Nations suffered a serious setback when the U.S. Senate refused to ratify the Treaty of Versailles, thus preventing the United States from taking a leadership role in this fledgling organization.

The potential for the League of Nations as an international forum for re-solving conflict and addressing issues was demonstrated successfully during several tense standoffs during the interwar years.[20] However, despite some clear successes, the limitations of the League were perhaps even more noteworthy. In particular, the League of Nations lacked the ability to enforce decisions or police noncompliant nations. This was especially true of the great powers, including Poland's refusal to abide by the League's decision in the Vilnius dispute (1920), the French occupation of the Ruhr (1923), and Italy's occupation of Kérkira (1923). Furthermore, the League took no action on several key international issues, further diminishing its standing. Examples included failure to act concerning the Japanese invasion of Manchuria (1931) and an inability to stop the Chaco War (1932–35) between Bolivia and Paraguay.

The League began to disintegrate with Germany's withdrawal (1933) and Italy's successful attack on Ethiopia in defiance of the League's economic sanctions (1935). In a further dooming action, Adolf Hitler remilitarized the Rhineland (1936) and denounced the Treaty of Versailles; in 1938 Germany seized Austria. Faced by threats to international peace from all sides—the Spanish civil war, Japan's resumption of war against China (1937), and finally the appeasement of Hitler at Munich (1938)—the final chapter of the League of Nations began. German claims on Danzig, where the League commissioner had been reduced to impotence, led to the outbreak of World War II. The last important act of the League came in December 1939, when it expelled the Soviet Union for its attack on Finland.

The U.S. refusal to join the League of Nations cannot solely be blamed for the forum's failure or the start of World War II, but it certainly was a significant contributor. Despite the experience of World War I, the United States chose a retreat to isolationism over adopting a role as a world leader.

During the interwar years, U.S. national security strategy focused on developing treaties and arms control agreements to prevent further conflict. Beginning with the Treaty of Versailles, which placed limits on the German armed forces, the United States and allies hoped to prevent further German aggression. The lack of cooperation between the major allies, primarily the United States, Britain, and France, contributed to the treaty's failure and ultimately to the German remilitarization.[21] Generally, these arms control agreements were focused multilateral treaties designed to establish limitations on specific actions or areas (such as arms holdings). They included no means by which to verify or enforce the treaties or provide any explicit consequences of failing to adhere to the terms of the agreements.

In what would be a harbinger of the events to unfold and the growth in outwardly focused national security, the U.S. military under the direction of the Department of War and the Department of the Navy established a Joint Board to develop a set of elaborate plans to defend U.S. interests from potential adversaries. The joint board consisted of the Army Chief of Staff, the Chief of Naval Operations, the Chief of the Operations Section of the General Staff, the Assistant Chief of Naval Operations, and the Chiefs of both the War Department and Navy War Plans Division. The plans were color-coded to correspond to different contingencies. As an example, the Orange Plan was a response to Japanese aggression.

In preparation for possible intervention in hostilities around the globe, the Joint Board in 1939 developed a series of five defensive plans, called the RAINBOW plans, to deal with several scenarios and potential adversaries.

> RAINBOW 1 was a defensive plan for preventing the violation of the Monroe Doctrine by protecting the U.S., its possessions, its maritime commerce, the portions of the Western Hemisphere from which the vital interests of the U.S. could be jeopardized. RAINBOWS 2 & 3 both emphasized the Pacific front in a two-ocean war. RAINBOW 2 called for the armed forces to "sustain the interests of the democratic powers in the Pacific, and defeat enemy forces in the Pacific." RAINBOW 3 envisioned a vigorous offensive in the Pacific to "insure the protection of the U.S. vital interests in the western Pacific by securing control there." RAINBOW 4 provided the Western Hemisphere defense on a more aggressive scale than RAINBOW 1 by including the dispatch of American task forces wherever necessary to South America or the eastern Atlantic. RAINBOW 5 emphasized aggressive transatlantic operations to defeat Germany and Italy in the eastern Atlantic, Africa and Europe.[22]

The significance of this effort should not be minimized. The degree to which the United States began planning these contingency operations indicates an emerging global focus and ongoing transition from our previous isolationist tendencies. The plans also reflected an industrialization of the application of military power. Preparations for military operations were being reduced to a set of executable plans highlighting the strategic set at the time as well as the forces and manner in which they would be employed. Developing these types of detailed plans would have been unthinkable prior to World War I. Given the increased interactions among nations and the increased complexity of war planning, the United States began developing these detailed contingencies in the event that our interests were threatened and a response was required. The stage for the emergence of the United States as a global power had been set at the end of this period, and the winds of war were once again blowing, given events in Germany and Japan.

Conclusions

- American leadership in global affairs is vital.
- Interactions between nations continued to expand as the capabilities for contact between nations, societies, and individuals increased.
- Isolationism is not a viable option for enhancing America's interests or promoting economic prosperity.

GROWTH OF THE UNITED STATES AS A WORLD POWER AND THE NUCLEAR STANDOFF, 1941–75

The next period encompasses thirty-four years, from the last year of the pre–World War II time frame to the end of the Vietnam War. During this time, fundamental changes occurred with regard to U.S. participation in world affairs and growth in global responsibilities. As one would expect, these sorts of changes resulted in significant and complementary changes in U.S. national security strategy.

In briefly examining this time frame, it is quite evident that the United States made extraordinary transitions, from being an isolationist nation to becoming the leader of a coalition that thwarted Fascist intentions to emerging as a nuclear power and the leader of democratic nations throughout the globe. Perhaps even more surprising is that most of this transformation occurred during the short seven-year period from 1941 to 1948. The manner in which this transformation occurred and the implications for U.S. national security strategy deserve considerable attention.

From 1941 to 1975, the types of operations for which the United States deployed forces increased, yet the activity level (i.e., number of operations per year) was at its lowest during any of the five periods under discussion. This categorization is somewhat misleading, as the number of conventional operations more than doubled and included World War II, the Korean War, and the Vietnam War. These instances of the use of force were lengthy, extremely high in intensity, and undertaken by large coalitions. They also required the hard power capabilities of the United States to be combined and coordinated in ways far greater than previously experienced in our history. The ability to combine the political, military, and intelligence capabilities of our nation supported with the economic wherewithal to execute our grand strategy was essential to our success during this watershed period in our history.

This period also included a significant change in the types of operations undertaken, as resistance or counterinsurgency operations became prevalent. During this period, the United States participated in operations in Lebanon (1958), Thailand (1962), Laos (1962), the Congo (1964), the Dominican Republic (1965), and the Congo again (1967).

A new type of operation emerged as a surrogate to the security operation: the noncombatant evacuation or NEO. The emergence of NEO really reflects an increased capability to protect citizens and property through evacuation rather than protection in place; six NEO operations occurred, including the evacuation of Cambodia and Vietnam. The Berlin Airlift is the lone (and first) humanitarian operation listed in the CRS data, and could easily have been listed as a security operation or even a conventional operation as it was really the first major event of the Cold War. Also notable during this period were the attack on

Pearl Harbor at the beginning of World War II and the Cuban Missile Crisis, two attacks or threats clearly directed against the U.S. homeland.

Not depicted in the CRS data set but key to U.S. national strategy are the global deployments as part of the Cold War disposition of forces. In the period following World War II, the United States stationed forces throughout the globe in what would today be called Support and Stability Operations or SASO. Major dispositions of forces were in Europe, particularly in Germany, France, the UK, and Italy. The Inter-German Border (IGB) separating West and East Germany became a focal point of the East-West standoff at the height of the Cold War. Forces were also stationed in the Pacific in China, Japan, and the Philippines following World War II and later in Korea following operations there.

Another category of deployment concerns the nuclear standoff and the resultant deployment of forces, both abroad and in the United States, to defend against this dangerous threat. This is discussed later in greater detail.

World War II

World War II resulted in a major turning point in U.S. national security strategy. Despite another somewhat reluctant entry into a world war, the U.S. contribution throughout the conflict and in achieving victory was unmatched. If one were to measure contribution simply by means of casualty rates or destruction of property, it could be argued that other nations paid a higher price. However, looking broadly at the war effort, no other nation was able to fight a global war on multiple fronts simultaneously with such decisive capability. Perhaps the most significant consequence of World War II was the emergence of America as a nuclear superpower with global responsibilities and a newfound understanding of its place in the world.

As with the treatment of World War I previously, it is beyond the scope of this work to present the military strategy, operations, or tactics that were employed during the course of the war. These events and decisions are discussed only in their relation to the development of U.S. national security strategy in the postwar era.

Arguably, the United States entered the war somewhat more prepared than in World War I, as indications and warnings of an impending crisis were evident for a lengthy period, beginning with German remilitarization in the 1930s, the bloodless conquests of Austria and Czechoslovakia in 1938–39, and the blitzkrieg into Poland and France in September 1939–40. By 1941, Hitler's aggression had consumed a large portion of Europe, including France, Poland, Luxembourg, the Netherlands, Denmark, and the Balkans. Despite Hitler's clear aggression and signaled intentions to continue his acquisitions, the American military-industrial complex had made little progress in transitioning to a wartime footing.

The Japanese bombing of Pearl Harbor essentially took away from the United States the strategic decision to enter the war. In effect, the United States ceded this decision to the adversary. Japan's attack on the United States and the Japan-Germany-Italy tripartite alliance ensured U.S. entry into this global conflict. Hitler's alignment with Italy and subsequent decision to support the Italians in North Africa, coupled with the German invasion of Russia, left the tripartite partners by the end of 1941 engaged in a global conflict on four continents with two separate fronts in Europe. America was reluctant no longer.

In a sense, World War II was the quintessential Industrial Age conflict. Despite earlier uses of the tank in World War I, the new armored capability came into its own during World War II. Large armored formations conducted decisive and rapid maneuvers to strategic and operational depths—the German forces using their blitzkrieg tactics demonstrated these new capabilities to the dismay of the Allies, penetrating hundreds of kilometers into Allied territory. Aircraft, which had debuted in warfare in World War I on a limited scale, now routinely patrolled the skies, provided ground support, and bombed strategic targets deep in the enemies' rear areas and industrial bases. Strategic bombing included attacks by hundreds of bombers along with fighter escorts conducting raids over enemy territory with great regularity. Large capital ships including battleships and aircraft carriers secured sea lanes of communication and provided support for advancing ground forces. The V-2 ballistic rocket was unveiled as a weapon of terror against the British populace. All around the globe, warring nations established strategic footholds and stockpiles of supplies and equipment. The ability to rapidly replace losses became a key measure of success.

In a single battle in North Africa, the Battle of El Alamein, the U.S. Eighth Army with a strength of 200,000 troops, 750 aircraft, and 1,000 each of tanks and artillery fought a German Panzer force of 100,000 troops, 675 aircraft, and 500 each of tanks and artillery. The totals reflected in this battle were certainly not unique and were representative of both the size of the formations and implements used to conduct World War II. In fact, battles on the Eastern Front on average were larger than those on the Western Front and resulted in considerably more casualties.

Advancements in Industrial Age weapons systems allowed dramatic increases in the ability to maneuver. These advances, coupled with new tactics integrating firepower and maneuverability, combined to minimize the occurrence of the stalemates experienced in World War I. The introduction of wireless communications also provided a greater ability to maneuver while remaining in contact with higher headquarters. As this was the first experience with the use of radio during ground operations, there were associated growing pains, yet the potential was clearly recognized.

Indeed, a major contributor to the successful U.S. role in the war was the ability to mass-produce everything from weapons and supplies to comfort items for the troops. In fact, even the ability to mass-produce soldiers and units was essential to the successful war effort. The U.S. advantage in industrial capacity resulted in a competitive advantage that no other nation could match. Comparing aircraft production during World War II demonstrates this significant U.S. advantage in industrial capability. From 1940 to 1944, German aircraft production increased from 10,826 to 40,593, or an increase of nearly 400 percent. Russia also achieved a complementary increase while Britain increased production by 300 percent. In this same time frame, U.S. aircraft production grew from 2,141 to 96,318, a staggering 4,800 percent increase.[23] Of course, it would be unfair not to acknowledge that German aircraft production was adversely impacted by the Allied bombing campaign, while the United States maintained a significant geostrategic advantage by being outside the main conflict area, thus allowing U.S. production to continue unfettered during this period. The same trends hold true for tank production during World War II, albeit the disparity was far less.[24]

Despite the enemy's role in one of the first major strategic decisions, the U.S. entry into the war, a host of other key strategic decisions made by U.S. leaders were critical to the execution of the war and the postconflict shaping of world events, including the future national security strategy of the United States.

Prior to entering the war, the United States decided on a strategy of "defeat Germany first." Even after this military strategy was determined, adjustments were required during the execution to slow Japan's advances in the Pacific. The overall magnitude of the global conflict prevented the United States from executing a simultaneous two-front offensive. The decision was largely based on the strategic calculation of which adversary presented the greatest long-term risk to the United States. Of course, the direct attack on Pearl Harbor by the Japanese and the national outcry for a response placed the "Germany first" strategy in jeopardy.

The major decisions dealing with the conduct of the war can be categorized as strategic military decisions, as opposed to national strategic decisions, and are thus beyond the scope of this book. As an example, the decision to participate in operations in North Africa prior to a major invasion of the European continent falls into this category. Decisions on where to land on D-day or how to conduct the island-hopping campaign in the Pacific also are more concerned with military strategy than with national strategy and are not elaborated on further in this analysis. Despite the fact that the postwar world was shaped by decisions such as the massive air campaign in both theaters to destroy the industrial base and will of the people or the naval campaign to choke the Japanese economy, these too are not considered as they are more closely related to military campaigning.

However, several strategic military decisions with significant implications for the postwar period warrant further investigation. The Allied decision to seek unconditional surrender from the vanquished powers was intended to ensure that these nations would be reshaped and restructured to the point that they would never again endanger Western democracies.[25] This decision also led to the postwar stationing of Allied forces, particularly U.S. forces, to assist in restructuring and reshaping governments and militaries. These deployments have lasted in Germany and Japan until the present day, although the disposition, structure, and rationale for their continued deployment have changed dramatically. Certainly Germany and Japan are now partners rather than defeated nations, and our forces are no longer necessary for ensuring stability within the borders of these nations.

Arguably, another strategic national decision concerns the development of the Combined Chiefs of Staff between Britain and the United States. This forum provided an opportunity to discuss and coordinate national priorities between the two powers. The CCS (as it was known) helped to keep the Allies focused on the same strategic goals. It was unfortunate that a similar structure could not have been developed between the United States and China to apply greater pressure on Japan in the Pacific and China-Burma-India theaters.

The Yalta Conference also clearly falls into the category of a key coalition (and by extension, a key national) strategic decision. In February 1945, Winston Churchill, Franklin D. Roosevelt, and Joseph Stalin met at the seaside Crimean resort town of Yalta to agree on a peace settlement for the European theater. Essentially, the leaders of the three major powers met to plan the final defeat and occupation of Germany. Under the provisions of Yalta, Stalin agreed to a Western military presence in Berlin after the surrender and to a four-power government (Britain, France, United States, and Soviet Union) over Germany. These agreements were certainly related to the Allied decision not to push to the Elbe toward the end of the war and set the stage for the Cold War period and the division of Europe.

Perhaps the most significant strategic decision was the dropping of atomic bombs on the cities of Hiroshima and Nagasaki. It is no exaggeration to state that these decisions remain were both strategically and militarily significant today. Since the dropping of the first atomic weapon and a second several days later, arguments both for and against this decision have been made. Proponents argue that the action saved as many as 1 million soldiers and untold casualties on the Japanese side, while opponents cite the brutal nature of the attack and the undue suffering it caused. Whichever side of the argument one is on, one clear outcome of the action is not in dispute; the dropping of the first atomic bomb ushered in the nuclear age. These two instances were the only time atomic weapons have been employed in the course of human history. Of course, that has not stopped state and nonstate actors from attempting to acquire these types of weapons.

The Aftermath

In the aftermath of World War II, a series of crucial changes occurred in relations between nations that would set the world on a dangerous and uncertain path for much of the next forty years. The differences between the Allies became quite clear in the waning months of the war, particularly between the Soviet

Union and France, Britain, and the United States. For the United States, it was not just the emerging differences that weighed heavily, but also the comprehension of the new global responsibilities of emerging alliance leadership. Events in the previous twenty-five years, including two world wars and a troubled peace brought on by the Treaty of Versailles mandated strong U.S. involvement in shaping world events in the postwar period.

As the United States set out upon this new path, four key events shaped the journey: the National Security Act of 1947, the policy of containment, the establishment of the United Nations, and the establishment of the State of Israel.

National Security Act of 1947

> SEC. 2. [50 U.S.C. 401] In enacting this legislation, it is the intent of Congress to provide a comprehensive program for the future security of the United States; to provide for the establishment of integrated policies and procedures for the departments, agencies, and functions of the Government relating to the national security; to provide a Department of Defense, including the three military Departments of the Army, the Navy (including naval aviation and the United States Marine Corps), and the Air Force under the direction, authority, and control of the Secretary of Defense; to provide that each military department shall be separately organized under its own Secretary and shall function under the direction, authority, and control of the Secretary of Defense; to provide for their unified direction under civilian control of the Secretary of Defense but not to merge these departments or services; to provide for the establishment of unified or specified combatant commands, and a clear and direct line of command to such commands; to eliminate unnecessary duplication in the Department of Defense, and particularly in the field of research and engineering by vesting its overall direction and control in the Secretary of Defense; to provide more effective, efficient, and economical administration in the Department of Defense; to provide for the unified strategic direction of the combatant forces, for their operation under unified command, and for their integration into an efficient team of land, naval, and air forces but not to establish a single Chief of Staff over the armed forces nor an overall armed forces general staff."[26]

Following World War II, President Truman and his key advisors turned to the pressing question of national security strategy in this postwar era. The United States recognized that a formal national security apparatus was required to support America's new role in global affairs. Several plans for developing the structure and organizations of national security were proposed, including plans developed by key governmental agencies. General Vandenberg, the early Director of Central Intelligence, developed a comprehensive plan focused on intelligence matters. The Joint Chiefs of Staff also had a plan in the works, obviously with more focus on military matters. Clark Clifford, the President's Special Counsel, was instrumental in developing the plans as well as in working to arrive at a compromise between the various actors.

The compromise plan was forwarded by President Truman to the Chairmen of the House and Senate committees on military and naval affairs in June 1946, including twelve points on which there was broad agreement. These points included the establishment of a Central Intelligence Agency that would operate under a Council of National Defense, an early designation for what would later become the National Security Council. This work formed the basis of the National Security Act of 1947.

The intent of the National Security Act of 1947 is very clear: to coordinate foreign and defense policy. This legislation was revolutionary, as it formally established the structure for the coordination and implementation of national security strategy. Key outcomes included the creation of a National Security Council (NSC), chaired by the President and including the Secretaries of Defense and State; the establishment of the Department of Defense, including delineation of the roles and responsibilities of the Secretary of Defense and staff; the establishment of the Chairman of the Joint Chiefs of Staff and his staff, and the roles and responsibilities of the Services; and the development of a national intelligence structure, including the Central Intelligence Agency.

While the National Security Act of 1947 was an important development in our new grand strategy and in the process of coming to terms with our emerging global role and responsibilities, an essential outcome of the legislation that received far less notoriety was the Key West Agreement of 1948, in which the Secretary of Defense, James V. Forrestal, chaired a capstone meeting of the new structures of defense including the secretary's staff, the Chairman's staff, and the four Services to agree to the roles and missions that each would fulfill. The result was a paper titled "Functions of the Armed Forces and the Joint Chiefs of Staff" that was issued in April 1948. For example, the Key West agreement established that the Air Force was responsible for strategic air warfare and the Navy for naval campaigning. The intent was to develop a comprehensive system of defense with minimal redundancies and an understanding by all responsible offices of the roles and missions of each.

During the subsequent sixty-year period, changes have been made to better organize the national security process; however, in large measure, the agreements reached in the National Security Act of 1947 remain in practice today.

Over time, Presidents have also altered the workings and composition of the NSC, but its basic charter has remained intact: "to advise the President on the integration of domestic, foreign, and military policies relating to national security and to facilitate interagency cooperation."

The interagency process was an important outcome of the National Security Act of 1947. The term Interagency refers to the grouping of departments, organizations and agencies within the U.S. government that cooperate and coordinate national policy. Members of the interagency deliberations on a particular issue vary on a case by case basis, and the grouping can be expanded in an ad hoc fashion to include other nongovernmental organizations and agencies that may be called upon to provide input on matters of special interest or to coordinate for a specific purpose. The coordination of efforts is supervised by the National Security Council (NSC). Interagency deliberations normally proceed from the working group to the deputies committee to the principals' level which includes the President, Vice President and cabinet level secretaries. The results of deliberations or decisions are passed between the levels as coordination is conducted and decisions reached.[27]

Almost immediately after its inception, Truman changed the original composition of the NSC by directing the Secretary of the Treasury to attend the meetings. In 1949, the NSC was reorganized, with the three Service Secretaries eliminated from the proceedings while adding the Vice President.

Over the course of the next four years, further changes were instituted as the emerging requirements of America's role in the post-WWII world were better understood. The challenges faced by the formation of NATO, the humanitarian and reconstruction requirements for Europe, the Soviet Union entering the nuclear age, and the Communists gaining control of China all mandated changes to the NSC. Some changes included the inclusion of the Director for Mutual Security (newly created by the Mutual Security Act of 1951), the Bureau of Budget, and the Psychological Strategy Board (PSB) (designed to manage covert psychological counterattack against the Soviet Union).

It was also during this period, with the aid of these new national security structures, that the United States began to execute covert actions. These operations were executed primarily by the Central Intelligence Agency and the military, although other agencies and organizations had specialized covert capabilities as well; as an example, the National Reconnaissance Office (NRO) had responsibility for electronic surveillance using satellites. As pointed out previously, the CRS data set does not account for these types of operations, despite the increased frequency with which they were conducted.

Over time, the interagency process under the control of the NSC continued to mature. The NSC development has not been stagnant, as the President's reliance on the council and its staff has fluctuated based on Presidential prerogatives. In the Eisenhower administration, a "systemic flow of recommendation, decision and implementation" was established.[28] Eisenhower was comfortable operating within this structure, while Kennedy reduced the influence and size of the NSC staff. Under the Johnson administration, the NSC tended to be a more personal staff. President Nixon wanted foreign policy to by directed out of the White House and thus reinvigorated the NSC.

With the development of a robust national security apparatus (at least in comparison to pre-WWII times), it should come as no surprise that the United States became more capable of participating in global affairs. The National Security Act of 1947 had established the structure and organizations that would support the formulation of policy for the next sixty years.

The Policy of Containment: NSC-68

As America emerged from World War II, it was evident that a new world order was taking shape, one unlike any that had come before it. In these new arrangements, the U.S. faced the prospect of having to share its status as a nuclear superpower with a hostile Soviet Union.[29]

The National Security Act of 1947 was the single document that established the structures and organizations that enabled national security strategy and policy development and execution. However, it was NSC-68, the policy of containment, that was the driving strategic document that set the course of U.S. foreign policy. George Kennan was a foreign service officer working in the U.S. embassy in Moscow in 1946 when he sent back to Washington an analysis of "Stalinist policy, its origins, its evils, and its dangers in his 'long telegram.'"[30] In a subsequent article published in *Foreign Affairs* in July 1946, Kennan wrote under the pseudonym of "Mr. X":

The United States has it in its power to increase enormously the strains under which Soviet policy must operate, to force upon the Kremlin a far greater degree of moderation and circumspection than it has had to observe in recent years, and in this way to promote tendencies which must eventually find their outlet in either the breakup or the gradual mellowing of Soviet power. For no Messianic movement— and particularly not that of the Kremlin—can face frustration indefinitely without adjusting itself in one way or another to the logic of that state of affairs.[31]

Through his work, Kennan had unveiled a strategy called containment. The concept met with a broad range of responses. Many within the administration still hoped for a cooperative relationship with Moscow and thus felt that containment would push the Soviet Union in the wrong direction. Others saw the direction in which the Soviet Union had been moving since even before the end of World War II and strongly advocated the ideas contained in the Mr. X article. The second camp prevailed, and NSC-68 was the outcome.

NSC-68 represented an evolution and refinement of an earlier strategy articulated in NSC-20/4, which was a broad policy paper on U.S.-Soviet relations based on Kennan's continued work. The original report recommended "'timely and adequate preparation' to combat the Soviet threat to our security."[32] However, NSC-68 made two significant enhancements, including proposing a higher level of effort to counter Soviet aggression and a significant emphasis on improving U.S. military capabilities.

In the end, the decision made by President Truman to implement NSC-68 was largely a result of an impending crisis. In 1947, Britain informed President Truman that it could no longer shoulder the burden of supporting Greece and Turkey in their struggle against Soviet pressure and a growing Soviet-supported insurgency. Truman responded with the Greek-Turkish Aid Program and later the Truman Doctrine, which declared U.S. willingness to "consider such aid as we could prudently make available to any country subject to aggression or intimidating pressure and prepared to act in its own defense."[33]

Essentially, NSC-68 amounted to an assessment of threats and response options for the President. It was never intended nor used as a statement of public policy and remained classified from its signing until 1975. The key question confronting the administration was what form a response to the overarching Soviet threat should take. Should a direct buildup of force be initiated? Perhaps attempts to negotiate with the Soviets should be made to reduce tensions and bring about a negotiated settlement.

In concert with the strategy of containment, the United States launched a series of initiatives including the Marshall Plan to aid in the economic reconstruction of Europe and directed programs for the economic recovery of Germany and Japan. Simultaneously, negotiation began for the establishment of the North Atlantic Treaty Organization (NATO).[34] Earlier the reader may have questioned why the establishment of NATO was not included in the grouping of key events that helped to shape the post–World War II period. Certainly, NATO has been and continues to be a vital part of our nation's security. However, my intent was to discuss NATO as a subset of the development of the strategy of containment, as its formulation is closely related to the foundations laid down by Kennan.

Since April 1949 with the signing of Treaty of Washington, NATO has been at the cornerstone of U.S. defense policy. Ten European nations, the United States, and Canada agreed to a collective security arrangement. At the heart of this arrangement was Article V, the collective security provision which really defines the alliance: "the Parties agree that an armed attack against one or more of them in Europe or North America shall be considered an attack against them all and consequently they agree that, if such an armed attack occurs, each of them, in exercise of the right of individual or collective self-defence" (see appendix D). Arguably, it is this portion of the treaty that has kept the alliance relevant for over sixty years.

NATO continued to expand and by 1952 included Greece and Turkey as members. The alliance continued to improve the structures and organizations that would ensure the common security of member nations. In May 1955, with the signing of the Warsaw Treaty between the Soviet Union, Albania, Bulgaria, Czechoslovakia, East Germany, Hungary, Poland, and Romania, the Cold War officially began, although the seeds of the East-West standoff were sown well before with decisions such as those made at Yalta and decisions at the end of the war concerning the final limits of the Allied advance in the West.

The standoff between NATO and the Warsaw Pact was both a political and military confrontation in which conventional and nuclear forces were available for planning and use. The United States had stationed forces with the capability for delivering tactical nuclear weapons in Europe and of course maintained a

growing strategic nuclear stockpile consisting of weapons that could be delivered by aircraft, submarine, or ballistic missile. France and the UK also had
nuclear-capable forces by the mid-1960s.

In this tenuous balance, the Warsaw Pact held a very significant advantage
in conventional force totals, while generally it was accepted that NATO had
higher-quality systems. NATO and other non–Warsaw Pact nations, by and
large, tended to see NATO as the defensive alliance while viewing the Warsaw
Pact as the aggressor. Of course, some events, such as the interventions in Korea
and Vietnam, caused some to challenge this view.[35]

The basis for the thoughts contained in NSC-68 was validated by a series of
Soviet acts of aggression, including the use of tanks to crush an antigovernment
rally in Hungary in 1956, the building of the Berlin Wall in 1961, elimination of
liberal reforms in Czechoslovakia with the Soviet assault in 1968, and the
continued development of Soviet nuclear capabilities.

Over the period from 1947 to the fall of the Berlin Wall in 1989 (or perhaps
the demise of the Soviet Union in 1991), the overarching strategic direction for
U.S. actions has been the policy articulated by George Kennan. The policies
pursued by the Soviet Union and the United States (through the strategy of
containment) led to a global competition that left few countries untouched. From
the handling of the Cuban Missile Crisis by President Kennedy in 1962 to the
wars to stop the spread of Communism including the Korean and Vietnam Wars,
the United States and by extension our allies have followed this strategy of
containment. In the case of both the Korean War and particularly the Vietnam
War, these conflicts in combination had a profound impact on U.S. commitment
of forces well into the 1990s.

While a detailed examination of the Korean and Vietnam Wars is well
beyond the scope of the book, these two major demonstrations of national resolve
and commitment of forces certainly deserve more than the brief mention in the
preceding paragraph.

The Korean War was the first major, though limited, war that the United
States fought on the continent of Asia in the era of global tension that followed
World War II. In many regards this was the formal confrontation between the
democratic world and Communist forces. The Soviet-sponsored government
of North Korea invaded the Republic of Korea on June 25, 1950, following a
period of heightened tension in which less forceful means were employed by the
North Koreans to compel the Government of South Korea to incorporate under a
single communist regime. Following the invasion, the United States, based on a
United Nations resolution, came to the aid of the South Koreans as part of a UN-
sponsored action to blunt the aggression and restore 38th parallel, the pre-war
border between North and South Korea.

The fighting was confined both in geographic terms as well as by the political decisions that placed significant restrictions upon military strategy and
operations, although not on the tactics employed by the forces in contact. In this

regard, the war was considered limited by all but the two Korean governments, which saw the war as involving survival interests and therefore used the full breadth of their capabilities. Despite the characterization of the war as limited, the battles on the ground were extremely ferocious for all the combatants.

As an emerging superpower, the United States learned some critical lessons as a result of the intervention. First and foremost was the high cost of unpreparedness. The military, which had only some five years earlier defeated Nazi and Japanese aggression, had turned into an occupation force. Many of the former draftees had left the Service and returned to civilian life. The force had also failed to provision its soldiers adequately and training was lacking. *This Kind of War* by T. R. Fehrenbach (Pocket Books, 1964) chronicles well the dismal state of the force in the early engagements of the war.

The second major lesson involved the role of a nation with a global strategy. Following World War II, U.S. efforts centered on countering the Soviet Union and its satellite nations. This delineation did not include the region to which we would find two major U.S. commitments in the post–World War II period. Consider that in January 1950, in a speech to the National Press Club in Washington, D.C., Secretary of State Dean G. Acheson announced an American defensive strategy in the Far East that excluded both Korea and Formosa (Taiwan).

The three-year war resulted in more than 142,000 American battle casualties. As a postscript, the tense standoff continues today along the Demilitarized Zone (DMZ) separating North and South Korea, and North Korea is acquiring a nuclear capability that would likely destabilize the region even further.

Clear similarities exist between the Korean and Vietnam Wars. In each, the initial involvement was largely based on the domino theory and thus was directly related to the East-West standoff. Both also involved the limited use of force and a constrained strategy. Based on concern about the potential for a broadening of the conflict to a direct superpower confrontation, the United States attempted to confine the conflict to North Vietnam and remain well clear of the Chinese border. Limitations also existed on operations in neighboring countries of Laos, Thailand, and Cambodia. This translated into battlefield success being measured in body counts and loss exchange ratios rather than in gaining and holding terrain. Unfortunately, the enemy proved elusive and quite resilient, which ultimately led to a U.S. strategic failure.

At the beginning of the war, North Vietnam was under the control of the Vietnamese Communists who had opposed France and who aimed for a unified Vietnam under Communist rule. The South was controlled by Vietnamese who had collaborated with the French. In 1965 the United States sent in troops to prevent the South Vietnamese government from collapsing. After some ten years of conflict involving the United States and over a decade more prior to that involving the French, the final scene that was played out across the globe was the U.S. evacuation of Saigon in 1975. Shortly thereafter, Vietnam was reunified under Communist control. During the conflict involving the United States, approximately 3 to 4 million Vietnamese on both sides were killed, in addition to another 1.5 to 2 million Laotiano and Cambodians who were drawn into the war. The war has the dubious distinction of being the longest in American history and was waged at a cost of over 58,000 killed and 300,000 wounded.

In many respects, the Vietnam War was waged by the United States as largely a conventional conflict, which failed to account for the insurgent nature of the war. Some initiatives were established to more fully address the true nature of the conflict, but those initiatives ultimately received mixed reviews both in terms of magnitude of support and overall effectiveness. Through the U.S. Agency for International Development (U.S. AID) and later with the Civil Operations (and) Revolutionary Development Support (CORDS) command, the United States attempted to address the root causes of the insurgency. In January 1970, CORDS was changed to the Civil Operations (and) *Rural* Development Support command. The advisory effort entailed assistance to the Government of Vietnam's pacification program, and was the Civil Affairs/Civil Military Operations joint command, consisting of military personnel and civilians. While the initial U.S. AID effort focused primarily on the police and security forces, by the end of the conflict CORDS had expanded to virtually all segments of Vietnamese infrastructure.

The manner in which the war was waged and the postconflict analysis, largely played out over the last twenty-five years of the twentieth century, were key to the manner in which the United States executed its foreign policy and security strategy during this period. Major themes that emerged were: political failures translate into military miscues; the importance of clear political and military objectives prior to the commitment of force; the failure to comprehend the nature of the conflict or insurgency; and an aversion to taking casualties. The implications of these themes are discussed further in the "Winning the Cold War, 1976–1989" section.

One criticism that is worthy of note is that the strategy of containment led in many ways to the incorrect impression that Communism was a monolithic threat—that is, that the Soviet Union and China were Communist allies or practiced the same brand of Communism and therefore had aligned their policies. Given this assumption, practitioners of U.S. national strategy further assumed that with cooperation between the Soviet Union and China, any nation that became Communist or even Socialist was either in or moving into this monolithic Communist sphere of influence. The term coined to describe this concept was the "domino theory," which postulated that the fall of one nation to Communism could, if not halted, lead to the communization of neighbor nations or even an entire region if left unchecked. Following the demise of the Soviet Union and its client states, we have come to realize that the degree of cooperation between these Communist states was not nearly as great as we once assumed.

The United Nations A significant lesson resulting from World War I, which was essentially relearned with the initiation of hostilities in World War II, was the need for an international forum for discussions between nations, maintaining order and discipline within the state system, resolving disagreements, and if necessary policing nations not in compliance with international laws. The League of Nations following World War I was intended to serve this purpose, but, as discussed previously, suffered from a lack of participation and credibility, which eventually led to its demise.

Following World War II, nations, in particular the United States, saw the need for an international forum of this sort. In response, representatives from fifty nations met in San Francisco in October 1945 to create the United Nations Charter. By the end of the conference, representatives from all fifty nations signed the charter; Poland, which was not represented at the conference, later signed as one of the original fifty-one member nations.

The preamble of the charter describes well the purpose of the United Nations:

> We the peoples of the united nations determined to save succeeding generations from the scourge of war, which twice in our lifetime has brought untold sorrow to mankind, and to reaffirm faith in fundamental human rights, in the dignity and worth of the human person, in the equal rights of men and women and nations large and small, and to establish the conditions under which justice and respect for the obligations arising from treaties and other sources of international law can be maintained, and to promote social progress and better standards of life in larger freedom.
>
> And for these ends to practice tolerance and live together in peace with one another as good neighbors, and to unite our strength to maintain international peace and security, and to ensure, by the acceptance of principles and the institution of methods, that armed force shall not be used, save in the common interest, and to employ international machinery for the promotion of the economic and social advancement of all peoples.[36]

The stated purposes of the UN are equally descriptive, compelling, and worthy of review:

- To maintain international peace and security
- To develop friendly relations among nations based on respect for the principle of equal rights and self-determination of peoples
- To cooperate in solving international economic, social, cultural, and humanitarian problems and in promoting respect for human rights and fundamental freedoms
- To be a center for harmonizing the actions of nations in attaining these common ends

Today, the UN has agencies dedicated to a large variety of international concerns and areas of cooperation, including finance reform, women's issues, humanitarian issues, environmental protection, and social development, to name a few. A variety of international provisions and laws have also been developed and agreed within this forum.

While the UN continues to work to fulfill its established roles, it has gained mixed reviews for its ability to develop cooperation or even take the lead on security issues. The UN has sponsored fifty-nine peacekeeping operations since 1948, including sixteen that were ongoing as of December 2004—these sixteen included almost 64,000 military personnel and civilian police. This list of fifty-nine also includes some that have received considerable scrutiny and harsh reviews, including Operation Restore Hope in Somalia and UN Protection Force (UNPROFOR) in Bosnia, which has gained the UN considerable criticism for its inability to stem the violence and restore order. Still, a UN mandate is in some respects considered by many nations to be a prerequisite prior to the employment of force for conflict resolution.

Other criticisms include the distribution of power, as the UN has five permanent members of the Security Council, giving these nations what many consider to be a disproportionate amount of power, especially given that these nations were selected based on their post–World War II stature, which in some cases is no longer a relevant measure, as with Russia.

Additionally, some have criticized the bureaucracy and costs associated with running the UN. As with any large organization, inefficiencies do exist. The organizational structure is hierarchical and tends in many cases to arrive at solutions that are at the lowest common denominator and perhaps not in the best interests of the United States. This has become particularly true with the explosion in the number of member countries over the past fifteen to twenty years. The UN uses a one country–one vote system, giving Uzbekistan the same voting power as the United States, which causes great angst on topics of vital or significant importance to the United States.

Cost has also become a major issue in several regards. First, the United States pays approximately one-third of the total assessment, and for some time was approximately $1 billion in arrears, based on a dispute over how the national assessments were developed. The second but related issue concerns the manner in which costly UN initiatives can be developed and approved through the UN deliberation process. In some cases, these programs or policies are against U.S. policy or desires; however, once they are approved by the UN, the United States bears a third of the cost.

As with any alliance or international organization that a nation joins, national sovereignty can potentially become an issue. The United States has always reserved the right to act unilaterally regardless of the UN position in areas of important or vital interest. This has caused and most certainly will continue to cause friction between the UN and the United States, as events associated with the U.S.-led coalition invasion of Iraq in 2003 have demonstrated.

Despite these concerns, the UN remains, as it was designed to be, the principal organization for maintaining cooperation within the international community.

Establishment of the State of Israel The establishment of Israel does not necessarily seem to fit into the same category as the Security Act of 1947, the policy of containment, and the establishment of the United Nations; however, its impact, particularly on U.S. national security policy, cannot be underestimated.

With the issuing of the Balfour Declaration by the British in 1917, which announced support in principle for a proposed homeland for the Jewish people in Palestine, the question of a Jewish state became a pressing issue. Following World War II, the British withdrew from their control of Palestine, and the UN partitioned the area into Arab and Jewish states, an arrangement rejected by the Arabs—it is this action that has resulted in a series of confrontations and wars.

Throughout the period from the founding of Israel in 1948 to the present, U.S. support can be characterized as virtually unwavering. Thus, the rationale for inclusion in this succession of key events in national security development is that the U.S. relationship with Israel and the resultant relationship with Arab nations in the region and more recently, globally, has helped to define a significant part of U.S. national security policy.

More to the point, the Arab point of view during this same period is that the U.S.-Israeli relationship always takes precedence over U.S.-Arab relations. This feeling of always being second has generated tremendous animosity within the Arab world and will continue to have an impact well into the twenty-first century. Furthermore, it is frequently cited within the Arab community as a significant cause of friction and mistrust of the United States in dealing with the Middle East.

The Growth of Global Economics and the Bretton Woods Agreement

Several key economic developments occurred during this period that have had the effect of stabilizing global economies and drawing the nations of the world closer together. While not listed previously as one of the four key events that shaped the Cold War period, economic developments certainly played a major role in this period and have been a driving factor in the rapid march toward globalization. The International Monetary Fund (IMF) and World Bank certainly fit into this category.[37]

The World Bank's mission is to fight poverty and improve the living standards of people in the developing world. It serves as a development bank providing loans, policy advice, technical assistance, and knowledge-sharing services to low- and middle-income countries to reduce poverty. In tandem, the IMF's work to stabilize currencies through the establishment of a link to the dollar certainly is a major contributor to the advent of globalization. Not to say that globalization would not have happened without this linkage, but rather that stabilizing currencies in this way set the world on a path toward economic integration.

Because of the key role of economics in shaping the outcome of the Cold War, it would have been a serious omission not to address the growth of the global economic system in this period. However, despite U.S. reliance on economics, no direct national security economic strategy has been developed complementary to the defense strategy.

Conclusions

- During this period, the United States established the structures and organizations that would significantly impact not only its ability to wage the Cold War, but would also propel it to superpower status.
- In the Industrial Age, economic capacity was directly related to military capacity.

WINNING THE COLD WAR, 1976–89

This period has been deliberately titled "Winning the Cold War," for it was in this time frame that the demise of the Soviet Union and Warsaw Pact began. The United States and our allies began a deliberate military buildup that in effect would overwhelm the Warsaw Pact. This period included the post-Vietnam evaluation of the commitment of forces and the military buildup of the Reagan years.

An appropriate summation of this period is that the hard power elements of our nation were engaged in a deliberate campaign to overwhelm the Communist threat. The political-military-intelligence organizations were keenly focused on defeating a determined ideological threat to democracy and our very way of life. The conflict was so pervasive that even events such as the Olympics were not immune from East-West tensions. The U.S.-Soviet hockey match in the 1980 Olympics provides ample evidence of the manner in which the standoff was perceived and executed.

President Reagan's delineation of the Soviet Union as the "Evil Empire" provided both the exclamation point to and the ideological basis for the conflict. The Cold War was not simply a traditional state versus state or alliance to alliance competition, but rather a conflict between good and evil.

From 1976 to 1989, U.S. forces were involved in a wide variety of different types of operations, participating in seven of the eight categories of operations. Conventional operations tended to be more limited and included Grenada (1983), Panama (1989), three incidents with Libya (1981, 1986, and 1989), and two incidents in the Persian Gulf (1984 and 1987–88) related to the free flow of oil in this region. Perhaps most notable during this period is that U.S. forces provided assistance in support of five counterinsurgency operations, including El Salvador (1981), Honduras (1983–89), Chad (1983), Panama (1989), and the Philippines (1989).[38]

Also of interest is the emergence of two other categories of operations, counterdrug and counterterrorism, with two operations listed in each. The numbers in these categories certainly can be misleading, as many of these types of operations are conducted by special operations or covert forces and are therefore not listed in the CRS data set. Also not specifically addressed within the data set was the global deployment of forces in accordance with our overall policy of containment.

In Europe, over 300,000 U.S. service members, primarily from the Army and Air Force, patrolled the borders between NATO and the Warsaw Pact. The NATO alliance continued to rely on a strategy of flexible response, which would make use of the full range of military conventional and nuclear forces in the defense of the European continent. The DOD contemplated how to fulfill the commitment to NATO to reinforce the continent with ten U.S. Army divisions in ten days along with the necessary naval and air forces. This exercise amounted to a very complex allocation problem as air, naval, and ground forces competed for strategic lift assets to get from the Continental United States (CONUS) to the theater.

Likewise in Korea, the Army and Air Force defended an uneasy armistice along the Demilitarized Zone (DMZ) between North and South Korea. Here the United States had stationed approximately 100,000 forces along the narrow DMZ. Reinforcement plans and yearly exercises were conducted to provide necessary support in the event of an attack by the North. The forces were part of a larger effort in coordination with South Korea to defend the territorial integrity of the southern half of the peninsula. U.S. and South Korean forces developed defensive plans to fight against much larger, although technologically inferior, forces to blunt a North Korean attack and restore the DMZ.

The Navy was involved in overseas deployments around the globe to ensure freedom of navigation, to protect U.S. interests, and to stem the spread of Communism. Naval contributions were essential in each of the war plans as well. They included protecting the lines of communication, delivering forces via sealift to a theater, direct support of ground forces, and maintaining air and naval superiority.

Each of the Services maintained both conventional and nuclear capabilities. There was considerably more than casual discussion regarding how to fight on a dirty battlefield created by the use of nuclear, chemical, or biological weapons. Soviet and Warsaw Pact capabilities and writings on military operations and tactics clearly established the intention to employ these types of weapons in support of their war plans.

The U.S. national security and by extension the military was organized around preparing for a three-front war with operations in Europe, on the Korean Peninsula, and in Southwest Asia against an Iranian threat. Of course, in combat war games and simulations, operations could be conducted individually or in various combinations. The scenarios also varied in terms of which action would come first. In the worst-case scenario, the operations occurred simultaneously and greatly stressed, in fact overwhelmed, the military. In each of the scenarios, the best the United States could hope to do was to fight to a stalemate, except in the European theater where the numerical superiority of the Warsaw Pact invariably caused a rapid conventional defeat and the necessity of using nuclear weapons to save the continent.

Covert operations and spying using military forces and intelligence capabilities were also highly prevalent and have been well chronicled in fiction and nonfiction works. These operations involved human and technical/scientific capabilities. In the end, it fell to analysts on both sides to separate out the capabilities from the intentions. It is relatively straightforward to count numbers of weapon systems or to define capabilities. While that does not mean that intelligence always gets it right, at least the process is relatively easy to understand. However, it is much more complex to determine the intentions of an adversary. What if the enemy has two divisions of soldiers and associated support on the border? Do they intend to use them and in what manner? These are the more difficult questions to contemplate.

Correlation of Forces and Means Methodology

The Soviets measured their international relations in terms of a "correlation of forces." For the West, the analogy would best be described in terms of the balance of power. The intent was to develop a ratio to allow for an assessment of the relative strength of the capitalist and Communist blocs. In this methodology, all aspects of national power could be and were considered, including political, economic, ideological, and military. The analytical technique was called the correlation of forces and means (COFM).

Initially, the methodology focused on military balance, but as the perception of what constitutes national power broadened, the political element of the equation took on a more prominent role.[39] In true Industrial Age fashion, the Soviets perfected a methodology for determining force requirements and capabilities. The power of a military force was directly related to the number and quality of weapons systems available to the commander. The Soviet methodology called for multiplying the number of weapons systems by their quality weight and then summing up all the systems' totals. COFM was applied to both conventional and nuclear weapons systems and became the basis for calculations at the strategic, operational, and tactical levels of war.

As an example of their use at the tactical level, the Soviets would perform the COFM calculations and then determine if they possessed the proper combat power to prevail in a certain operation. If they were on the offensive, the COFM called for a minimum of a 3:1 ratio of forces across the front and a 6:1 ratio in the strike sector, or area of intended penetration.

Included in the methodology was the use of timelines for the conduct of operations. Commanders at various levels were expected to maintain a certain pace and level of expenditure based on the type of operation and the enemy being faced. In some respects, the effect of the COFM was to take decision making out of the commanders' hands and reduce warfare to an industrial engineering problem, thus minimizing the human factors. This is in direct contrast to the notion held for years and written about extensively by military theorists that warfare was a very human experience requiring competent, thinking, courageous soldiers and leaders at all levels.

Requirements for the Soviet nuclear arsenal also made extensive use of the COFM. By measuring their capabilities against those of the West, particularly the United States, they were able to determine the number and types of each system required. Indeed, the concept of deterrence that was practiced by the United States and Soviets was initially based on the concept of mutually assured destruction, making the cost of a nuclear war so high as to prevent it from occurring. However, two wild cards caused the Soviets concern with regard to the nuclear standoff. The first was the French withdrawal from the NATO integrated military command structure. As the French had nuclear weapons and an expressed policy of using these systems to defend the French homeland from a possible Warsaw Pact invasion, the Soviets had to consider not just the NATO (really the U.S.) response, but also the French actions. Second, the updated NATO policy of flexible response signaled to the Soviets that NATO nations were ready to risk a nuclear confrontation in response to Warsaw Pact aggression and, most important, to launch a first strike in response to Warsaw Pact conventional aggression.

For the United States, the Cold War and the period of strategic deterrence saw many within the national security policy arena measuring security in terms of numbers, throw weights, megatons, and ability to survive and respond to a first strike. The mix of systems and their means of launch (e.g., intercontinental ballistic missiles, intercontinental bombers, or submarine-launched ballistic missiles) was even a matter of keen debate. The dialogue took on almost a surreal quality, more akin to a religious discussion. In the end, the U.S. strategic nuclear arsenal at the height of the Cold War numbered approximately 7,000 warheads, in contrast to well over double the number in the Soviet arsenal.

Throughout this period of the strategic deterrence framework, a series of measures were implemented to reduce the threat of a miscalculation. Perhaps the most famous of these measures is the Washington-Moscow hotline, which provided for an open telephone line between the capitals. Others include arms control agreements and other transparency measures such as Open Skies, which allowed controlled overflights of each of the signatory nations according to very specific rules.

The Nuclear Age and the competition between Warsaw Pact allies and NATO allies had another interesting effect. During this period, there was clear competition to acquire allies or client states, either by mutual consent or through coercive action. However, with the stakes so high in terms of small conflicts potentially escalating into strategic nuclear confrontations between the superpowers, a series of proxy wars were fought. Examples include Cuba, Afghanistan, El Salvador, Nicaragua, and Angola. These are certainly representative and reflect only a small subset of the nations involved in this superpower competition. The common thread was support in the form of "advisors," weapons systems, ammunition, and supplies. In this way, a Cold War was waged for almost forty years from the late 1940s to 1989.

Arms Control Agreements

Arms control agreements have been and remain today a cornerstone of national security policy for the United States. As a matter of policy, the United States has sought to achieve national security objectives through negotiated settlements. Over the course of our nation's history, we have negotiated hundreds of bilateral and multilateral agreements.

During this period in history, the arms control agreements that were negotiated or remained in force were seen as key to our security. Several key agreements between the United States and Soviet Union during this period include the Strategic Arms Limitations Talks (SALT) I, Anti-Ballistic Missile or ABM, SALT II, and Intermediate Nuclear Force (INF) treaties.[40] Other measures were also taken to reduce the risk of miscalculations. An example is the establishment of the Nuclear Risk Reduction Center, which facilitated exchange of information.

Multilateral arms control agreements were also important for protecting U.S. security concerns. In this period, treaties that were negotiated or in force included the Nuclear Non-Proliferation Treaty (NPT), Confidence and Security Building Measures in Europe (CSBE), and the Conventional Forces in Europe (CFE) treaties.[41]

Talks were held on a variety of different national security and defense matters, including virtually all classes of weapons and behavior. Many of these discussions were held within the framework of the UN. In fact, in 1979, the UN established a Conference of Disarmament for this express purpose.

The interwar period after World War I had provided valuable lessons about the need for not only arms control agreements, but also for verification of any agreements reached. Verification was intended to allow all sides to gain confidence and assurance that each was adhering to the terms of the agreements. Failure to incorporate an implementible verification regime signified the end of any potential arms control agreement. It was not enough to sign an agreement signaling an intent to limit weapons totals or behavior; there must also be a way to ensure that all parties were adhering to the terms of the agreement.

National Security Strategy Reforms

Several events in the 1970s and early 1980s led to calls for reform in national security in the United States. The national catharsis resulting from the Vietnam War clearly weighed heavily on national political and military leaders. Questions included: How could a third world nation such as North Vietnam defeat a superpower? How could the U.S. Army, which was never defeated on the field of battle, lose the war and fail to achieve its stated objectives? How do we as a nation prevent this from happening again? These were issues of significant debate. The failed rescue of the U.S. hostages held captive in Iran for the last year of the Carter Presidency and the accompanying dissection of why the mission had been aborted was another key driver of the need for defense reform.

Indeed, President Reagan ran on a platform that included the need for a significant defense reform. One author notes, "Recall that Reagan was elected, in part, as a result of the perceived failure of the Carter administration to address equipment related inadequacies within the post Vietnam American military. The perception of a 'hollow force'—one with only a mere shell of combat power was widespread."[42]

To this end, President Reagan appointed the Blue Ribbon Commission on Defense Management, chaired by David Packard, to examine ways to improve overall defense management, including the crucial areas of national security planning, organization, and command.[43] An anecdotal story of a soldier deployed on combat operations in Grenada needing to use a commercial telephone to call his home station to request support was a sort of last straw.

Public Law 99-433, dated October 1, 1986, better known as the Goldwater-Nichols Department of Defense Reorganization Act of 1986, was the result. Goldwater-Nichols represented the most significant change to the defense structures of this nation—and by association the national security policy of the United States—since the National Security Act of 1947. The legislation is titled "Defense Reorganization," and provisions in the code call for submission by the President of an annual report on the national security strategy of the United States. Thus it really amounted to a national security reform document as well.

The first of these National Security Strategy documents to be submitted, dated 1988, lists five national interests:

1. The survival of the United States as a free and independent nation, with its fundamental values intact and its institutions and people secure

2. A healthy and growing U.S. economy to provide opportunity for individual prosperity and a resource base for our national endeavors

3. A stable and secure world, free of major threats to U.S. interests

4. The growth of human freedom, democratic institutions, and free market economies throughout the world, linked by a fair and open international trading system

5. Healthy and vigorous alliance relationships

To protect these interests, the document began to define the superstructure necessary to ensure national security. For example, the NSS further identified five major objectives and subordinate objectives essential to national security.[44] Additionally, the 1988 NSS also listed the elements of national power or the means of the strategy as follows: Moral and political example, military strength, economic vitality, alliance relationships, public diplomacy, security assistance, development assistance, science and technology cooperation, international organizations, and diplomatic mediation. Hence, in the first several pages of the document, the ends, ways, and means of U.S. national security strategy were established. This 1988 NSS is also noteworthy as it reflects the first time that the United States had formally established a grand strategy. Even the strategy of containment, despite its far-reaching implications, was not as comprehensive in its treatment of national security strategy.

Examination of the interests and objectives provides significant insight into the linkages between achieving these stated goals and the use of force. It is quite clear that there is a strong, even dominant military competent in each; furthermore, without the ability to back up the statements of interest or objectives with force if necessary, they are simply platitudes.

For example, the second objective, concerning the global economy, lists three subordinate objectives. Two of the three have direct military components, such as "ensuring access to markets, resources, and energy" or ensuring "minimal distortions to trade." Neither of these could reasonably be expected to be guaranteed without a strong military capable of enforcing these conditions should they be threatened.

The linkages between achieving our stated national security strategy and the other elements of power are not nearly so clear. While the document discusses the importance of economic prosperity, there is little definition of the economic ways and means for achieving this stated goal. Thus this early NSS is really more concerned with the traditional elements of power, politics and defense, than with looking more broadly at the other components of national power.

The Debate on the Use of Force

After the U.S. experience in Vietnam, a nearly continuous debate ensued to examine under what conditions the use of force was appropriate and how forces should be used to best effect.

The general sense after Vietnam was that failures in execution were political rather than military or battlefield failures. The strategic miscues and inability of senior political and military leaders to forcefully speak out against the Vietnam War is well documented in a book written in 1998 by an Army officer, H. R. McMaster. The book, *Dereliction of Duty*, provides ample evidence of what can happen to a strategy that is not supported with the appropriate ways and means to achieve the stated goals.

In 1986, largely in response to the Vietnam experience, Secretary of Defense Caspar Weinberger and his staff developed a six-point checklist to identify the conditions under which the use of force was appropriate. The checklist was presented to Congress in the Secretary's February 5, 1986, message. It included the following provisions:

- U.S. forces should only be committed to combat in defense of interests vital to our nation or our allies.

- U.S. forces should only be committed in numbers adequate to complete the mission.

- U.S. forces should only be committed when we have clearly defined political and military objectives.

- The relationship between objectives and forces committed should be continually reassessed and adjusted if necessary.

- U.S. forces should be committed only when there is a reasonable assurance of support from the American people and Congress.

- U.S. forces should only be committed as a last resort.

For each of these provisions, one can relate the rationale to the experiences and lessons learned from the Vietnam War. In the aftermath of the conflict, a general, almost pervasive, feeling by many foreign policy analysts, military leaders, and soldiers that had fought in the conflict was that America had lost its way in the war.

Missions were often vague or thought to be irrelevant. One day, units would be ordered to capture a piece of terrain, only to abandon it the very next day. The object of many of the missions was "search and destroy," an operation designed to wear down and attrite enemy forces. But the enemy was elusive. Despite heavy and mounting casualties, the enemy always seemed to return to fight another day. Even heavy bombing raids did little to interdict the flow of supplies down the Ho Chi Minh Trail or to kill the enemy.

On the U.S. side, casualties mounted with little tangible result. By war's end, over 58,000 U.S. Soldiers, Sailors, Airmen, and Marines had been killed. The only lasting images seemed to be the photos of the evacuation of Saigon at the war's end. The manner in which the war was waged had failed to account for the enemy's center of gravity and thus failed to provide a linkage between the battlefield or the tactical operations and the overall strategy.

The constraints placed on the forces executing the missions were in many ways symbolic of the manner in which the entire war was conducted. Political will to win was another area where significant deficiencies seemed to exist. Forces were not generally permitted to pursue enemy forces into Cambodia or Laos, despite the enemy's use of these areas for refuge. There was significant concern about penetrating too deeply into North Vietnam for fear that this action could bring China into the war, and perhaps lead to a global confrontation.

As the war drew on, support from within the United States fell sharply. Debates raged as the nation became polarized by the experience. Another key outcome of the Vietnam experience was a piece of legislation that was enacted in 1973, the War Powers Act, which required Congressional notification of any commitment of force within sixty days. While it was signed into law in 1973, the first applications of the law were in the post-1976 period.

Given these sorts of experiences, U.S. leaders sought to prevent ever again going to war in these limited conditions and without the support of the American people. The Army's reaction in particular sheds light on how this experience impacted on defense policy. As part of the restructuring of the armed forces following the Vietnam War, the Army was restructured to ensure that any future major commitment of forces could not be undertaken without the Reserve Component, to ensure support from the American people.

Military Restructuring and Modernization

This period included a significant military buildup, which saw the DOD budget increase by over 45 percent[45] and the capabilities of the Department and all Services improve by orders of magnitude. The Army fielded the "big five" systems, which included the Abrams tank, the Bradley infantry fighting vehicle, the Multiple Launched Rocket system, the Blackhawk utility helicopter, and the Apache gunship helicopter. The Navy fielded new aircraft carriers, new and improved ballistic missiles, and fast attack submarines. Meanwhile, the Air Force fielded the B-1 and B-2 bombers, F-15 and F-16 fighters, and new aerial refueling tankers and strategic airlift that improved the global reach of the United States and the ability to deploy forces.

The new equipment fielded throughout DOD represented generational improvements in the overall capability of U.S. forces, although not a revolutionary leap in capability. The new systems were designed at the height of the Cold War with the intent of defeating the main Cold War adversary, the Soviet Union and its client states.

Perhaps the most defining new program initiated or fielded during this time frame was the Strategic Defense Initiative or SDI. The program was designed to develop a protective missile shield over the United States and our allies, an extremely contentious program from its inception. First, there was the issue of the ABM treaty. A capability such as this would fracture the system of strategic deterrence that had been in place between the Soviet Union and United States, giving the United States a decided advantage with regard to defending against a Soviet nuclear attack. Second, the plan had significant technical issues. Experts debated whether SDI was even feasible, given the technological capabilities of the period. A third issue was the practicality of developing a comprehensive defense shield. Some compared SDI with the French Maginot Line, which was easily defeated by the Germans at the beginning of World War II. Fourth and finally, the potential costs of developing this defense capability would be staggering. Despite much debate, President Reagan formally announced the program and the intent to develop a defense shield for the United States. The Soviet reaction was predictable and the rhetoric hinged upon the impact of SDI on the ABM treaty. However, another extremely important concern was the Soviets' recognized inability to compete to develop a costly and technologically advanced complementary capability or counterforce.

The deployment of the Intermediate Nuclear Force, Pershing II missiles and air-launched cruise missiles, also had a significant impact on the Soviet and Warsaw Pact psyche, if not the balance in the theater. In terms of war fighting, the weapons represented a small increase in capability, but with regard to establishing a link between the defense of Europe and the U.S. strategic nuclear arsenal, their value was virtually incalculable. The elimination of these systems a short time later through negotiation in the INF treaty gives credible weight to the assertion that the presence of these systems caused the Soviets great concern.

During this time, NATO and the United States revised their thinking and plans for the defense of Europe. Until the early 1980s, the alliance planned to defend Europe using a concept called the active defense. In this doctrine, the intent was to establish battle positions from which the defense would be executed. As the defense became untenable, ground forces would continue to fall back into supplementary battle positions. Naval and air forces would resist the advancing Warsaw Pact threat, while ground forces attempted to slow the advance while awaiting reinforcements. The U.S. commitment of ten Army divisions in Europe in the first ten days was intended to be the initial wave of reinforcements.

The concept of active defense was replaced in the early 1980s with AirLand Battle. This concept, developed by the Army's Training and Doctrine Command or TRADOC was briefed throughout all levels of our government and to the NATO allies. It became the basis of a new, more offensively oriented doctrine that incorporated fire and maneuver to strike the enemy at critical points to the depth of their formation. The doctrine also incorporated "the strength of Western man, to exploit his innovativeness, independent thinking, flexibility, and adaptability."[46] Essentially, the doctrine called for integrated and extended battlefields. Integrated refers to the joint application of combined arms taking advantage of the synergy between ground maneuver elements consisting of tanks, artillery, infantry, and helicopters with fighter and bomber aircraft. Extending the battlefield referred to taking the fight to the enemy. Instead of fighting forces in direct-fire range in close battle, the notion was to attack deep into the enemy's rear to destroy and disrupt forces and operations.

The Impact of Economics

With the push during the 1970s to increase Soviet influence and power around the globe coupled with increasing military expenditures to keep pace with the United States, the Soviet Union began to show signs of increased economic stress. While a significant result was obviously the impact on the Soviet people, another was long-term prospects for sustaining this type of political-military competition. By the time President Reagan came to office in 1981, the cracks were beginning to show.[47]

The competition for allies and satellites became impossible for the Soviet Union to sustain during this period. Their command economy was falling further behind the West in terms of production and economic measures such as GNP and per capita income. Not nearly as measurable, but certainly recognized, was the inability to compete in technological and engineering advances, particularly in the field of information technologies. The true cost to the Soviets and their allies of maintaining this political and military machine could not really be discerned, as many of the true measures of cost did not apply. However, it was clear that this adventurism demanded a more robust economy.

Each acquisition or case of engagement further exacerbated the problem. The final straw was the Soviet foray into Afghanistan in the late 1970s. After what appeared to be a quick military operation, the long insurgency began, fueled by U.S. intervention in the form of military aid and covert operations. Over time, the Soviets were forced to withdraw after suffering a severe political and military defeat.

Conclusions

- The strategy of containment served to mobilize the collective efforts of the West and was central to the winning of the Cold War.
- There are limits to American power—certainly the American experience in Vietnam provided ample evidence of this fact.
- U.S. industrial capacity and technological advantages allowed the mass production of weapons and capabilities that overwhelmed the Soviet ability to compete.

- The role of economics in the demise of the Soviet Union and Warsaw Pact was significant.
- Defense reform was needed to allow for more coordinated use of force.
- The emergence of the early stages of the Information Age and the technological enhancements related to information technologies certainly signaled to the Soviet Union that they could not compete in this new arena.

4

INTO THE INFORMATION AGE

THE POST–COLD WAR ERA

TWO DEFINING EVENTS have shaped the post–Cold War era. First was the demise of the Soviet Union and Warsaw Pact. The confrontation that had been foremost on our national security agenda since the late 1940s was now alleviated. While the demise had been forecasted by many, the rapidity with which the Soviet Union and Warsaw Pact dissolved was certainly not widely predicted. The fall of the Berlin Wall is perhaps the most recognizable icon for the beginning of the period. The defining event of the later portion of this period is the terrorist attacks of 9/11 and the postattack examination of virtually all aspects of the failures and organizational deficiencies that either contributed to or allowed these attacks to be perpetrated against the United States. The responses to these attacks in terms of changes in the U.S. government have been equally significant.

The post–Cold War era is also a period in which a new phenomenon has emerged—globalization.[1] The relationship between the Information Age and globalization is clear and unmistakable. The homogenizing and compressing of peoples and societies is in large measure due to the information technologies that have emerged and helped to fuel the process.

The effect of the disintegration of the Soviet Union and Warsaw Pact and the integration of the world through globalization has led to great uncertainty and instability around the world. It is analogous to throwing a rock into the water, causing ripples that travel outward from the point of impact. Over time, the turbulence will dissipate and the body of water will return to its steady state.

However, in the initial phases, the rock hits the surface of the water with a violent impact.

The rapid implosion of the Soviet Union left a vacuum in terms of security policy and strategy around the world. Former satellites and client states that had once received political, economic, and military support now joined the ranks of the nonaligned nations. Some nations with strong political and economic prospects were able to move forward rapidly. Examples include Poland and the Baltic states of Latvia, Lithuania, and Estonia. Others such as Angola or Uganda have not fared as well, due as much to ethnic strife as to their limited economic prospects. In the case of Poland, the economy experienced a growth of 4.5 percent from 1990 to 2001. In contrast, the Democratic Republic of the Congo has seen its economy cut 5.1 percent over the same period.[2]

The fall of the Soviet Union also left the world with a single superpower and, oddly enough, a vacuum where U.S. national security policy had once been. For years, the United States had political structures and defense capabilities to match or defeat Soviet and Warsaw Pact capabilities. The demise of this threat also left the United States with a largely unchecked ability to engage throughout the globe.

With the Soviet and Warsaw Pact threat waning, questions began to surface about the rationale for the U.S. military. What size force should we have? Is the military still relevant? In what types of operations should or could the military be used? In the end, the country declared a peace dividend, and the armed forces were greatly reduced. As an example, the active-duty Army went from 760,000 to 480,000 soldiers. The other Services saw similar reductions, although the Army was most strongly impacted by this personnel downsizing.

The national security debate began with the fall of the Berlin Wall and continued throughout much of this period until the events of September 11, 2001. National Security Strategies were published in 1991, 1996, 1997, 1999, and 2002 in accordance with the law passed by Congress as part of the Goldwater-Nichols Defense Reorganization Act. The 1991 version focused on the demise of the Soviet Union and Warsaw Pact. In 1996, the debate was about the use of force (i.e., the military) for other than vital or humanitarian interests. The 1997 and 1999 versions saw little change from the 1996 version. With the publishing of the 2002 NSS following 9/11, the United States responded with a strategy of preemption.

Examining the frequency and types of operations to which the United States committed forces using the CRS data yields some useful insights. The period from 1990 to the present includes the greatest number of instances of the use of force abroad. However, some notes must be made to clarify the data. First, with the passing of the War Powers Act and the resultant requirement for the President to notify Congress of any commitment of U.S. forces, there are now multiple entries related to a single operation. Examples include Bosnia, in which yearly entries are noted beginning in 1995 with the initial deployment of forces as part of the NATO-led peacekeeping mission. Multiple entries are also listed with respect to conventional operations such as those in Iraq, where the United States has conducted several named operations such as Desert Fox (1998) or enforcement of the no-fly zones. Despite these flaws, the data indicate major deployments or combat operations in Desert Shield/Desert Storm (1990–91), Somalia (1993–95), Bosnia (1994–95), Kosovo (1999), Iraq (1992–present), and Afghanistan (2001–present). The number of peace and humanitarian operations has also continued to grow, with over forty of these types of operations during this period.

The first major action of this period is also noteworthy for another reason, as it is considered by some to be the first major operation of the early Information Age or at least using information technology capabilities on a large scale. In August 1990, the forces of Iraq, led by Saddam Hussein, invaded the neighboring country of Kuwait. The response to this unprovoked aggression was a U.S.-led effort to protect Saudi oil fields and free the kingdom of Kuwait. The Bush administration put together a broad multinational coalition, including Arab nations, engaging in Operations Desert Storm and Desert Shield.

These operations were also noteworthy as they were the first major conventional operations following the demise of the Soviet Union and Warsaw Pact. Under the Cold War system, the chance of a nuclear confrontation and simply the diversion of forces would have made this sort of large-scale deployment of forces nearly impossible without introducing unacceptable risk. However, with the Soviet Union no longer a threat and even some former adversaries assisting the coalition against Saddam, this operation to liberate Kuwait and protect Saudi Arabia could be undertaken.

The operations against Saddam also served as an example of the overwhelming superiority of U.S. forces. The equipment, systems, and procedures developed to combat the Soviet Union and Warsaw Pact had proven their worth. Even allied forces such as the French and British had not kept pace with U.S. developments in defense. This was particularly true in high-tech fields such as aviation and intelligence.

Information Age technologies were used almost exclusively by U.S. forces alone. For the first time, formations were guided by GPS. Targets were engaged by precision guided systems with great effect. Satellite systems beamed communications throughout the battlefield. Intelligence gleaned from space or from within the theater was sent to the United States, processed, and beamed to combat commanders on the ground within the theater almost instantaneously.

Almost as rapidly as the coalition defeated Saddam Hussein and the Iraqi Army, events unfolded in Somalia that served to remind us of the potentially deadly consequences of committing forces where the mission is ambiguous and the forces not properly equipped for the mission at hand. Initially, the operation in Somalia was a humanitarian mission designed to deliver needed food to a badly war-ravaged people. Over time, the mission transformed from humanitarian operations to a security mission, and finally to combat operations. Despite a change in the objectives, the necessary adjustment to the ways and means did not occur, causing a mismatch of troops to task. In October 1993, a battle raged in the streets of Mogadishu following an ill-fated attempt to capture the notorious warlord, Mohamed Farah Aideed. Shortly thereafter, U.S. forces left Somalia, and debates once again ensued concerning the use of force. In particular, the question of using force for less than vital interests was considered. The unsuccessful operation in Somalia resurrected discussions about peacekeeping and peace enforcement operations conducted under UN command and control.

With several operations throughout the Balkans to stabilize the region, the debate about the use of force for other than vital interests has largely subsided. However, these operations have also assisted in the maturation of thinking on how force can and should be used. In Bosnia and Kosovo, given the right set of circumstances, including a war-weary society, decisive NATO force, significant authority provided by a robust UN mandate, an operation under competent NATO command and control, and NATO perseverance, the operations have been successful.

A topic that has received considerable scrutiny during this period is peace operations. The UN categorizes peace operations as peacekeeping or peace enforcement. The distinction is that in peacekeeping, there is generally a peace to keep and thus the means of enforcement are not as coercive, while peace enforcement tends to require a more robust application of force using decisive military means. Perhaps the most highly publicized remark concerning the use of the military for these operations was recounted by Colin Powell in his memoirs. At one point in deliberations concerning commitment of force in Bosnia, Madeline Albright asked, "What's the point of having this superb military you're always talking about, if we can't use it?"[3]

Experience indicates that peace operations are extremely complex and require a mix of both military and nonmilitary capabilities to achieve success, including establishing and maintaining security and nation-building activities. In countries where peace operations are conducted, there are usually issues with regard to reestablishing one or more of the following: the rule of law, the political process, economic viability, the educational system, basic services, or the human rights of the society.

By implication, then, the military must have partners from within the Interagency that are able to deploy in concert to provide rebuilding capabilities rapidly on the heels of the establishment of a stable and secure environment. Failure to do so can have dire consequences, as the expectations of the populace are generally quite high.

The discussion of national security in this period would not be complete without a mention of the Nunn-Lugar Cooperative Threat Reduction (CTR) program designed to eliminate nuclear weapons from the states of the former Soviet Union. Since 1991, the $400 million per year Nunn-Lugar program has deactivated 6,072 nuclear warheads. It has destroyed 515 ballistic missiles, 441 ballistic missile silos, 115 bombers, 399 submarine-launched missiles, 408 submarine missile launchers, and 27 strategic missile submarines. It has sealed 194 nuclear test tunnels. More than 20,000 scientists formerly employed in WMD programs have been employed in cooperative, peaceful endeavors.[4]

DEFENSE RESTRUCTURING TO MEET THE CHALLENGES OF A NEW WORLD

With the end of the Cold War, several initiatives were undertaken to restructure the military. Essentially, national security strategy and military planning had always been threat based. That is, a threat was examined to determine the vulnerabilities it caused to U.S. national security. Based on these assessments, a strategy was developed including the ways and means required for achieving the stated national security goals.

However, with no enemy to size the U.S. national security effort against, the DOD turned to a capability-based formulation of national security and defense strategy. This amounted to developing a general set of capabilities that could be employed as necessary to achieve national security policy. As one might imagine, this is a significantly less precise way to calculate national security requirements. Whereas before, one could use analysis and simulations to assess U.S. and allied capabilities against the Soviet Union and Warsaw Pact, now less specific threats resulted in a general set of capabilities that would have application in a variety of theaters. For the Korean theater, however, this was not a major issue as the force required was more easily defined because it remained a focused effort with a defined threat.

The first comprehensive review following the demise of the Soviet and Warsaw Pact threat was President Bush's 1991 NSS, which described a "minimum essential military force—the Base Force." This new strategy envisioned "continued forward presence, prepositioning of military equipment overseas and the need to contain regional threats, including possibly a limited conventional threat to Europe."[5]

The "new" strategy drew considerable criticism, primarily from those who felt that it did not adequately address the enormous changes underway. These critics believed that many of the Cold War assumptions, policies, and practices were left in place by this strategy. On the other hand, some believed that the Soviet Union and Warsaw Pact could still reconstitute and that they had retained formidable capabilities even if their intentions had changed. Some believed that a resurgent Soviet threat was possible.

The second effort at defining a new strategy, the Bottom-Up Review (BUR) undertaken in 1993 by Secretary of Defense Les Aspin, called for retaining the capability to fight and win, without allies, two major regional wars simultaneously.

Following these first two efforts, a formal requirement was established to examine the DOD strategy, force structure, modernization, and infrastructure on a periodic basis. On September 30, 1996, President Clinton signed the DOD Fiscal Year 1997 Authorization Act, which contained the Military Structure Review Act of 1996, which codified this requirement. This act calls for providing Congress with a Quadrennial Defense Review (QDR), "at the beginning of each newly elected Presidential administration." While the intent of the legislation is pure, its implementation has not resulted in substantial reform. As an example, a defense pundit wrote of the 1997 QDR, the first of these submissions:

> On May 19 the Defense Secretary Cohen released the results of the Defense Department's Quadrennial Defense Review (QDR). It was the Pentagon's third attempt to construct a post-cold war military strategy, and like its predecessors, it failed to weave forces and budgets into a coherent military policy. By avoiding the hard decisions, the Pentagon made it easier for reactionary elements in the military-industrial-congressional complex to protect their parochial interests at the expense of our fighting forces and the taxpayers who pay for them. The Pentagon struck out, and the contractors are now in the batter's box.
>
> It re-affirmed the strategy of being preparing to fight two major regional wars nearly simultaneously, but it also committed the military to a strategy of global engagement, wherein a large portion of our forces are deployed overseas in peace-keeping operations such as Bosnia, Haiti, and no-fly zones over Iraq, etc. Although the QDR made a few minor changes in force structure, most notably a reduction of 15 warships and a transfer of one Air Force fighter wing to the reserves, it retained the main elements of the Defense Department's combat power: 10 active Army divisions, 3 active Marine divisions, 12 carrier battle groups, 12 amphibious ready groups, 20 active and reserve Air Force tactical fighter wings, and 187 strategic bombers.[6]

Generally, the assessment of previous QDR submissions is that they have been highly politicized and conservative and have not resulted in the needed reforms. Overall, little change proposed by or resulting from the QDR system has been enacted. The best predictor of funding, forces, and organizations remains the current levels or structure. In general, most changes are made on the margin, with little stomach for taking on the hard issues that are at the core of the DOD. For example, questions such as the value of one Army division versus one Air Force fighter wing versus one Navy aircraft carrier do not get addressed directly.

If one believes that the allocation of resources or means provides insight into strategy, then one would have to question whether the "Services Percentage Share of DOD Budget" in table 3 shows any change in strategy in the transition from the Cold War to the post—Cold War era. The table includes data from 1980 to 2003. As a reference, 1980 is included, followed by 1989, the year that the

TABLE 3. Defense Spending

Year	Army	Navy	Air Force	Defense-wide
1980	24.4	33.1	29.3	13.3
1989	27.0	33.7	32.5	6.9
1993	24.7	31.5	27.8	14.2
1997	25.5	31.2	30.1	14.6
2001	25.4	31.3	30.9	13.9
2002	23.5	28.7	31.0	20.4
2003	24.0	28.6	28.2	19.2

Berlin Wall came down. The remainder of the years listed are the QDR years. The data indicate that the total obligation authority (TOA) or budget for the Services remained fairly constant for the period 1980-2001. After this point, the Navy and Air Force TOA dropped by 2 to 3 percent. Also of note is the rise in defense-wide spending, which reflects the growth in agencies such as the Defense Threat Reduction Agency (DTRA) or the Defense Health Program (DHP).

Given that the end of the Cold War should have resulted in a significant change in strategy, one would anticipate that resources would also change significantly. However, this does not appear to have been the case. Looking farther into the TOA at weapons programs also does not indicate a large change in the major systems to be procured. As an example, the Air Force is continuing to buy the F-22 and participate in the Joint Strike Fighter (JSF) program despite having air campaign capabilities that are generations better than those of any other nation. The important question really is what mix of capabilities is required to ensure the security of the United States, rather than what advanced tactical fighter is the optimum platform for air-to-air or air-to-ground roles?

Of equal concern with the QDR methodology should be the potential for incremental changes based on projections of strategy and operations that could have dire consequences. For example, the major question facing the panel during the 2001 QDR was whether to reduce the Army from ten to eight active divisions. Today that question seems rather unenlightened, given participation in operations in Iraq and Afghanistan, steady-state operations in Korea, engagement in Asia and Latin America, and recovery from combat operations. In contrast, the discussion for 2005 is about increasing the Army to the equivalent of fifteen active-duty divisions (i.e., going from thirty-three to forty-eight brigades).

At the end of the first Gulf War, there was recognition of an impending Revolution in Military Affairs (RMA). Much work has gone on during the ensuing period to deal with increasing the efficiency and effectiveness of the Joint Force. In particular, efforts have been made to transform the Services.

At its core, transformation is really about bringing the military into the Information Age. Military transformation includes a series of efforts to ensure that the Services develop systems and procedures that will enhance the overall performance of the DOD. The DOD established an Office of Force Transformation in October 2001 to "challenge the status quo with new concepts for American defense to ensure an overwhelming and continuing competitive advantage for America's military for decades to come."[7] The office is led by one of the brightest minds in military theory today, Vice Admiral (Ret.) Arthur Cebrowski. For years, Cebrowski has pushed the notion of "net-centric warfare" to describe the military's movement toward the Information Age. To describe these concepts, the DOD transformation office writes the following:

> The world is shifting from the industrial to the information age, characterized by complex, non-linear, and inherently unpredictable challenges. In order to maintain and increase a competitive advantage in this environment, we are witnessing fundamental changes in how militaries organize, fight and interact with each other and with non-military organizations.
>
> Network Centric Warfare, a maturing theory of Information Age Warfare, provides a foundation and framework for militaries to shape and operate in this new environment.
>
> Militaries around the world recognize that operating in the information age calls for robustly networked forces to share information and collaborate across time and space. This entails a shift to agile, innovative and creative decision making from the top out to the "edges" of the organization. This creates a tension requiring significant innovation in technical, social, cultural and organizational processes and procedures designed for success.[8]

As the military transformation concept has matured, the goal has changed from developing interoperability between the various components to gaining Joint interdependence. The distinction between these terms is that interoperability implies that the Services can operate in the same environment, but that seams may still exist. As an example, ground and air forces could be interoperable if close air support can be delivered effectively in support of ground forces. Joint interdependence "purposefully combines Service capabilities to maximize their total complementary and reinforcing effects, while minimizing their relative vulnerabilities."[9] For example, the Army could reduce indirect-fire artillery units and rely on the Air Force for a large portion of its indirect fire. Of course, this interdependence will require an information sharing and networking capability that is real-time, robust, self-healing, and assured.

In thinking about transforming to an Information Age force, the Army has developed the concept of "see first, understand first, act first, and finish decisively." The notion is that information will be a driver that will allow for seeing the three-dimensional battle space and analyzing and synthesizing the information to create an understanding of the situation. With this picture and understanding of the battle space, the force will have the capability to take the first action and finally finish decisively, achieving assigned missions, operational imperatives, and strategic goals.

Another defense reform initiative is the Beyond Goldwater-Nichols Study published in March 2004 by the Center for Strategic and International Studies. This initiative was undertaken by the Washington-based policy think tank to take a broad view of defense reform in the new strategic era. The major topic areas for the recommendations included rationalizing organizational structures in DOD, joint procurement of command and control capabilities, a more effective resource allocation process, strengthening civilian professionals in defense and national security, improving interagency and coalition operations, and strengthening congressional oversight.

The study looked to build on the previous Goldwater-Nichols Act and create even more efficiencies and effectiveness within the DOD, particularly with regard to eliminating seams between the Services and the Combatant Commanders in the field. The study also proposed streamlining command and control relationships and eliminating redundancies. An area receiving considerable scrutiny was the resource allocation process, which continues to be a target for defense reform initiatives.

Phase I of the study has been completed and the results are briefly presented above. Phase II is ongoing with an approximate completion date in 2005.

An internal initiative for defense reform was initiated in March 2003 by Secretary of Defense Donald Rumsfeld. The study was called the Joint Defense Capabilities Study (JDCS) and had a charter to do the following:

- Optimize capabilities across the department, not within the components
- Support both near- and far-term joint war fighting and enterprise (non-war fighting) needs
- Base decisions on open and explicit analysis
- Shorten the response time for innovation, decision making, and implementation
- Allow senior decision makers to make major risk decisions "up front"

A significant outcome of the Joint Defense Capabilities Study is the restructuring of the Joint Strategic Planning Process and the development of the Program Objective Memorandum (POM) or five-year defense plan. The changes that have been incorporated have put more effort into developing the defense strategy and have reduced the amount of time spent on the budget and program (i.e., resources). The notion is that since strategy should drive resources, more time should be spent with strategy development.

Other initiatives that were proposed included combining staffs such as the Office of the Secretary of Defense and Joint Staff, and in the Services consolidating the staff for the Secretary and Chief of each Service. Some of these

TABLE 4. Proposed Defense Reform Initiatives

Major Process	Existing Problems	End-State Attributes
Strategy	• Multiple documents • Joint needs and guidance not integrated, prioritized, or fiscally informed	• Single translation of NSS into department objectives, priorities, and risk tolerance • Conceptual framework and focus for planning and capability development • Resource-informed strategic planning guidance
Planning	• Defense planning guidance (DPG) is provided late and is not fiscally constrained • DPG is developed by OSD • The DPG makes little, if any, provision for trade-offs among components	• "Jointness" is born at the beginning of the process • Joint programming guidance is provided early and is fiscally constrained: Developed collaboratively, with extensive involvement by combatant commanders and components; Articulates a single statement of joint needs that reflects decisions on trade-offs among components
Resourcing	• Components' programs cannot comply with all of the requirements of the DPG • Adversarial, labor-intensive process • Senior leadership forces "jointness" into the process at the end, with great effort • Gaps and redundancies in joint capabilities render the defense program cost-ineffective	• Collaborative, efficient process produces early decisions • Senior leadership attends to issues of compliance and executability
Execution and accountability	• Focus on expenditure/adherence to regulations • Prolonged and complicated process to produce new capabilities • Human capital planning and costs are not addressed • Logistics and acquisition cycle time and support are not timely or cost-effective • Execution data not useful for decision making	• Focus on performance/results • Reduced cycle time so that capabilities are developed to meet emerging needs • Human capital managed strategically • Full costs (acquisition and logistics sustainment) considered and continually refreshed • Execution reporting provides feedback to planning and resourcing processes

organizational recommendations have not been well received, either within the DOD or by those within the defense community who think that the initiatives may swing the balance of power too heavily in one direction. For example, the proposal to combine the Office of the Secretary of Defense and the Joint Staff would leave the Chairman of the Joint Chiefs of Staff (CJCS) with a reduced ability to serve as the principal military adviser to the President.

In the final report, dated December 2003, a table was provided that looked at the problems and desired end-state attributes for the major processes including strategic planning, resourcing and execution and accountability (table 4). This table provides a good summary of the study.

Another key outcome was the direction to produce Strategic Planning Guidance (SPG). Previously DOD only produced Defense Planning Guidance (DPG) as the programming and budgeting guidance before developing a POM. In an effort to ensure linkage between the strategy and the programming and budgeting, a specific document, the Strategic Planning Guidance, was included. Based on this strategic guidance, more detailed programmatic and budgeting direction is provided in the follow-up Defense Planning Guidance.

This fifth period has been replete with discussions dealing with defense reform initiatives—this is especially true for the latter years of the 1990s. The discussions have examined issues from national security strategy and policy down to equipment procurement reform, and include everything in between. Many of the findings and recommendations, particularly for the more recent analyses, are currently being vetted.

Unfortunately, the same condition does not exist for the other elements of national power. There has been little reform to better respond to the challenges posed by the post–Cold War environment. Despite an increase in operations such as nation building, which are clearly broader than defense, little has been done to expand the contribution of the nontraditional or soft power elements of national power. Indeed, in these other areas an almost laissez-faire approach has been taken. Several initiatives that look more broadly at the other elements of power are presented below.

BROADENING NATIONAL SECURITY TO THINK BEYOND DEFENSE

The discussion over the last few pages has focused exclusively on transitioning to the Information Age as it pertains to the military. This was done deliberately, as my intent was to transition from the discussion of the Cold War with the strong focus on political-military interaction to a more balanced treatment of national security. In making the transition, three efforts or initiatives warrant further investigation.

First is the inclusion of economics within the national security framework under the Clinton administration. The second initiative was a comprehensive analysis of national security issues as part of a three-year effort from 1999 to 2001 as part of the U.S. Commission on National Security/21st Century, better known as the Hart-Rudman Commission. The final major initiative is divided into two parts, the immediate changes made in the aftermath of the terrorist attacks on September 11, 2001, and the 9/11 Commission Report. Before reviewing each, a disclaimer is in order. The reader is likely at this point to be dismissive of my argument, thinking that indeed economic tools have been and currently are very much in use today. These arguments do have validity. However, it is really the level of participation, which seems small in comparison to the political-military, that is in question.

Clearly, economic development has fueled the development of the United States as a world power and in turn the national security strategy of our nation. With only 5 percent of the world's population, the United States produces nearly one-fifth of the world's output of coal, copper, and crude petroleum. U.S. agricultural capability is also quite robust, producing nearly half of the world's corn; nearly one-fifth of its beef, pork, mutton, and lamb; and more than one-tenth of its wheat. The United States owes its economic position more to its highly developed industry than to its natural resources or agricultural output, but this development would have stagnated without access to new markets and sources of raw materials. Unfettered access, in turn, requires the ability to ensure free transit of waterways, protect U.S. citizens and property across the globe, and enforce international law, if required. Our national security tools, fueled by economic development and the drive for further economic growth, have certainly provided the resources and drive, respectively, that have led to the corresponding growth in defense capabilities. But few, if any, would point to economic prosperity as a national security tool.

Another example is the use of foreign aid, which assists in supporting developing counties. Total expenditures, not including Department of Defense, are approximately $15 billion per year for these humanitarian and developmental programs. However, this figure does not include resources such as those allocated for one-time purposes such as the reconstruction of Iraq, which is covered in a supplemental appropriation. For example, what about foreign aid, such as that provided to Israel and Egypt to the tune of $2.7 and $2.0 billion per year, respectively?[10] This aid is at times tagged for certain purposes such as defense; in other cases it is fairly open ended. In other cases, such as Pakistan, the United States has provided debt forgiveness. These are clearly uses of the economic tools of our nation in a deliberate way to gain favor with foreign governments and their people.

The use of Normal Trade Relations (NTR) status, formerly known as Most Favored Nation (MFN) status, has also been used to identify and reward those nations that are part of the international community of nations in good standing.

The delineation of normal trade relations was based on the United States join-ing the General Agreement on Tariffs and Trade (GATT) in 1948. With this agreement, the United States extended Most Favored Nation status to all other countries on a bilateral basis. The status was also extended to some countries that did not join GATT. However, in 1951, the U.S. Congress directed President Harry Truman to revoke Most Favored Nation status from the Soviet Union and other Communist countries. Today, nearly all nations have Normal Trade Re-lations with the United States. Those that do not, such as Iran and North Korea, are the exception.

What about the use of embargoes or blockades? Clearly, these tools have an economic component. However, both of these methods are really coercive measures with more of a military component, designed to punish another nation or bloc of nations (as in the case of the Cold War).

There clearly are numerous examples of the use of economics as tools of foreign policy throughout our nation's history, primarily in the period since World War II. However, in assessing their use, it is worth noting that the total resources involved are quite small in comparison to the other national security tools in use, and that potentially economics could be more adequately incor-porated into the national security strategy toolkit. This concept is discussed in more detail later.

The National Economic Council

The National Economic Council (NEC) was an initiative by the Clinton administration to integrate and coordinate his administration's economic poli-cies. As described in *An Assessment of the National Economic Council*, by Kenneth Juster and Simon Lazarus, "The NEC may not have been a radical departure from the past, but it clearly was a new approach, located in the White House, with a broad charter covering both international and domestic policy and a top-level manager, the assistant to the president for economic policy."[11]

Other Presidents had attempted to incorporate economics into national security policy, as in Truman's inclusion of the Secretary of the Treasury in NSC meetings. However, largely because President Clinton was elected on a platform of needing to reenergize the economy, this initiative is noteworthy. The most common slogan from this period in election campaigning was, "It's the economy, stupid."

The NEC was created based on the conclusions of two prominent com-missions which recommended that in the post–Cold War world, economics needed a more prominent role. Examples of key outcomes from the NEC include the development of a five-year deficit reduction plan, a recommendation to press for enactment of the North American Free Trade Agreement (NAFTA) giving international trades issues higher profile, and working to link public investment programs with social programs.

Despite some successes, the institutionalism of the NEC and the development of an economic national security strategy do not appear to be on the horizon. In fact, the Commission on National Security/21st Century, to be discussed shortly, recommends the abolishment of the NEC. This proposal does not signal that the economic component of national security strategy will not be considered, but rather that the commission has a different proposal for dealing with developing a national economic strategy.

The U.S. Commission on National Security/21st Century

This commission was a three-part effort to examine national security challenges, opportunities, and issues in this new century as well as proposing recommendations and adaptations for addressing future U.S. national security strategy.

Phase I was conducted from July 1998 to August 1999 and examined the evolution of the world over the next twenty-five years, until 2025. It produced a comprehensive document that examined "global trends in scientific, technological, economic, socio-political and military security domains and the interplay of these developments on U.S. national security."[12] Phase I included an executive overview as well as an exhaustive review of the scientific, technological, economic, sociopolitical and military security assessments for each region of the world. The findings provide a detailed set of potential scenarios that frame several outcomes. In addition, a global trends section developed several future scenarios for the world in the 2025 period, along with implications of advances in technology. The major themes and implications of the Phase I study appear below.

Phase II, from August 2000 to April 2001 developed a potential national security strategy for the United States for the 2025 time frame. In construction and tone, it is very similar to previous national security strategies published by the White House.

Included in the document are a set of key objectives. The Phase II report, titled Seeking a National Strategy and dated April 15, 2000, lists six major objectives, provided below.

These objectives are worth reviewing for several reasons. First and foremost, they are largely based on the core values on which the United States was founded. As a result, they are somewhat impervious to change. For comparison, the 1991 NSS lists four interests, including (1) the survival of the United States as a free and independent nation, with its fundamental values intact and its institutions and people secure; (2) a healthy and growing U.S. economy to ensure the opportunity for individual prosperity and resources for national endeavors at home; (3) healthy, cooperative, and politically vigorous relations with allies and friendly nations; and (4) a stable and secure world, where political and economic freedom, human rights, and democratic institutions flourish.

U.S. Commission on National Security/21st Century
Major Themes and Implications
September 15, 1999

1. America will become increasingly vulnerable to hostile attack on our homeland and our military superiority will not entirely protect us.
2. Rapid advances in information and biotechnologies will create new vulnerabilities for U.S. security.
3. New technologies will divide the world as well as draw it together.
4. The national security of all advanced states will be increasingly affected by the vulnerabilities of the evolving global economic infrastructure.
5. Energy will continue to have major strategic significance.
6. All borders will be more porous; some will bend and some will break.
7. The sovereignty of states will come under pressure, but will endure.
8. Fragmentation or failure of states will occur, with destabilizing effects on neighboring states.
9. Foreign crises will be replete with atrocities and the deliberate terrorizing of civilian populations.
10. Space will become a critical and competitive military environment.
11. The essence of war will not change.
12. U.S. intelligence will face more challenging adversaries and even excellent intelligence will not prevent all surprises.
13. The United States will be called upon frequently to intervene militarily in a time of uncertain alliances and with the prospect of fewer forward-deployed forces.
14. The emerging security environment in the next quarter century will require different military and other national capabilities.

A comparison of the 1991 interests and objectives with those contained in the commission's report generally indicate that the basic ends of the strategies are close, if not in one-for-one correspondence. Key themes in both include defense of American values, territory, and people, vigorous relations with allies, promotion of stability and security, respect and promotion of human rights, and economic prosperity. The second major reason for their inclusion is that they form the basis for the recommendations and principles developed in part II.

Phase III of the commission's activities, from April 2000 to February 2001, recommends changes in the U.S. government (particularly in the Executive and Legislative branches) to respond effectively in the 2025 time frame for enhancing America's security. The full set of recommendations is included in appendix B. However, an analysis that groups and assesses the focus of the recommendations is provided in table 5. For the analysis, many of the recommendations could have been considered to have multiple components and thus could have been counted in several categories.

Proposed National Security Objectives from the U. S. Commission
on National Security/21st Century

First, to defend the United States and ensure that it is safe from the dangers
    of a new era.

Second, to maintain America's social cohesion, economic competitiveness,
    technological ingenuity, and military strength.

Third, to assist the integration of key major powers, especially China, Russia,
    and India, into the mainstream of the emerging international system.

Fourth, to promote, with others, the dynamism of the new global economy
    and improve the effectiveness of international institutions and international
    law.

Fifth, to adapt U.S. alliances and other regional mechanisms to a new era in
    which America's partners seek greater autonomy and responsibility.

Sixth, to help the international community tame the disintegrative forces
    spawned by an era of change.

An example is recommendation 6, which states, "The Secretary of Defense, at the President's direction, should make homeland security a primary mission of the National Guard, and the Guard should be organized and properly trained, and adequately equipped to undertake that mission." In the analysis, the initiative was characterized as "domestic" focus and the "homeland defense" element of power.

The overarching conclusion is that the focus of the fifty recommendations was on restructuring the U.S. government, particularly the National Security Council, DOD, State Department, and the Intelligence Community. Simply put, most of the initiatives were focused domestically, while only two directly involved foreign initiatives.

One could argue that any initiative to restructure the State Department is a foreign-focused recommendation. This was not the manner in which the analysis was conducted. Rather, a more narrow view was taken. As an example, a foreign focus would include the development of overseas initiatives to promote a better understanding of the United States but would not include the restructuring of the State Department.

The questions resulting from this analysis really are these: Should we be concerned about the lack of focus on change or efforts outside the United States? Do we believe that retooling the internal organizations and processes of this nation will be enough to ensure U.S. security? If the answer is yes to both, then we must implement these initiatives immediately. However, if the answer to one or both is no, then a more comprehensive analysis is in order.

Another important conclusion is that most of the recommendations deal with the habitual national security strategy elements of political and military (and by

TABLE 5. Analysis of Recommendations from the U.S. Commission on National Security/21st Century

	No. of Recommendations	Focus		Element of Power										
		Foreign	Domestic	Foreign Policy/Political	Defense/Military	Homeland Defense	Intelligence	Legal	Science and Technology	Economic	Cultural	Human Rights/Liberties	Education	Informational
Securing the Homeland	7	2	7	1	3	7	3	2						
Recapitalizing America's Strengths in Science and Education	6		6						4				3	
Institutional Redesign	25		25	8	15	3	7	3	1	4	1			
The Human Requirements for National Security	7		7	4	2			2			1		1	
The Role of Congress	5		5	5	2	2	2							
	50	2	50	18	22	12	12	7	5	4	2	0	4	0

extension intelligence and legal) issues. The distinction to be drawn is that the recommendations tend to address perceived flaws or failings in the structure of the U.S. national security apparatus rather than looking more broadly at other elements of power as they relate to national security policy. Few issues were targeted other than traditional national security elements such as economics, culture, education, or even information.

The lack of direct focus on information and gaining information dominance, given the emergence of the Information Age, is certainly a shortfall that requires more attention and is addressed as part of the recommendations in part II. Despite this critique, the report remains one of the most articulate and descriptive accounts of the future challenges the United States is likely to face in 2025.

The Post-9/11 Examination

Shortly after the publication of the final report from the U.S. Commission on National Security/21st Century, the United States was brutally attacked by al-Qaeda, a terrorist group headed by Osama bin Laden. On September 11, 2001, using hijacked civilian aircraft as missiles, attacks were perpetrated against the World Trade Center towers and the Pentagon by three airplanes. A fourth crashed in a field in Pennsylvania after passengers stormed the plane's cockpit.

Events of 9/11 generated many questions and a desperate search for answers. How could this tragedy have occurred? Could it happen again? Were there cues that were missed by the various intelligence agencies? How can we improve homeland defense and better protect U.S. citizens? With the desire to answer these and the many other questions surrounding the incident, Congress and the President created the National Commission on Terrorist Attacks upon the United States (Public Law 107-306, November 27, 2002). The result was the 9/11 Commission Report, published in July 2004, almost three years following the terrorist attacks. However, this intervening period was not a time of inaction or simple reflection. In-depth consultations resulted in a series of Presidential Decision Directives; strategies to address subordinate issues impacting on our nation's security; Congressional consultations; and finally legislation making profound changes in the structure of the U.S. government.

The Immediate Response

Shortly after the 9/11 attacks, the Homeland Security Act of 2002 was passed. This legislation established the Department of Homeland Security (DHS) with seven missions, including the following: (1) prevent terrorist attacks within the United States; (2) reduce the vulnerability of the United States to terrorism; (3) minimize the damage, and assist in the recovery, from terrorist attacks that do occur within the United States; (4) carry out all functions of entities transferred to the Department, including by acting as a focal point regarding natural and manmade crises and emergency planning; (5) ensure that the functions of the agencies and subdivisions within the Department that are not related directly to securing the homeland are not diminished or neglected except by a specific explicit act of Congress; (6) ensure that the overall economic security of the United States is not diminished by efforts, activities, and programs aimed at securing the homeland; and (7) monitor connections between illegal drug trafficking and terrorism, coordinate efforts to sever such connections, and otherwise contribute to efforts to interdict illegal drug trafficking.[13]

The Homeland Security Act also established a Homeland Security Council (HSC), intended to be complementary to the NSC established in the National Security Act of 1947. Many of the duties and organizational structures in the HSC parallel those of the NSC. The function of the HSC is to advise the President on homeland security matters. The HSC membership consists of the President, Vice President, Secretary of Homeland Security, the Attorney General, Secretary of Defense, and other individuals as may be designated by the President.

With regard to composition, the difference between the NSC and HSC membership is the Secretary of State in the NSC and the Secretary of Homeland Security and the Attorney General in the HSC. The legislation also allows for the convening of both the NSC and HSC simultaneously, at the prerogative of the President.

As with most legislation of this magnitude and influence, significant reporting requirements are embedded that cut across numerous departments of the U.S. government. For example, there is a requirement to report on improvement in immigration services, specifically with regard to the backlog of people awaiting ruling on their citizenship applications.

Essentially, with the enacting of this legislation, the United States has developed complementary and competing structures for foreign and domestic defense and security. The issue was directly addressed within the body of the first National Strategy for Homeland Security (NSHS), published in July 2002. In the last line of the excerpt below, the relationship between the NSS of the United States and the NSHS is clearly equal, with no stated precedence between them. The development of the HSC was not without controversy, as some argued that the separation of security and defense in this manner creates a seam to be exploited rather than streamlining and consolidating essential security and defense roles and missions.

The NSHS lists three strategic objectives: (1) prevent terrorist attacks within the United States; (2) reduce America's vulnerability to terrorism; and (3) minimize the damage and recover from attacks that do occur. Evaluating these three objectives and comparing them to the NSS of 2002, the most recent national strategy formulation, indicates the degree to which they overlap. While redundancy is not necessarily a bad thing to ensure a high degree of success (for example, using multiple computers for polling on the space shuttle) in organizations and bureaucracies, negatives such as unhealthy competition, lack of coordination and synchronization, or failure to address seam issues are certainly possible outcomes.

The consolidation of the effort of eleven of the fourteen cabinet-level departments, including State, Defense, Justice, Transportation, Energy, Treasury, Interior, Agriculture, Commerce, Health and Human Services, Veterans Affairs, and several other essential subordinate agencies, such as the CIA, Environmental Protection Agency, and Federal Emergency Management Agency, was a necessary first step to improving the security of the United States. However, it would be disingenuous not to also acknowledge that the manner in which this consolidation occurred created a seam precariously down the center of the issue between foreign and domestic security and defense, and brought the management

Homeland Security and National Security

The Preamble to the Constitution defines our federal government's basic purposes as " to form a more perfect Union, establish justice, insure domestic Tranquility, provide for the common defense, promote the general Welfare, and secure the Blessings of Liberty to ourselves and our Posterity." The requirement to provide for the common defense remains as fundamental today as it was when these words were written, more than two hundred years ago.

The National Security Strategy of the United States aims to guarantee the sovereignty and independence of the United States, with our fundamental values and institutions intact. It provides a framework for creating and seizing opportunities that strengthen our security and prosperity. The National Strategy for Homeland Security complements the National Security Strategy of the United States by addressing a very specific and uniquely challenging threat–terrorism in the United States–and by providing a comprehensive framework for organizing the efforts of federal, state, local, and private organizations whose primary functions are often unrelated to national security.

The link between national security and homeland security is a subtle but important one. For more than six decades, America has sought to protect its own sovereignty and independence through a strategy of global presence and engagement. In so doing, America has helped many other countries and peoples advance along the path of democracy, open markets, individual liberty, and peace with their neighbors. Yet there are those who oppose America's role in the world, and who are willing to use violence against us and our friends. Our great power leaves these enemies with few conventional options for doing us harm. One such option is to take advantage of our freedom and openness by secretly inserting terrorists into our country to attack our homeland. Homeland security seeks to deny this avenue of attack to our enemies and thus to provide a secure foundation for America's ongoing global engagement. Thus the National Security Strategy of the United States and National Strategy for Homeland Security work as mutually supporting documents, providing guidance to the executive branch departments and agencies.

There are also a number of other, more specific strategies maintained by the United States that are subsumed within the twin concepts of national security and homeland security. The National Strategy for Combating Terrorism will define the U.S. war plan against international terrorism. The National Strategy to Combat Weapons of Mass Destruction coordinates America's many efforts to deny terrorists and states the materials, technology, and expertise to make and deliver weapons of mass destruction. The National Strategy to Secure Cyberspace will describe our initiatives to secure our information systems against deliberate, malicious disruption. The National Money Laundering Strategy aims to undercut the illegal flows of money that support terrorism and international criminal activity. The National Defense Strategy sets priorities for our most powerful national security instrument. The National Drug Control Strategy lays out a comprehensive U.S. effort to combat drug smuggling and consumption. All of these documents fit into the framework established by the National Security Strategy of the United States and National Strategy for Homeland Security, which together take precedence over all other national strategies, programs, and plans.[14]

and resolution of issues up to the President or Vice President level, rather than where it resided prior to 9/11, within a staff element such as the NSC. The manner in which the President chooses to fulfill this responsibility will significantly impact on whether this seam will have operational significance. Furthermore, it is highly unlikely that potential adversaries will respect this sort of distinction in the execution of their plans.

To continue with this train of thought, the rationale for how this issue unfolds is based largely on the legal basis for the treatment of people, according to whether they are citizens or guests in our country, or whether they are noncitizens outside the United States. The issue is one of sovereignty and is at the very heart of the Constitution and Bill of Rights.

Still, to place an artificial boundary on such a critical aspect of our nation's security and defense seems somewhat imprudent. Perhaps now is a point in our nation's history to reexamine some of the limiting legislation concerning the use of the military on U.S. soil and the monitoring of people and organizations within the United States. These issues are further addressed in part II.

The 9/11 Commission

The 9/11 Commission Report, published on July 22, 2004, is a lengthy, thorough, and awesome account of the nation's unpreparedness. The implications reach across the United States and foreign governments, law enforcement agencies at all levels, the Intelligence Community, the DOD, emergency preparedness organizations or first responders, and even our society in general. The report is noteworthy for its completeness as well as for its recommendations. Embedded in the later chapters of the report are forty-one recommendations to address the shortfalls identified during the commission's tenure. These recommendations are a focus for this analysis.

In assessing the report, one must also consider that the lengthy time between the attacks and the publishing of the findings caused some of the "recommendations" to be implemented prior to the publication of the report. Even where changes to our national security system have been implemented, they may not have been done so exactly in accordance with the published recommendations.

Using the same methodology as described above for the U.S. Commission on National Security/21st Century, each of the recommendations has been characterized as a foreign or domestic focus according to the elements of power that it encompasses. The intent was to try and judiciously categorize the recommendations into the various elements and be more, rather than less, restrictive. The full analysis for each of the recommendations is provided in appendix C.

The results have been summarized in table 6, which compares the recommendations from the National Security/21st Century and 9/11 commissions in terms of their focus and the elements of power.

TABLE 6. Comparison of Recommendations from Commission on National Security and the 9/11 Commission

	No. of Recommendations	Focus		Element of Power										
		Foreign	Domestic	Political	Defense/Military	Homeland Defense	Intelligence	Legal	Science and Technology	Economic	Cultural	Human Rights/Liberties	Education	Informational
9/11 Commission Recommendations	41	15	28	11	17	24	29	25	0	7	8	9	8	8
National Security/ 21st Century	50	2	50	18	22	12	12	7	4	5	2	0	4	0
	91	17	78	29	39	36	41	32	4	12	10	9	12	8

The 9/11 report provides a more balanced treatment of the recommendations with regard to foreign versus domestic focus, yet still about two-thirds of the recommendations are focused on domestic initiatives. Given that the attacks occurred on the homeland, this is certainly understandable. However, taken together, the combination of the recommendations shows an almost exclusive focus on internal restructuring.

Examination of the analysis of the elements of power indicates the trend toward recommendations to alter traditional elements, including the political, military, intelligence, and legal areas. Few initiatives are targeting the softer elements of power and fewer still are looking at the use of softer elements of power overseas to influence foreign audiences.

As an example, only five of the recommendations from the 9/11 Commission dealt with economics. Of these five, none truly focused on economics directly, but rather alluded to economic programs, as in recommendation 2: "the United States should be willing to make the hard choices too and make the difficult long-term commitment of the future of Pakistan. Sustaining the current scale of aid to Pakistan, the United States should support Pakistan's government in its struggle against extremists with a comprehensive effort that extends from military aid to support for better education." Knowing that the United States has forgiven much of Pakistan's debt, and this statement leads to the conclusion that economics is being used to advance U.S. interests, but perhaps more can and should be done using the economic element of power.

The same is true for the other nontraditional elements of power. Consider the recommendation, "Where Muslim governments, even those who are friends, do not respect these principles, the United States must stand for a better future. One of the lessons of the Cold War was that short-term gains in cooperating with the most repressive and brutal governments were often outweighed by long-term setbacks for America's stature and interests." This statement receives credit for all elements of power except homeland defense and science and technology as is certainly relates to the other categories, despite not providing specifics for implementing this recommendation.

Most of the recommendations tended to be quite direct and highly focused on the military, intelligence, and law enforcement elements. Consider the recommendation, "Targeting travel is at least as powerful a weapon against terrorists as targeting their money. The United States should combine terrorist travel intelligence, operations, law enforcement in a strategy to intercept terrorists, find terrorist travel facilitators, and constrain terrorist mobility." The point is not that these are not valid recommendations or that they should not be implemented. In fact, all are worthy of consideration, at a minimum, and most should be incorporated into a comprehensive strategy for implementation.

Rather, the point is to make a directed analysis of how the other elements of power could be included in a comprehensive package for improving our national security. Taken in combination, the 9/11 Commission and the Commission on National Security/21st Century are both significant efforts that need to be considered, broadened, and then implemented within a complete and overarching national security package.

Two other topics that warrant consideration in the framing of a broad new national security strategy are the Patriot Act and the most recent NSS published in 2002.

The Patriot Act was enacted on October 24, 2001, in reaction to the 9/11 terrorist attack. Generally, laws have been established that provide the government greater authority with regard to intelligence and legal issues. Debates have raged on both sides. Some feel that the legal reforms have given the Federal Government too much latitude and thus have adversely impacted on civil liberties, while others argue that they do not go far enough. In any case, the provisions of the Patriot Act will be reexamined and are likely to be modified as part of this review.[15]

The 2002 NSS has much in common with its predecessors; however, there is one large difference. The tone of the document is decidedly more urgent and the focus is on using all means to defeat terrorism. This version remains, like earlier versions, a reflection of the principles and values on which our country was founded.

The strategy is summed up under "2002 National Security Strategy." The eight major objectives and the strategic concept for each are provided. The inclusion of specific initiatives represents another difference in this strategy.

2002 National Security Strategy

Champion aspirations for human dignity

- Speak out honestly about violations of the nonnegotiable demands of human dignity using our voice and vote in international institutions to advance freedom
- Use our foreign aid to promote freedom and support those who struggle nonviolently for it, ensuring that nations moving toward democracy are rewarded for the steps they take
- Make freedom and the development of democratic institutions key themes in our bilateral relations, seeking solidarity and cooperation from other democracies while we press governments that deny human rights to move toward a better future
- Take special efforts to promote freedom of religion and conscience and defend it from encroachment by repressive governments

Strengthen alliances to defeat global terrorism and work to prevent attacks against us and our friends

- Direct and continuous action using all the elements of national and international power; our immediate focus will be those terrorist organizations of global reach and any terrorist or state sponsor of terrorism which attempts to gain or use weapons of mass destruction (WMD) or their precursors
- Defending the United States, the American people, and our interests at home and abroad by identifying and destroying the threat before it reaches our borders; while the United States will constantly strive to enlist the support of the international community, we will not hesitate to act alone, if necessary, to exercise our right of self-defense by acting preemptively against such terrorists, to prevent them from doing harm against our people and our country
- Denying further sponsorship, support, and sanctuary to terrorists by convincing or compelling states to accept their sovereign responsibilities. We will also wage a war of ideas to win the battle against international terrorism. This includes:
- Using the full influence of the United States, and working closely with allies and friends, to make clear that all acts of terrorism are illegitimate so that terrorism will be viewed in the same light as slavery, piracy, or genocide–behavior that no repectable government can condone or support and all must oppose;
- Supporting moderate and modern government, especially in the Muslim world, to ensure that the conditions and ideologies that promote terrorism do not find fertile ground in any nation;
- Diminishing the underlying conditions that spawn terrorism by enlisting the international community to focus its efforts and resources on areas most at risk; and
- Using effective public diplomacy to promote the free flow of information and ideas to kindle the hopes and aspirations of freedom of those in societies ruled by the sponsors of global terrorism.

Work with others to defuse regional conflicts

- The United States should invest time and resources into building international relationships and institutions that can help manage local crises when they emerge.
- The United States should be realistic about its ability to help those who are unwilling or unready to help themselves. Where and when people are ready to do their part, we well be willing to move decisively.

Prevent our enemies from threatening us, our allies, and our friends, with weapons of mass destruction

- Proactive counterproliferation efforts.
- Strengthened nonproliferation efforts to prevent rogue states and terrorists from acquiring the materials, technologies, and expertise necessary for weapons of mass destruction (WMD).
- Effective consequence management to respond to the effects of WMD use, whether by terrorists or hostile states.
- To support preemptive options, we will:
  1. build better, more integrated intelligence capabilities to provide timely, accurate information on threats, wherever they may emerge;
  2. coordinate closely with allies to form a common assessment of the most dangerous threats; and
  3. continue to transform our military forces to ensure our ability to conduct rapid and precise operations to achieve decisive results.

Ignite a new era of global economic growth through free markets and free trade

- Pro-growth legal and regulatory policies to encourage business investment, innovation, and entrepreneurial activity
- Tax policies–particularly lower marginal tax rates–that improve incentives for work and investment
- Rule of law and intolerance of corruption so that people are confident that they will be able to enjoy the fruits of their economic endeavors
- Strong financial systems that allow capital to be put to its most efficient use
- Sound fiscal policies to support business activity
- Investments in health and education that improve the well-being and skills of the labor force and population as a whole
- Free trade that provides new avenues for growth and fosters the diffusion of tehnologies and ideas that increase productivity and opportunity

Expand the circle of development by opening societies and building the infrastructure of democracy

- Provide resources to aid countries that have met the challenge of national reform.
- Improve the effectiveness of the World Bank and other development banks in raising living standards.
- Insist upon measurable results to ensure that development assistance is actually making a difference in the lives of the world's poor.
- Increase the amount of development assistance that is provided in the form of grants instead of loans.
- Open societies to commerce and investment. Trade and investment are the real engines of economic growth.
- Secure public health.
- Emphasize education.
- Continue to aid agricultural development.

Develop agendas for cooperative action with other main centers of global power

Transform America's national security institutions to meet the challenges and opportunities of the twenty-first century

• Our military must:
1. Assure our allies and friends
2. Dissuade future military competition
3. Deter threats against U.S. interests, allies, and friends
4. Decisively defest any adversary if deterrence fails
• We must also ensure the proper fusion of information between intelligence and law enforcement.
Initiatives in this area will include:
1. Strengthening the authority of the Director of Central Intelligence to lead the development and actions of the nation's foreign intelligence capabilities
2. Establishing a new framework for intelligence warning that provides seamless and integrated warning across the spectrum of threats facing the nation and our allies
3. Continuing to develop new methods of collecting information to sustain our intelligence advantage
4. Investing in future capabilities while working to protect them through a more vigorous effort to prevent the compromise of intelligence capabilities
5. Collecting intelligence against the terrorist danger across the government with all-source analysis

More detail has been provided with regard to specific programs or goals for each of the major objectives. This is a useful inclusion as it represents a higher degree of fidelity with regard to elements other than the traditional areas of power (i.e., political-military).

So now the question becomes which organization or agency within the U.S. government has responsibility for implementing each of the eight objectives and the goals established under each. Perhaps more important, do they have the necessary resources to accomplish the goals laid out in the strategy? Another useful consideration is the question of whether the seams created by the delineation of foreign and domestic defense and security in the 2002 versions of the NSS and the NSHS should remain or be eliminated by the merging of the NSC and HSC.

CONCLUDING THOUGHTS

The period from 1898 to the present has seen dramatic change in both the perspective and the capability for national security in this country. The United States has matured from an isolationist and youthful nation, with a clear and declarative focus on internal matters and protection against incursion by others into the Western Hemisphere, into a global power with both capabilities and outlook that extend well beyond our borders. In each of the periods examined above, the United States has become more integrally involved in setting the course for the nations of the world and, when necessary, policing others. U.S. leadership now dominates world affairs in a way unlike any nation in the whole of history.

In 1898, U.S. national security was focused on protection of interests at home and abroad through enforcement of the Monroe Doctrine. In a single year, with the incursion into Cuba and shortly thereafter into the Philippines, a new era in U.S. strategy emerged. The United States demonstrated the capability for and early designs on global leadership.

The post–World War II period and the launching of the strategy of containment signaled a major turning point in U.S. grand strategy. Large, massed military formations, the nuclear triad, and RealPolitik became the terms of the day. Even following the demise of the Soviet Union, the United States has largely pursued a strategy of containment. Many of the expressions of strategy during this post–Cold War period have had their roots in this strategy: attempting to contain the spread of nuclear material and technologies; operations in the Balkans to contain the spread of instability in Europe and manage the implosion of former Communist regimes and satellites; and even the limited operation to drive Saddam Hussein and the Iraqi Army out of Kuwait and protect Saudi Arabia and the postconflict sanctions regime were designed to contain Saddam. In some cases, we have used other terms such as support and stability operations instead of containment, but the implications are the same.

This transformation in U.S. national security has not been wholly altruistic, nor has it followed a deliberate path. Certainly our allies and arguably the world have benefited, but the motivation remains largely one of self-interest. The desire for economic prosperity has driven a complementary change in the political, military, social, cultural, and now information capabilities of our nation. In turn, these changes have collectively contributed to the U.S. status in the world today as a hyperpower.

Figure 2 captures the evolution of the U.S. national security strategy transition over time. Depicted on the diagram are the transitions from the Preindustrial to the Industrial to the Information Age as well as some of the major events that precipitated changes to our national security. The figure shows that the political and military components have been the predominant elements of our national security strategy, with a small contribution by the economic element. This does not imply that economics have not been important. In fact, as previously articulated, they have been really the driver for the development of U.S. power in terms of the rationale for global interaction and for allowing our nation to build these significant national security capabilities.

While other elements have made a contribution, in examining our national security strategy and relations with other nations, the political-military

FIGURE 2. Evolution of U.S. National Security Strategy

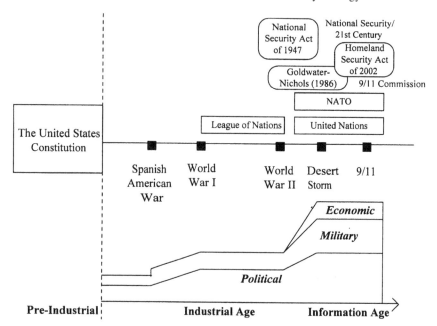

relationships have been where the energy of the government has been. The focus has been on the use of "hard power" to achieve national security objectives and thus our grand strategy. For these areas, the U.S. has developed well articulated National Security Strategies (NSS) which focus on the political-military while making mention of the other elements. For the military, a National Military Strategy (NMS) further identifies the "Strategy" for achieving goals in these areas. However, there is no corresponding coherent strategy for the other elements.

The National Security Act of 1947 and the Goldwater-Nichols Defense Reform Act of 1986 reflect the two most recent and definitive legislative formulations of national security policy. However, they are also over fifty-five and fifteen years old, respectively, and in many respects reflect Industrial Age thinking. In addition, the two most recent analyses are highlighted in figure 2 as well: the U.S. Commission on National Security/21st Century and the 9/11 Commission. The diagram also depicts the 2002 NSS as it is the most recent overall expression of national security strategy. In addition, the NSHS is included due to both its pivotal role in addressing key threats to America in the period following 9/11 and its complementary and competitive relationship with the more traditional security documents.

As the transition to the Information Age continues, opportunities exist to move away from the Industrial Age and containment to an Information Age strategy. In this new era, full-spectrum, complex operations will be the predominant type of actions that the U.S. undertakes. These operations will involve considerably more capability than the Foreign Service, military, and Intelligence Community collectively have and a more coordinated and integrated approach to U.S. grand strategy.

In part II, my intent is to develop a set of principles to be followed in the development of a comprehensive national security strategy for the Information Age. The key themes to be addressed are as follows:

1. The current definition and application of strategy, and national strategy in particular, are inadequate. They must be revised to more fully account for the move into the Information Age. Strategy has been defined as the linking of *ways* and *means* to achieve *ends* while mitigating *risk*. In the future, we must factor *environment* into any reasonable discussion of strategy.

2. The United States must rebalance its national strategy by rebalancing its ways and means. It is nearly impossible to have a discussion of national strategy without defaulting to military relationships, rather than a more effective means of addressing all major elements of national power in a balanced manner. In the preconflict relationships between nations, states, and world actors, nonmilitary ways and means can and should be preeminent. However, our current national security strategy remains heavily weighted to the political-military, with little direct focus on the other elements of power. In the Information Age, the nonmilitary elements of power will dominate, with particular emphasis on information.

3. The U.S. government must be reorganized to more appropriately respond to the challenges of the Information Age. Inherent in this discussion is the harmonization of efforts between the Departments of Defense and Homeland Security. In addition, the DOD must undergo a holistic review and restructuring to develop the capabilities that will be required. This will mean divesting those capabilities that no longer fit into current strategy, operations, and tactics. The difficulty will be eliminating systems, procedures, and platforms that may have great capability, but are no longer effective within the defense system of the future.

Part II

THINKING DIFFERENTLY ABOUT NATIONAL SECURITY

5

DEVELOPING A U.S. NATIONAL SECURITY STRATEGY FOR THE INFORMATION AGE

THE PRECEDING DISCUSSION CONCERNING the aftermath of the terrorist attacks of September 11, 2001, provides important insights into this highly charged period. The expectation was for swift military responses to those responsible and a rapid reaction to alleviate the organizational and procedural miscues that allowed the attacks to occur and contributed to their success.

In the intervening period between the terrorist attacks and the announcement of the 9/11 Commission's analysis and recommendations, many both in and out of government initiated changes designed to protect against perceived weaknesses in their systems. Cabinet-level departments, other government agencies, state and local governments, and even those responsible for private and public infrastructure were making sweeping changes. The natural reaction was to read about the ongoing adaptations and have confidence that the government was making the necessary changes to secure America and its citizens, then and in the future.

While not trying to be alarmist, I would make the opposite case. Today, changes are being made in the structure and operation of the government that are, in the near term, exposing seams in the critical armor of the nation's security and defense capabilities. Certainly, individual cabinet-level agencies are making changes within their organizations and processes to streamline their systems. Unfortunately, many of these changes are occurring within the stovepipes of the respective organizations with little cross-talk between agencies, or worse still, dismantling systems that have weaknesses, but not replacing them with viable substitutes.

Consider the case of the Intelligence Community (IC), which is now led by a National Director for Intelligence or NDI. Unfortunately the structure of the IC remains very much in doubt, with clear conflicts between the NDI and subordinate elements. For example, the CIA in the past developed and provided to the President the President's Daily Brief (PDB). The NDI is currently not structured or manned to allow for the development of such a comprehensive product, but now has the responsibility for it. Who will be the lead in the presentation of the material? The NDI, by position, runs the IC, a role the Director of Central Intelligence (the Director of the CIA) once fulfilled. If both the NDI and CIA Director, are in the PDB meeting, who will have primacy? What about oversight of the special reconnaissance teams that the DOD established? Are they subject to the same level of oversight as the rest of the IC? These are important questions that must be addressed in a coordinated manner if the necessary intelligence products and capabilities are to be in place to thwart any potential threats to U.S. national security.

Likewise, the Department of Defense is undergoing a significant restructuring of its forces. This transformation as it is called will incorporate changes in all aspects of the force from the organizations to the doctrine and training, and will raise cooperation across the Services to new levels. These changes are centered on advances in information technology and other fields, which are allowing changes in the structure of the operational forces. Net centric warfare is permitting real time communications of voice, video, and data across vast distances, allowing virtual communications where none existed in the past. Across the Services, changes are underway to facilitate operations across the spectrum, including humanitarian, peace enforcement, and combat and everything in between. But these changes are largely being developed in isolation with little or no cooperation within the Interagency. In the next complex operation requiring a broad range of capabilities from across the elements of power, how will non-DOD and even nongovernmental organizations be able to effectively participate? How will they even be able to communicate?

A similar issue concerns ongoing initiatives in the Department of State where a new office is being established to assist in managing the aftermath of war and stabilizing countries torn by civil strife; the new office is called the Office of the Coordinator for Reconstruction and Stabilization. Areas of needed expertise would include political administration, law enforcement, and economics, as these are areas that frequently require immediate attention in the aftermath of any intervention in troubled states. While this concept looks to have great promise, perhaps a more useful approach would be to look holistically at postconflict stability from a U.S. government perspective rather than have the State Department make a set of changes in relative isolation from other departments making similar changes. For example, in the Department of Defense there are similar initiatives to enhance selected capabilities for Support and Stability Operations (SASO) by increasing civil affairs, military police, and psychological operations forces to name a few.

My assessment is that these initiatives must be developed under a coordinated, deliberate process just as the National Security Act of 1947 was based on deliberations and negotiations by all of the Interagency. To allow separate organizations to transform themselves from their current states toward an objective that is loosely formulated within the NSS or HSS will not have a high probability for a successful integration of U.S. government capabilities. Even oversight by the Executive or Legislative Branches is unlikely to force individual departmental or agency transformation efforts to result in a coherent system for executing a twenty-first century, Information Age NSS. An even lower probability exists that these individual and internal deliberations will result in the creation of a new organization like the NSA of 1947 did with respect to the National Security Council, the Central Intelligence Agency, or the Department of the Air Force.

In part I, the emerging environment and the development of U.S. national security strategy were discussed in some detail to provide a foundation for the development of a set of principles and considerations for a new national security strategy for the Information Age. The purpose of part II is to present these principles and considerations for the reader. An obvious question then is, why not just develop a new national security strategy within the book?

Given the complexity and enormity of the task, it is well beyond the scope of this work, or any single person for that matter, to develop and present a complete U.S. national security strategy. Any attempt to do so would inevitably result in a less than acceptable outcome, as what is truly required is a comprehensive, broadbased analysis of the Information Age and a corresponding dialogue among leaders from across the elements of power to arrive at a new U.S. national security strategy. To date, this has not occurred, although several significant efforts in the last five years have been invaluable and will even form the basis for this strategy development.

Instead, the central proposal in part II is the development of a National Security Act of 20XX. This legislation would be complementary in outcome but even broader in scope than its predecessor, the National Security Act of 1947, which launched the strategy of containment and set the course for U.S. strategic thought for well over fifty years. In fact, the National Security Act of 1947 and the policy of containment remain today, even after the demise of the Soviet Union, the preeminent drivers of U.S. national security policy. A new national security act would not only replace this Cold War, Industrial Age framework, but also bring our strategy into the Information Age (figure 3). Perhaps most important is that legislation of the type being proposed would prepare the United States to meet the challenges and harvest the opportunities of this new era.

This chapter examines the elements of a new U.S. national security for the Information Age. It begins with an examination of how national strategy or grand strategy formulation must change and concludes with some very specific recommendations for implementation of a new strategy.

FIGURE 3. Making the Transition to the Information Age

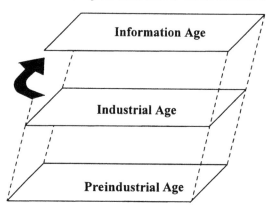

In the first section, the expansion of the definition of strategy is considered. The second section examines the need for rebalancing the way in which we consider U.S. national strategy, and includes the proposal for a new national security act that does for the Information Age what George Kennan and the policy of containment did for the Cold War. Finally, in the third section, a critical examination of some changes required of DOD to adapt to the Information Age is conducted.

A NEW WAY OF THINKING ABOUT NATIONAL SECURITY STRATEGY

The current definition and application of strategy, and national strategy in particular, are inadequate. They must be revised to more fully account for the move into the Information Age. Strategy has been defined as the linking of *ways* and *means* to achieve *ends* while mitigating *risk*. In the future, we must factor *environment* into any reasonable discussion of strategy.

For years, policymakers have used the concept that strategy is a linking of means and ways to achieve stated ends. However, it is my strong conviction that the currently accepted formulation of national security strategy, addressing ends, ways, means, and risk, is no longer sufficient for a complete discussion of strategy.

The lengthy discussion of the geo strategic environment in the previous section was meant to describe the principles that will separate the Industrial Age from the Information Age in terms of strategy development, in particular U.S. national security strategy formulation, as well as to convince the reader that the

---

Principles for the Information Age

1. Globalization is a real force (and growing).
2. The world is getting smaller.
3. The nature, character and conduct of conflict are changing.
4. The world is becoming increasingly complex.
5. There is greater availability of means.
6. There will be less freedom of action; someone will always be watching (or listening or reading).
7. There is a tenuous relationship between engagement and risk.
8. Asymmetry in conflict will be the norm, not the exception.
9. The United States cannot have too many allies.
10. There are some combinations of development of nations and alliances that may naturally threaten the United States
11. It's a matter of when not if.
12. It's the economy, stupid.

---

environment must be specifically considered in a future strategy formulation. The twelve principles discussed previously are listed together to highlight the distinctions between the Industrial and Information Ages.

If there is one overarching theme, it is that the homogenizing of societies through globalization will make the development and application of coherent national security strategy more difficult and complex in the Information Age. There will be less flexibility to act and each decision will inevitably be met with critiques and discussion both for and against U.S. policies. There will be instances where the United States can lead, but not force or coerce as this will likely cause repercussions or elicit a negative response, thus threatening our national security. An example is democratic reforms and liberalization of closed societies. We can and must serve as a role model for developing nations and can even use carrots and sticks as positive and negative incentives, but the internal development of a country must proceed at the pace best suited to each nation.

Thus, the rationale for including the environment explicitly in future formulations of the strategic equation is this. Ends, ways, and means all apply to the country developing the strategy. The ends are the desired outcomes from the perspective of the country developing the strategy. The means are the resources and the ways are the processes or techniques that will be employed; but both of these are also "owned" by the country developing the strategy. So where do we consider how the strategy will be received internationally? Or whether, in the case of conflict, the desired ends are even feasible for the country?

It almost goes without saying and certainly has become cliché that the Information Age will create both opportunities and challenges with respect to the commitment of national security assets. But herein lays the real issue. The degree to which this new age presents opportunities will depend largely on how the United States decides to apply resources and in what ways (i.e., the means and ways of the strategy). Using the old Cold War, Industrial Age formulations will prevent the United States from becoming a true Information Age power, and even puts at risk our global position as a hyperpower.

To this end, a broad rethinking of our national security strategy is in order. This dialogue must include an evaluation of how, when, and for what purpose we should commit the elements of national power. Inherent in this discussion are the roles and missions of the organizations and agencies within the U.S. government and how they will each contribute to our national and homeland security and defense.

The discussion must begin with a determination of what type of philosophy the United States will follow. Will the United States be internationalist or isolationist? What about being interventionist? Or should we have a realist approach to the world? Will we decide to work as part of the global community to engage in dialogue and resolve issues? Or will we decide to go it alone? The decision in this case is unilateralist versus multilateralist. These are significant questions of national policy that must be debated and considered. Granted this is a somewhat academic exercise, as the past hundred years or so has made clear that U.S. values, power, and interaction have been and will continue to be essential to global development and stability.

Regardless of which path we choose to follow or even if the choice is to use different approaches in different parts of the world, the United States must develop a more methodical view of national security strategy. To this end there are five key factors or considerations to guide the development of a new security strategy: foundations, transparency, perspective, legitimacy, and balance.

Foundations

The United States has been and will continue to be a nation based on values and ideals. This remains an essential part of our national character. It follows then that a future national security strategy will also be ideologically based.

As a result, foundations will, by necessity, continue to be a cornerstone of U.S. national security strategy. The question is really to what degree the United States is willing to compromise its ideals to achieve less-than-perfect foreign policy outcomes. The phraseology may immediately cause some to recoil and say that we will never compromise on such fundamentals, but this is not a realistic approach to security.

In fact, overreliance on ideology is extremely dangerous and can lead to disastrous outcomes. We must be willing to compromise to get the "best" rather than the "optimum" solution. In developing a strategy, we must determine what we are trying to achieve. The goals must be stated clearly and then the path to achieve these goals developed and implemented.

In *America Unbound*, the authors state, "The essence of the Bush strategy, therefore, was to use America's unprecedented power to remake the world in America's image."[1] This, if a true reflection of the strategy, would be an infeasible outcome. The special conditions under which the United States formed and evolved are not present anywhere else in the world, so the thought that a cookie-cutter approach whereby similar nations can be stamped out is simply not realistic. However, the notion that democratic institutions and rule of law can be established in formerly authoritarian or nondemocratic nations is indeed a reasonable and desirable goal, and certainly one worth pursuing in the future.

Failure to rely on the foundations can lead to equally disastrous outcomes. Consider the case of Bosnia. If the goal had been only to stop the fighting in Bosnia, it would have failed to address the underlying causes of the killing and instability in the Balkans, and most certainly would have been only a temporary fix to the problem. Rather, the approach the United States took was to establish four broad policy goals, which included stopping the killing, alleviating the humanitarian crisis, establishing a multiethnic state, and reintegrating Bosnia back into the European community. The real lesson concerns the need to promote values and ideals through strategies and policies to achieve reasoned, well-articulated outcomes.

Transparency

The Information Age will provide unprecedented transparency. Actions can and will be seen and evaluated in real time, sometimes with little true analysis to provide the context for what is seen on television screens or heard on the radio. While our intentions may be righteous, the execution of each and every policy will be played out and, more important interpreted across the world. As a result, transparency will also serve to limit flexibility. We will need to be mindful that a covert action only remains so if not discovered, at least during the operation.

The means for promulgating this new transparency will be the information technologies that are leading to higher degrees of globalization, interaction among global actors, economic prosperity, and political freedoms. An early example of the use of transparency techniques is Radio Free Europe which targeted individuals living behind the Iron Curtain. Messages were broadcast in native languages to get the maximum exposure to the oppressed peoples of these Communist regimes. For many, Radio Free Europe was the only exposure to democracy that they had and the only source of hope for greater political and religious freedoms, and greater economic prosperity.

Transparency will also lead to greater accountability by leaders and individuals. Unfortunately for some, transparency entails explaining actions and taking responsibility for failures and miscalculations. Authoritarian figures will no longer be able to hide their oppressive ways from their societies. Small wonder that authoritarian governments and leaders fear the proliferation of information technologies that lead to political awareness and, by extension, liberalization, democratization, and economic development. Given the relationship between transparency and democracy, for dictators and tyrants that strive to control their people, transparency would signal the beginning of the end. What does or should this portend for future U.S. strategy and policy formulation?

Consider the case of Cuba. It is worth asking how this rogue nation might look today if we had forced more transparency through interaction rather than isolation. If years ago the United States lifted sanctions and increased interaction between our nations, would Cuba still be an authoritarian regime today? What would be the impact of flying over Cuba dropping televisions and satellite receivers by parachute? Could Fidel Castro have survived such an onslaught? Any new strategy that is articulated will most definitely need to account for this increased transparency as a result of globalization and the Information Age.

Perspective

Along with transparency, perspective will be important to the development of new strategies for the Information Age. The United States must become more attuned to looking at the world and issues from the perspective of others in addition to a simple calculation of national interest. Given that the Information Age will allow large segments of the world's population to see and interpret U.S. actions and policies in real time, more attention to at least understanding how actions will be interpreted is essential.

At the extreme, this issue begs the question, "Should this moderate U.S. behavior?" To use a military analogy, it is possible to win all the battles and still lose the war. If each decision is measured strictly based on U.S. interests, building coalitions and attracting allies will be difficult if not impossible. Therefore, in the short term perhaps national interest alone will be an adequate measure, only if vital interests are at stake. However, if there are decisions that are in the near-term perhaps less than optimal for U.S. interests, but will collectively provide greater benefit to allies or globally, then perhaps we should find a way to embrace them. This is by no means to suggest that the United States should give up its leadership role or accept policies that are clearly against its interests, but we must find ways to accept compromises or even suboptimal solutions on some occasions and to be able to explain our positions to the rest of the world if our actions are not well understood.

Consider some of the positions the United States has taken in recent negotiations and try to see how some of these positions could be interpreted by non-Americans. We recently unilaterally withdrew from the Antiballistic Missile or ABM Treaty. Does this signify that we are going to take an aggressive first-strike stance with respect to nuclear confrontation? What about the Kyoto Treaty? As of September 2004, 84 parties had signed and 125 parties have ratified or acceded to the Kyoto Protocol. The United States was not one of these nations. Why would one of the world's most industrialized nations and the world's leader not sign an accord to protect the environment while limiting greenhouse gases that are believed to contribute to global warming and numerous second- and third-order environmental impacts? What about the International Criminal Court (ICC)? The U.S. administration has refused to send this treaty to the Senate for ratification. Why does the United States not support an international court that would have criminal jurisdiction over individuals accused of genocide, crimes against humanity, or war crimes?

At first blush, all of these initiatives seem to be extremely useful and would contribute to international rule of law, stability, and safety. However, the United States, as the world's leader, has determined not to participate in these treaties out of enlightened self-interest. Each of the actions (or inactions) has not been explained sufficiently to convince the world of the appropriateness of our position. With mass media available to dissect each and every twist and turn, the United States seems to have put its interests above the common good. However, in each case, there are rational reasons why the treaties were not in the best interest of the United States or are no longer relevant in their current form.

But many people see significant incongruence in some of our positions that requires addressing. The United States has been and remains a beacon leading the way to freedom, democracy, and respect for human rights. This democratic and benevolent notion of the United States seems to be in direct contrast to the other United States that has abrogated the ABM Treaty and refused to sign and ratify the Kyoto Protocol and ICC. While no sovereign nation in compliance with international law should be forced to commit to a treaty or behavior not within its interests, the legalities and technicalities associated with this position are lost on a world that increasingly views the United States with suspicion. Perhaps for some, the final straw was the "unprovoked" attack by the U.S.-led coalition against Iraq in March 2003. Many have forgotten or do not care about the years of sanctions, the previous use of WMD by this brutal regime both against its own people and in warfare against Iran, and have long since forgotten about the original sin, the invasion of Kuwait by Iraq in August 1990.

An important aspect of the concept of perspective is to avoid "mirror-imaging" when examining policy options. This term refers to looking at alternatives based on one's own perspective rather than understanding the conditions and sensitivities of other actors that will color the way they act in like conditions. In the Information Age, with mass media and information cycles measured in minutes and hours as opposed to days and weeks, mirror-imaging policy is destined for failure. The notion that policies that work in the United States can be directly applied to other nations fails to account for the special circumstances of the growth of our nation.

Finally, a useful Information Age analogy for describing the difficulty of understanding U.S. policies is that in some regards, the United States is talking in digital while the world is listening in analog and vice versa. We need to re-evaluate how our strategy and policies are perceived across the globe. We must find a way to ensure that the messages we are sending are being correctly understood throughout the community of nations and by the peoples of the world.

Legitimacy

Along with perspective, legitimacy is now even more important in the Information Age. Each action undertaken by the United States is likely to be judged and evaluated down to the last detail. Is the action legal? Is it logical and reasonable? Do others support the action, and, if so, are they a broad-based coalition or two or three outlier nations?

A key to this notion of legitimacy is the determination of whether the actions are perceived to be self-motivated or for the greater good. If the action is only in self-interest or is perceived as self-interest, then legitimacy will be hard to achieve.

Of course, there are exceptions, and an interesting case is the U.S. operations in Afghanistan in the wake of 9/11. Less than three weeks after the terrorist attacks, the United States along with a small number of close allies struck at the Taliban and al-Qaeda. The action was seen almost universally as legitimate as it was in self-defense and reflected preventative or preemptive war to destroy a determined enemy that had already attacked the United States, but it was undertaken largely out of self-interest. Over time, the relation of operations in Afghanistan to the global war on terror was rationalized and a broader set of multilateral actions launched to deal with this threat.

Unfortunately, consequences are also important in a military campaign assessing legitimacy. The bombing of the Chinese Embassy during the Kosovo Air Campaign in 1999, while it did not cause us to halt the campaign, certainly called into question the targeting process and even the legitimacy of the campaign. Likewise, engagements where civilians have become casualties from either air or ground forces in Iraq have caused significant problems for the United States and the coalition and have seriously undermined the legitimacy of operations, at least for those directly or indirectly targeted.

Related to legitimacy is a need to consider the views of the community of nations. America has been accused of being unwilling to listen to or consider the input of others. Most particularly in the aftermath of 9/11, but also at the height of the Cold War in dealings with NATO, other members at times felt that their opinions were largely ignored. The French reaction in the mid-1960s was to withdraw from the integrated military command structure, which at the time was a threat to NATO solidarity.

Any future formulation of U.S. national strategy must deal with the issue of establishing legitimacy for our actions. In the near term or in specific circumstances, the community of nations might be willing to allow a breach of legitimacy, but as a long-term policy, illegitimacy will be negatively considered and will jeopardize U.S. leadership and dominance in the world.

Balance

A new strategy must not be an all-or-nothing proposition. For example, a strategy to stop all trade and shut our borders because we cannot absolutely protect all ports and border crossings would be dead on arrival and would actually compromise the nation's economic viability and in turn, our long-term security.

Any new strategy must strike a delicate balance between the elements of power internally and competing interests around the globe. We certainly do not want to completely seal the borders for the sake of security, which would essentially eliminate trade and reduce economic prosperity and growth. At the same time, having completely open borders with no controls would leave the United States far too vulnerable to a host of threats, including illegal immigration, infrastructure security, safety, public health problems, and economic poaching.

Externally, the balance must be such that American interests are protected but not at the expense of other nations. We will need to work in concert with others for the collective good on some issues. An example could include the Ottawa Treaty, the Convention on the Prohibition of the Use, Stockpiling, Production and Transfer of Antipersonnel Mines and on Their Destruction. Given the human tragedy associated with landmines around the world, how can we balance the U.S. need for security in places like the Demilitarized Zone (DMZ) in Korea with the need to eliminate this class of dangerous weapons?

Perhaps the most important aspect of balance is to ensure that America avoids taking a short-term view of individual decisions and events against an enemy (and even in a world) with a longer-term view. There is a tenuous balance between actions taken for short-term and long-term gain. Sometimes, events such as Pearl Harbor or 9/11 scream for a swift, immediate, and unilateral action as a matter of principle. But the numbers of these types of action are few and far between. Most actions taken in foreign affairs and national security have longer time horizons and can and should be measured in that way.

ORGANIZING FOR COMBAT

Today the United States is perhaps less secure than in any time in our nation's history. With the number and type of threats greatly expanded, the old notions of national security need to be fundamentally examined to determine what works and what needs to be discarded or revised. With the transition in our national security apparatus from the Industrial Age to the Information Age, the way we think of national security strategy needs to change accordingly. Typically, hard power has been the coin of the realm. We measured security in terms of tanks or numbers of military personnel under arms. In some respects, issues such as economic development and social systems were seen as necessary for society and equally important for the promotion of our political and military power, but not necessarily part of our national security equation. They were seen as precursors or means to address national security concerns, but not necessarily ends. These notions must be reexamined.

The debates over operations in Iraq invariably center on what the military did and how the battle was waged. The military's success in combat operations was predictable and serves to illustrate the overwhelming capabilities of the U.S. military. On the other hand, military failures certainly occurred. An example was the failure to halt looting in the aftermath of the rapid fall of the Iraqi government. In this regard, troop strength was an issue, as there were not enough troops to secure key Iraqi facilities and structures. However, the inability to stop the looting was also directly related to the U.S. government's failure to adequately plan for Phase IV or postcombat operations and reconstruction. Despite failings in the military's plan, an even larger share of responsibility for the postcombat performance, including allowing the conditions for an insurgency to form, is directly attributable to the overall handling of the postconflict phase by the U.S. government. Thus the inability to rapidly deliver needed capabilities to the theater at a critical time immediately following combat operations coupled with the failure to understand the nature of the conflict doomed the operation to become a long, protracted, low-intensity conflict. The structure of the force and national capabilities deployed certainly were not adequate for the nation building that was envisioned.

The most important question really is, "Who said that nation building is the responsibility of the U.S. military?" Clearly, the military has a role and has invested much thought in this topic. It is not possible to go to any officer training school, even at the junior levels, without discussing the theory and conduct of low-intensity operations, of which nation building is a subset. At the major military training centers, such as the National Training Center (NTC) and Joint Readiness Training Center (JRTC) for the Army, and Twenty-Nine Palms for the Marines, the capabilities for fighting and winning in these low-intensity environments have been recently incorporated and are now trained and evaluated.

Where is the complementary training for the other elements of power represented in the other cabinet-level agencies? Only over the last few years have interagency players begun to participate in these exercises. Clearly, more than simple participation is required. An intellectual and physical investment must be made whereby the contributions of our national elements of power are melded into a cohesive force able to contribute to the achieving of our collective national security goals and objectives.

The Information Age will see a significant rearranging of how the world thinks of power and portends changes for how the United States must adapt its thinking to be successful in this new age. Soft power issues such as global economic prosperity, education, respect for human rights and women's rights in particular, public affairs and diplomacy, and the overarching relationship of information will become coequal partners with the hard power political-military arms of national security in this new age. This transition is depicted in figure 4. The triangle (Δ) symbol is meant to signify that other inputs were involved in the formulation of national security strategy but did not meet the threshold of significance to be listed separately. For example, as previously discussed, economics factored heavily into the "defeat" of the Soviet Union and Warsaw Pact, but the focus was the political-military standoff. This is obviously a judgment and open to interpretation and debate.

Some will undoubtedly make the argument that the national security strategies that have been published have all presented adequate discussion of

FIGURE 4. National Security Strategy Elements

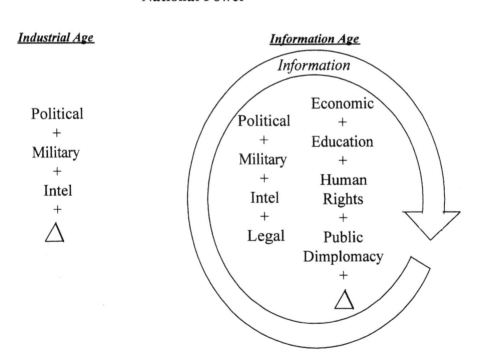

these areas. My response is that while the ends for these soft power elements are presented within the NSS, the means and ways to achieve them have not been articulated in the same manner as for the political and military components. The result is the one-sided formulation of strategy that exists today, with one basic set of hard power tools.

Notice that in the Information Age portion of figure 4, the word legal has been added to the hard power elements. In recognition of their growing importance, economics, education, human rights, and public diplomacy are expressly highlighted. A case could also be made that other components such as health, science and technology, or the environment should be added to figure 4. While I have not done so in the figure, I would not take offense to such additions, as they are in keeping with the general notion of expansion of the way we think and act on national security issues.

Stated directly, it is imperative that the United States develop Information Age structures within the government that cut across the full range of the elements of national power. But what does this mean in practice? Perhaps the best example comes from the Department of Defense.

Based on the NSS published by the White House, the DOD publishes several strategic documents. First, the Chairman of the Joint Chiefs of Staff publishes a National Military Strategy (NMS) which relates the guidance from the White House in the NSS to the military for implementation.

The Secretary of Defense also publishes strategic guidance in a series of documents beginning with the Strategic Planning Guidance, which provides "resource"informed strategic objectives, key assumptions, fiscal priorities and acceptable risks."[2] Following the Strategic Planning Guidance, the Secretary of Defense publishes a Joint Programming Guidance (JPG) which identifies metric-based, outcome-focused capability needs for selected major Joint requirements and assesses competing options and fiscally constrained programming guidance. For a number of years, the Secretary of Defense only had a single Defense Planning Guidance rather than two separate documents. This Defense Planning Guidance was used to provide direction for programmatic funding and resourcing for each of the Services (i.e., Army, Navy, Air Force, Marines) and the Defense Agencies (e.g., Defense Threat Reduction Agency).

The real point is that the DOD publishes a series of documents that lay out defense strategy including the ends, ways, means, and risk. These products are published as part of the budget cycle in the case of the Strategic Planning Guidance and Joint Planning Guidance, and in response to the NSS in the case of the National Military Strategy.

In addition to the cyclic publications, the DOD underwent a significant reorganization following the 1986 Goldwater-Nichols Defense Reform Act, discussed earlier. The focus of Goldwater-Nichols was on the ways to ensure that the resources allocated (i.e., the means) are put to the proper use and able to achieve the stated objectives or ends.

If this focus was not enough, the Commission on National Security/21st Century and the 9/11 Commission reports published in 1999–2002 and 2004 respectively also provided critiques and recommendations for better application of defense (and intelligence) assets to more effectively use these elements of national power. Additionally, a follow-up to the Goldwater-Nichols Act is being discussed that would further streamline operations and clarify command relationships.

But most of this reform and strategic guidance is directed toward the DOD. What do the other elements of power do to ensure linkage to U.S. national strategy and policy? The answer, unfortunately, is very little. Most departments of government do not coordinate their efforts with an eye toward national security. Nor do most of the departments focus their efforts outside of the United States.

The Department of Agriculture, for example, is keenly focused on internal concerns. A trip to the Department of Agriculture Web site allows one to browse topics such as agriculture, education and outreach, food and nutrition, laws and regulations, marketing and trade, natural resources and the environment, research and science, rural and community development, travel and recreation, and USDA employee services. Further into the site is a section on homeland security, with a focus on threats to food stocks. The same is true for other departments such as Commerce.

Perhaps another relevant question is how to focus the efforts of these cabinet-level departments to assist in alleviating U.S. security concerns at the source, in areas outside of the United States. In many cases this would be an expansion of responsibilities and missions, but these agencies certainly have expertise in areas where State and Defense have little expertise and thus could contribute in a more significant way to national security. For example, education is emerging as a significant concern of the global war on terror (GWOT). Many schools in Islamic areas of the world focus on technical or religious studies, with little education in the liberal arts. These shortfalls in education directly relate to the lack of debate or dialogue allowed between teachers and students. On the surface, this does not appear to be a major issue, until one understands that a lack of debate in the educational process can translate into an inability to engage in meaningful dialogues later with respect to other issues such as democratic institutions, rights of women, and religious tolerance. The issue of education in democracy takes on a whole new importance given that democracies have a history of not going to war against each other.

How are these efforts coordinated with other government agencies? In truth, the U.S. government operates its departments fairly autonomously, with integration through informal coordination or in the Interagency (IA) with the NSC staff in the lead. The result is that most of the coordination between cabinet-level departments and other specialized agencies is on an ad hoc basis related to specific tasks rather than full-time or fused coordination. Another way to look at cooperation between the agencies is that interaction is on an issue-by-issue basis.

In some regards, the notable exceptions are State, Defense, the Intelligence Community, and Justice, which have had close cooperation for some time. However, even this cooperation is mostly limited to particular issues. The reason closer ties developed between these agencies and departments is that the formalized coordination to resolve Cold War issues forced regular deliberations at the working group, deputy principal, and full NSC levels.

Even where one would expect coordination to occur on a regular basis and to delve into the smallest details, it does not occur adequately. The 9/11 Commission report provides ample evident of failure to communicate and coordinate between the Central Intelligence Agency, the Department of Justice (including the FBI), and the military intelligence-gathering agencies. The coordination that one would expect between airline screeners that work for the Department of Transportation and the law and intelligence organizations was very spotty before 9/11. Some of this has been attributed to competition between various agencies, especially within the Intelligence Community. However the cultural and self-imposed isolation of the various organizations and agencies is at least as much to blame. Even after 9/11, efforts have been focused on fixing deficiencies rather than conducting a comprehensive examination of threats to the United States and then developing a strategy to address the issues.

In this Interagency system, issues are considered at the lowest levels based on an agenda set by the NSC staff. After issues are debated and reach either a consensus view or a point of impasse, they are passed to the next level for similar deliberation. This process continues until an issue rises to the appropriate level for decision. Some issues may not make it to the full NSC as they are deemed not to be at that level of interest or decision. In this interagency system, the results of deliberations are passed up to the next level and guidance tends to be passed down.

But this system of deliberation is very linear and results in discrete coordination rather than full-time close cooperation and sharing of information. The current NSC system therefore suffers from an Industrial Age hierarchical model. As we move to the Information Age, new ideas such as information fusion, building a synergy across a complete set of policies, and harnessing the complete range of national security capabilities must begin to seep into the lexicon.

The discussion to this point has focused on the role of the Executive Branch of government; however, this is somewhat misleading. Congress's role in the development and execution of an NSS must also be considered to gain a full understanding of our national strategy. While the Constitution gives the President the responsibility of Commander-in-Chief of the Army and Navy, it also gives Congress the responsibility for providing "for the common Defence and general Welfare of the United States," and "organizing, arming, and disciplining, the Militia." To this end, Congress has exercised varying degrees of oversight throughout our nation's history and has developed a set of processes, structures, and mechanisms to allow for fulfilling these requirements.

The power of the Congress in national strategy has varied over time, largely dependent on the personalities and desires of the Executive and Legislative Branches. At times, the Executive branch, the President and Cabinet, have been dominant, as after 9/11, while at other times the Legislative branch has set the tone and to some extent the agenda for national security strategy. Arguably, an example of this condition comes from the early part of the first Clinton administration, as Congress exercised considerable oversight and direction.

Even when there is a healthy balance, Congress has the ultimate power of the purse and has levied significant reporting requirements on the Executive Branch to allow for fulfilling this role. The number of oversight committees today and the significant growth over time of the professional staff clearly has its roots in the ability of Congress to make informed decisions about the spending of our nation's resources.

Legislation such as Goldwater-Nichols demonstrates the ability of Congress to legislate and control large segments of the national security arena. While the President is the Commander-in-Chief, the role of building the defense and security apparatus is clearly a Congressional responsibility. So while it was President Truman and his advisors who began the deliberations that led to the National Security Act of 1947 and the restructuring of national security strategy, Congress developed the legislation that made the National Security Act of 1947 a reality.

THE NEED FOR A NATIONAL SECURITY ACT OF 20XX FOR THE INFORMATION AGE

A statement in the third Presidential campaign debate between President Bush and Senator Kerry provides ample evidence of the type and complexity of the threats that this country is likely to face and the magnitude of the solutions that will be required. The moderator asked a question in which he cited "8,000 illegal aliens crossing into the U.S. each day."[3] This issue has implications and solutions that go well beyond the realm of security and touch virtually all elements of national power.

This single issue affects numerous departments, including the Department of Homeland Security, Department of Justice, DOD, and Department of Transportation, to name a few. But these are just the obvious ones. If an illegal immigrant has worked on a farm over the last seven days, the Department of Agriculture would be concerned as well. If the illegal immigrant had been exposed to an infectious disease, the Department of Health and Human Services would have great interest. The scenario could be expanded almost indefinitely to demonstrate the potential impact on virtually all government departments and agencies.

Some may argue that the Homeland Security Act of 2002 does for homeland security what the National Security Act of 1947 did for national security, and thus the scenario above is a homeland security issue alone. The overarching criticism of this assertion is that the NSS and NSHS are two distinct documents, albeit with some significant overlap, coming from two distinct organizations, the NSC and HSC. A formal system exists for considering issues and adjudicating differences between organizations' positions and for reaching a decision—it is called the interagency process and is run by the NSC. To develop a separate or even second process to support domestic security and defense would not be in the best interests of the nation.

As we enter the twenty-first century and the Information Age, the United States has overwhelming military power and near-complete freedom of maneuver on the traditional battlefield. No other friend or foe can compete with regard to military capabilities and operations. But unfortunately, there are few traditional battlefields on the near horizon today, while a growing number of complex operations are developing. Even in Iraq, where the operation began with traditional combat, it quickly devolved into a more complex, nontraditional conflict involving a variety of elements of national power to be coordinated and applied in concert. However, this capability to coordinate does not exist within the United States today.

Therefore, the United States must begin development of a new national security act. This document must be broad and sweeping in the same way that the 1947 version was. The strategy must include a clear and compelling vision for the United States and include the *ends*, *ways*, *means*, *risk*, and *environment* of the strategy. But unlike its predecessor, it must include the entire government. The new national security act should establish as its goal to chart the course for the United States for the twenty-first century and the Information Age. It must also bring into alignment the organizations and processes for foreign and domestic security and defense this includes combining NSC and HSC roles and functions.

As a way of thinking about participation by all elements of government, the "spectrum of conflict," which the military typically uses to discuss operational planning, has been adapted and a depiction of the manner in which planning and operations should change superimposed on it. The military and intelligence have been grouped together as have the political and legal elements due to the close relationships between these pairs of national power contributors. In fact, all four of these traditional hard power elements are quite closely related and have been used in a fairly coordinated manner since the inception of National Security Act of 1947, at least in the case of political, military, and intelligence elements. The legal element has more recently emerged with the end of the Cold War and the growing use of the UN to establish violations of international law or highlight national security concerns. On the other hand, it could be argued that for years, it has been our policy to negotiate by way of arms control and other legal agreements to promote U.S. interests abroad, which certainly is the use of the legal element to promote national security interests. Figure 5 provides a conceptual

FIGURE 5. Spectrum of Operations

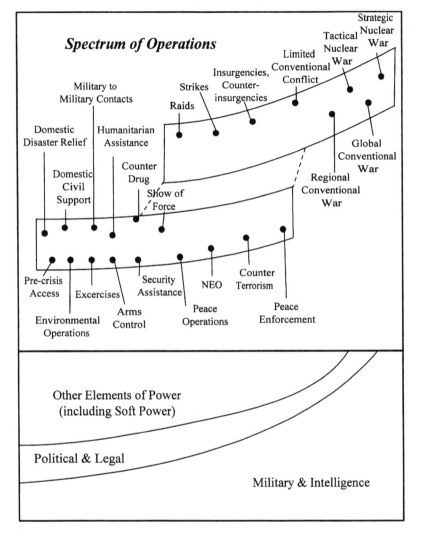

examination of the relative contribution that each element should make at different points along the spectrum—it is meant to be illustrative and in no way definitive, as specific operations may require more of less of each of the elements, depending on the situation on the ground.

At the lower end of the spectrum, each element has a role to play in promoting U.S. interests abroad. On a daily basis, one would expect to see diplomats, nation-building assistants, educators, financial consultants, and soldiers, to name a few from across the government, working shoulder-to-shoulder in operations such as humanitarian assistance. Toward the middle of the spectrum, which includes counterdrug, show of force, raids, and peacekeeping operations, the military role begins to dominate, although military power alone will most likely not lead to a successful policy outcome. The issue that caused the United States and allies to intervene in a peacekeeping operation likely has its roots in some political, economic, or cultural fracture point that will need to be addressed in a more fundamental and long-term manner, perhaps through education and promotion of democracy. At the highest end of the spectrum, which includes open conflicts such as regional, conventional, or nuclear war, the contribution of the military is certainly preeminent, yet again some of the traditional hard power elements remain essential for conflict termination and transition to the lower points on the spectrum as the situation allows.

The goal obviously is to keep relations at the lower ends of the spectrum, working in a cooperative manner with other nations, the example being security assistance. Although this may not always be possible and conflict may ensue, invoking higher levels of the spectrum, the ultimate goal remains an eventual return to normal peacetime interaction. Given this desired outcome and the contribution that the full mix of capabilities provides at the lower levels, it follows that no matter where the United States finds itself engaged along the spectrum, planning, if not action, should be ongoing at all times by virtually all of the elements of power.

Certainly it is beyond the scope of this book or even one single agency to develop this new security document. As a minimum, the new national security act should build upon the seminal work of the Commission on National Security/21st Century, the 9/11 Commission findings, the NSHS, and the most recent NSS, which goes further than any of its predecessors in charting a way ahead.

But any new formulation of national strategy must also examine security within the context of the Information Age. This implies recognition of the differences between the Information and Industrial Ages—the differences are fundamental and go well beyond simply having greater processing speeds. Cultural changes to adapt to the new environment will be required. Organizational changes will need to be broad and sweeping as well. The manner in which information is acquired, processed, analyzed, disseminated, and shared must be examined to ensure that we are gathering the right information in the right place at the right time.

Several recommendations for the formulation of a new U.S. national security strategy for the Information Age follow.

1. *Theory, doctrine, exercises, and curriculum must be developed to guide the U.S. national security apparatus.*

Much of today's theory, doctrine, exercises, and curriculum are based on hard power elements, most particularly the military. A concerted effort must be undertaken to develop a broad national security education and training system that incorporates the military and may even in large measure utilize military facilities and doctrine, but rationalizes the other elements into a coordinated national security policy team.

For the application of national security, most especially for crisis response, a trained full-time team with clear doctrine based on appropriate theories is imperative; we must get away from the pickup team mentality in which the team is developed and trains after the crisis begins. Over the course of the past decade or so with experiences in Somalia, Haiti, Bosnia, Kosovo, Afghanistan, and Iraq, to name a few, we have seen time and again the importance of a coordinated, broad-based response, but more must be done to institutionalize the efforts.

Prior to operations in Haiti in 1994, the deputies for the agencies responsible for providing support conducted an Interagency "rock drill" to coordinate and deconflict participation. In military terms, a rock drill is a step-by-step review of the plan for an operation prior to its conduct according to the phases of the operation. Part of the process is to develop branches and sequels to provide the capability to respond to unforeseen circumstances. The rock drill also ensures that all participants know their roles and have the means available to accomplish their assigned objectives.

Even this effort prior to the Haiti operation was not adequate, as much of the planning had already been done by the State Department and DOD prior to the rock drill and thus, instead of a holistic plan being developed that fully integrated the elements of power, the lesser elements (i.e., non-State and DOD) were harmonized at the end of the process, resulting in points of coordination, but not a single seamless effort.

The development of theory, exercises, and curriculum should not be used only to facilitate crisis response mechanisms. On a daily basis, planning and operations should be ongoing based on the theory, exercises, and curriculum. For example, if we had a Foreign Education Department under the Department of Education, it could be looking at maintaining and expanding educational programs around the globe. In developing their programs, the department could gain access to valuable information from across agencies that could be of great use in coordinating efforts and improving foreign educational systems in such endeavors as liberalization and democratization of societies.

2. *There must be a complete reevaluation of the national security apparatus, including the structure of the government organizations and agencies that are responsible for national security strategy planning and implementation.*

Based on the theory and doctrine of national security strategy resulting from the recommendations above, the structure of government organizations and agencies must also be modified. Developing the appropriate integration, coordination, and synchronization measures to facilitate cross-agency cooperation are of particular importance in this effort.

Both the Commission on National Security/21st Century and the 9/11 Commission addressed changes needed within the U.S. government. Most of these changes focused on the NSC, State Department, Intelligence Community, and DOD, the traditional national security structures. For example, recommendations from the Commission on National Security/21st Century for the State Department included provisions for developing and executing more responsive and coordinated policy by putting the U.S. Agency for International Development (U.S. AID) under the State Department, reorganizing the State Department, and creating a single integrated foreign operations budget. A recommendation likely to be controversial was the professionalization of the core of ambassadors, in contrast to the mix of political appointees and Foreign Service-trained individuals that serve today.

To assist in developing coherent regional strategies, the commission recommended that the State Department reorganize with five regional under-secretaries; today the structure of the department actually hinders the development of regional strategies. Ambassadors serve as the president's emissaries in each country in which they are stationed; policies are developed by country rather than by region. Harmonization does occur at State Department headquarters, but the ambassadors are largely free to take this guidance and implement it as they see fit, which does not always result in a coherent, single, regionally focused strategy. Under a regional undersecretary, directive guidance could be issued to better coordinate activities within regions. Using a dual reporting chain, ambassadors could still report directly to the President in the emissary role, yet receive daily direction from the department on regional issues.

Not contained in either report are recommendations for most of the other cabinet-level departments and key agencies. These too must be examined to determine what support they currently provide to national security strategy and how they can be reformed to more fully respond to the emerging Information Age environment. For each area where U.S. interests are at stake, an analysis should be conducted to determine how these departments fit into the overall national security strategy. The natural outcome must be that we will come to grips with the seams between organizations that currently exist, many of which can be eliminated or minimized based on information technologies that allow quick rapid and accurate sharing of critical knowledge.

The role of Congress must also be considered. While the overall manner in which the Congress functions in national security is adequate, issues exist with respect to resources and oversight. With regard to resources, the use of a supplemental to handle long-term operational commitments causes the DOD, for example, to use resources allocated for other activities to pay up front and then receive reimbursement. This causes an opportunity cost as priority programs sometimes must be slowed so that DOD can pay up front for immediate needs. Congress has been reluctant to have an operational account. However, the change in operational requirements must be accommodated to some degree. With regard to oversight, the 9/11 Commission expressed concern about the number of oversight committees maintained by Congress. The Department of Homeland Security staff complained at one point that they were spending a large percentage of their time preparing for duplicative Congressional consultations rather than working on the important issues of the day.

3. *Development of an Interagency Fusion Center that fuses the elements of power is necessary.*

The U.S. government must develop a fully manned, full-time Interagency Fusion Center to address the day-to-day business of coordinating efforts as well as crisis action management. It is not sufficient to have an Interagency process that brings in representatives for specific coordination at discrete points in time.

Policy and planning will remain essential elements, but we must also make the Interagency capable of execution at the strategic, operational, and tactical levels. Inherent in this requirement is the development of deployable capabilities to respond in a coordinated manner either inside or outside the United States. Today, few agencies have any capability to conduct operations outside the United States.

What I envision is an Interagency operations center where key information is shared and actions coordinated across the U.S. government. Organizations should represent a broad cross section of the government, with the ability to add other organizations as required. Standing members of the Interagency Fusion Center should include all cabinet-level departments and other specialized organizations such as the Centers for Disease Control and Prevention, CIA, and FBI.

Some may argue that the NSC staff is performing this mission today. In many respects, this is true, but it is also a misuse of the staff. The NSC was intended to be a policy-level organization and not an executing agency. The difficulties associated with trying to manage policy formulation and execution and the potential pitfalls clearly were contributing factors in the Iran-Contra affair.

We must solve the intelligence gap. It is imperative that we find a way to provide information to the persons, places, and levels where it is needed without compromising the sources and methods. The balance between the protection of intelligence information and the need to protect sources and means is an ongoing debate within the Intelligence Community, but it cannot be allowed to continue. Real and enlightened leadership will be essential to eliminating this roadblock and ensuring that the Intelligence Community does not contribute to another 9/11 or allow vital information to languish due to organizational infighting or bureaucracy.

We must learn to think, act, and allocate resources in real time. There is an opportunity cost associated with failing to act or acting too slowly. Mastering the decision cycle will be essential to future U.S. national security. Windows of opportunity will open for brief periods and will close just as rapidly. Consider Iraq, where there was a strategic opportunity immediately following the major combat operations when the fused application of diverse elements of national power likely could have stemmed the insurgency in its early stages. By late July 2003, a couple months after major combat operations ended, that window was closed and the insurgency was in full bloom. What if the other elements of power had executed their portions of the mission with the same rapidity and expertise as the military in these initial phases of the operations? Would an insurgency have developed at all, or would it have been eliminated in the early phases?

The Interagency Fusion Center must also consider how to incorporate NGOs which can be very useful in resolving conflict and alleviating the conditions that lead to conflict. The NGOs fill a vital capability gap and provide services that go well beyond what governments can do. This source must be harnessed to its fullest capability.

4. *We must conduct a comparison of requirements and capabilities across the U.S. government.*

Inherent in the development of a comprehensive U.S. national security strategy must be a complete evaluation of the requirements for national security. An old adage says, "He who tries to protect everything, protects nothing." What are the critical points and interests that the United States must protect? Certainly, with a total area of 9.63 million square kilometers of land and sea to protect,[4] it is not feasible to secure it all. Nor is it feasible to secure the entire 19,924 kilometers of coastline or the 12,034 kilometers of land boundaries. These figures do not even begin to address U.S. interests abroad, including embassies, corporations, and military installations outside the United States.

A serious discussion of security requirements must take place. For each of the elements of power, the requirements for interaction nationally and globally need to be examined and the capability gaps identified. For key areas, the United States must develop a defense in depth and in detail. What this means is that our national capabilities must be comprehensive and cut across the full range of the elements of national power. A likely outcome of this assessment is the identification of areas where we have overinvested and a number of key areas where underinvestment is the issue. The analysis is also sure to reveal entire areas where divestiture of capabilities would be appropriate and even necessary to developing a more reasonable security system.

Included in this discussion must be the capabilities (and unfortunately the requirements) that allies both can provide and require for security. Alliances and coalitions will be essential to U.S. national security. Interactions between peoples will increase as a result of globalization, and thus the United States will become more rather than less reliant on allies and coalitions.

5. *Development of a national Red Team capability is essential.*

A key deficiency in the U.S. government is the lack of a Red Team to assist in developing courses of action and evaluating proposed actions. The term

Red Team has its roots in military training and is related to providing an opposing force (OPFOR) to add to the realism of war games and to provide a thinking adversary to train against. The Intelligence Community also uses the term to describe analysis to gain understanding and perspective of what the threat might do given a certain set of circumstances. The idea is that a Red Team would be allowed the latitude to develop out-of-the-box threats and solutions.

This proposed organization would bring invaluable insights to the development of national security alternatives and options for implementation. The group as envisioned would need to be apolitical, independent, multidisciplinary, and highly skilled in the members' individual disciplines. It would need to have access to the latest in analytical capabilities, automation, and access to a variety of classified and unclassified source material. Perhaps most importantly, a Red Team would need to have a culture to think and interpret based on their individual judgments.

A likely criticism of such a proposal is that the CIA already has the capability and charter to conduct this sort of analysis. This is only partly true, as the focus of the CIA's efforts is foreign intelligence and a true Red Team effort would need to look at foreign and domestic threats and policy alternatives. Furthermore, the CIA and its the Director of Central Intelligence have become highly politicized and are not fully able to represent dissenting or nonmainstream views.

Given the global nature of the Information Age, an important charter of this new organization would be to ensure consistency in policy and allow for a harmonization of major policy initiatives, both around the world and in the United States. There is no intent to have this organization try to run the government or approve policies and strategies; rather, it should conduct a form of independent analysis and assessment.

6. *Bring network-centric capability to the lowest levels of government.*

An important aspect of transitioning the U.S. government to network-centric operations is to understand the environment as we move from Industrial to Information Age. Most important, the premise is that in the Information Age, virtually everything is known (or will be known) by someone. The key is to make the right information available at the right time to the right person. The border patrol guard needs to be able to access the complete fingerprint database (in real time) to allow rapid and accurate checks of individuals or even Interpol information. The history of a container at the port, including a verification of contents, perhaps through electronic sensor means, should be available on demand.

There must also be absolute interface between departments that allows the lowest levels of the security apparatus, whether that is the border guard, port stevedore, or National Guard soldier guarding the power plant, to access databases, communicate with higher headquarters, submit spot reports, and conduct required analysis of the situations that are encountered. It also means conducting exercises of the systems to ensure accuracy and timely reporting, understanding of the systems and capabilities that are in place, and the continued perfection of procedures.

The military describes this concept as "seeing first, understanding first, acting first, and finishing decisively." Imagine the advantages for the security system of having a border patrol agent with the capability to spot anomalies, conduct a rudimentary analysis, notify higher headquarters, and freeze the action before a breach of security occurs.

The ability to see first can be augmented through improving processes, use of sensors, and biometric identification systems, to name a few. After acquiring the initial information, a synthesis must occur in which situational understanding is achieved. This involves analysis and improvements in procedures to determine the importance of seemingly disparate pieces of information. As the situation develops, there is freedom to act and to continue until the action concludes decisively. The military has concluded that this is the promise of network-centric operations and the move to the Information Age.

Information reform is another aspect of competition in the Information Age. As we determine ways to protect vital information and networks against intrusion and tampering, multilevel security must be established that allows individuals with the requisite clearances and need to know to have access to classified or sensitive information.

7. *Avoid the temptation to implement all ninety-six recommendations of the 9/11 Commission and Commission on National Security/21st Century directly.*

It is imperative that we undertake a comprehensive look at national security. The direct implementation of all ninety-six initiatives may not yield the results expected and can even leave us with policies that work against each other, or perhaps even derail other U.S. programs that are on track and functioning properly.

As an example, President Bush created a Department of Homeland Security in 2003. This action had broad bipartisan support and appeared to be a wise response to the deficiencies that allowed 9/11 to occur. But an unintended consequence of this action was to divide U.S. national security into foreign and domestic security run by the DOD and the Department of Homeland Security, respectively. If that is not complex enough, some assets are shared jointly, for which arrangements on training, chain of command, and employment need to be negotiated between the heads of two cabinet-level departments. Examples include the Weapons of Mass Destruction-Civil Support Teams (WMD-CST) and some highly classified Special Operations Forces (SOF). Essentially, what the establishment of a Homeland Security Department did is to create another seam that a potential adversary could exploit and that must be comanaged by the two departments.

Despite the development of a new seam, the creation of a Department of Homeland Security was on balance the right action, if even only in the short term to develop immediate-response capabilities and coordinate actions across the

United States to better protect the nation. The point, though, is that it is not in the best interests of the United States to take a series of uncoordinated steps in an effort to enhance security in a way that may actually compromise security in the long run. Therefore, my theme is that a comprehensive strategy for national security is required rather than a series of hodgepodge arrangements that could result in confusion and a lack of unity of command and effort. We are taking baby steps toward the end state, which is a stable and secure America, but each step has potential unintended consequences.

8. *Learn to focus the nontraditional elements of power (soft power) externally as well as internally.*

> If the only tool you have is a hammer, everything looks like a nail.
> Anonymous

National security implementation has tended to use hard power focused externally, rather than to use all of the elements of power in a coordinated fashion. The result is that the United States is highly proficient in the application of the political, military, intelligence, and now legal aspects of national security. Unfortunately, we have failed to develop complementary systems in the elements of soft power. Here is the dilemma. The hard power elements will continue to have relevance in the globalized Information Age, but the soft power elements will have increasing importance to national security.

It follows then that we must continue to invest in hard power to ensure security, provide for deterrence, and, should deterrence fail, have the capability to engage and destroy threats. However, we must develop a complementary system that harnesses the collective capabilities of soft power to better coordinate these efforts. In one sense, I am talking about short-term and long-term investment systems. Hard power is short term. It is swift, direct, and can be brutal, while soft power works long term and focuses on winning hearts and minds. There is little near-term gratification in the application of soft power and the process has many ups and downs, but we must make the investment.

Demographics will continue to be a key point of friction. Population trends, especially in the undeveloped and developing world, will result in large youthful populations that must be given something productive and fulfilling to occupy their energies, or the result will be large disenfranchised, unemployable populations that will likely lead to instability and conflict. The key here is education.

Education must become the weapon of choice for the second wave. We must encourage broad liberal education across societies equally for men and women. While a cross section of society can engage in religious education and the sciences, liberal arts and the study of comparative religions must also be included in the curriculum. Students must be encouraged to develop critical thinking skills and move away from rote memorization. This is not to say that men and women need to sit side-by-side in class. Cultural differences would likely make this impossible in the near term until democratization and liberalization have begun to grow. The important aspect is teaching students how to think rather than what to think—the forum is less relevant.

Harnessing the power of the youthful populations through education and training will not only result in a liberalization of these developing societies, but will have the added benefit of enhancing economic prosperity. In short, economic deprivation is a major contributor to instability and conflict.

But what do the U.S. Departments of Education and Commerce do to support the process of democratization and liberation around the world? More important, what should they be doing to support these initiatives? The Department of State and DOD are, in many cases, the faces of Americans overseas in developing areas and areas of conflict. But neither of these two agencies has a core competency in education and commerce. The Foreign Service has officers with broad capabilities, most with training in international relations. There are few trained economists or educators. The same is true for the military, which has civil affairs units with limited expertise in these areas, but certainly not to the level found in the Departments of Education and Commerce.

We must develop a cadre of deployable individuals and government units capable of interacting with nations and local populations with a focus on capturing the hearts and minds of the second wave before it becomes necessary to deploy hard power forces to respond to instability or resolve conflict.

We must also develop more creativity in using the elements of power. As an example, it is in our national interest to give $2 billion in foreign aid to Egypt yearly. Perhaps we should go a step further and offer an additional $1 billion for use in targeted areas or for "good behavior."

9. *Develop a comprehensive plan for the security and defense of the nation's infrastructure.*

National security and defense were once the exclusive domain of the Foreign Service and military. However, with terrorists targeting the private sector and critical infrastructure, we must make a concerted effort to protect these assets and to respond in the event of an attack, which by necessity makes the private sector a nontraditional partner in defense and security. The importance of protecting critical infrastructure mandates separate treatment here, for visibility if for no other reason.

With 85 percent of the nation's infrastructure, including communications, transportation, finance, energy, and computer networks in the private sector, the implications are clear and unmistakable. On a comparatively small and temporary scale, the blackout along the East Coast in 2003 demonstrated the potential implications of a more serious terrorist attack.

Beginning with the development of a comprehensive strategy for private-sector security, the underlying policies, programs, and procedures must also be established for providing an adequate level of security, mounting a defense if required, and, finally, reconstitution in the event of an attack.

Survivability, liability, and economics represent vital areas of concern as well. The survivability of personnel in an emergency situation, whether a natural disaster or terrorist attack; liability of the private sector for failing to adequately prepare and respond to potential threats; and finally, the potential economic loss associated with a mass casualty scenario must all be factored into any equation of national security requirements.

Initiatives would in all likelihood be implemented through a mix of laws enacted by national, state, and local legislatures, and voluntary compliance. Some important initiatives would certainly include building interoperability, competence and confidence in security, and defense and response capability. Key components will undoubtedly include training and exercises, essential to developing these capabilities. In the event an attack occurs, the training of individuals and industry can reduce loss of life and property if procedures are in place and rehearsed in advance.

Perhaps the most important aspect of interoperability will be the development of information sharing at all levels. Classification of sensitive material will be a concern, but techniques to distribute essential information must be developed to allow better situational awareness. Technology and communications provide two other examples of where cooperation can and must be increased.

Included directly in all future NSS submissions must be the vulnerability assessments for civilian infrastructure and proposed techniques for increasing security at key facilities. Standards and metrics for assessing the preparedness of critical civilian infrastructure protection must be included to determine if progress is being made over time.

The Department of Homeland Security is working to develop and, where programs already exist, expand key areas of cooperation. One of these areas, public-private partnerships, will be a linchpin for ensuring security. Most U.S. citizens are in the private sector and represent a large, untapped pool of "intelligence sensors" that can provide early warning or assist in providing information that when combined with other information could result in the thwarting of a terrorist attack. Procedures and capabilities must be established that facilitate this public-private cooperation.

10. *A serious discussion of the trade-offs between security and civil liberties must occur.*

The potential for trade-offs between security and civil liberties is likely to be an unpopular topic of discussion. On one end of the spectrum will be civil libertarians such as the American Civil Liberties Union and even many right-wing antigovernment individuals (or at least those concerned that Big Brother is watching them) who will be hesitant to provide personal information to the government, while at the other end will be those who will propose measures in the interest of national security that will essentially eliminate the very freedoms that we as Americans hold sacred.

Neither alternative is acceptable. The key will be to navigate a middle path, which balances the need for security with the rights and freedoms of the individual. One way to ensure this balance is to encourage voluntary compliance with programs, providing built-in benefits for those participating.

An example is a national identification or ID card. Suppose that this card would contain biometric data and other critical information that would allow access to a variety of venues including mass transportation, shopping malls, and national parks, across country for example. Those individuals having the cards, thereby submitting to some invasion of privacy, would be rewarded with immediate access, while those not participating could still gain access but would need to go through additional checks and further scrutiny.

Even with voluntary compliance, this is likely to be a highly emotional subject. Questions will include these: How much security is enough? How much are we willing to pay for the added security? How much risk is appropriate? Is there such a thing as an acceptable loss? Trying to secure everything will not be feasible or desirable. Thus, as a nation, we must make honest assessments and develop solutions that provide reasonable levels of security and global interaction at equally reasonable levels of funding.

It will always come down to this. The more the American people are willing to trade their individual rights and freedoms for security, the greater the ability to secure the public will be. But this is the catch: the enemy wins when individual freedoms and liberties are eroded.

REBALANCING NATIONAL CAPABILITIES

Tomorrow's adversary will be more like the type we are seeing in Iraq and Afghanistan today rather than the traditional foe. We can expect to oppose a highly dispersed, networked enemy that fights asymmetrically. This adversary will maximize chaos, attack infrastructure, and inflict casualties on the coalition forces that it fights as well as the local population. Time and local public opinion will both be on the side of the enemy and will be invoked as often as possible. Unfortunately, this will become the standard, rather than the traditional force-on-force confrontation that the United States has shown great proficiency in conducting.

Deputy Secretary of Defense Paul Wolfowitz has clearly summed up the challenges the United States will face in confronting these new threats (see box). He identified the broad nature of the response that will be required to secure America and the patience that this response will entail. The unfortunate aspect is that the remarks were made by the Deputy Secretary of Defense rather than by the Secretary of Commerce, Secretary of Education, or even the Secretary of

> ### Remarks at the 2004 Eisenhower National Security Conference as delivered by Deputy Secretary of Defense Paul Wolfowitz, Ronald Reagan Building and International Trade Center, Washington, DC, September 14, 2004
>
> To be successful, once again, in defending our society and our freedom, four basic principles must guide our strategy in combating terrorist fanaticism.
>
> First, we must recognize that the struggle will be a long struggle. We will win it, but victory will not be marked by anything as dramatic as a signing ceremony on the U.S.S. *Missouri* or the collapse of the Berlin Wall.
>
> Second, we must use all the instruments of national power, including military force, but not solely or even primarily military force.
>
> Third, we must wage this war in multiple theaters, including here in our own country. But we must sequence our efforts and focus our energies in the right places at the right times. We can't take on every problem all at once.
>
> Fourth, and perhaps most important, we need to understand that this is an ideological as well as a physical struggle. We have to do more than simply kill and capture terrorists. As President Bush said in his very first State of the Union message a few months after September 11, we must work to build, and I quote, "a just and peaceful world beyond the war on terror and particularly in the Muslim world."

State. Perhaps another cause for concern is the obsessive focus on Muslims and Islam. If history has taught us anything, it is that new threats will emerge and that may be a great surprise. The 9/11 attacks fall into this category—at least the sophistication and planning that went into the attacks and went undetected or unrecognized for their potentially devastating consequences.

The sad truth is that even if the Secretary of Commerce or Education had made these comments, there are few programs and little funding to translate these thoughts into action and finally into a reality. As a nation, we have not dedicated the resources or effort to the longer-term efforts to create a world with broad support and a favorable opinion of the United States. Over the past ten to fifteen years, the negative trend has continued at an alarming rate, particularly in certain areas around the world where poverty, conflict, and instability are rampant, such as Africa, Asia, and throughout the Islamic community. Indeed, we have reached out when it was in our perceived national interest, but much of the world has not been the beneficiary of this support.

As further evidence of the overreliance on hard power, particularly the military, consider that in the Central Command area of operations, which includes

Afghanistan and Iraq, in August 2004 there were almost 216,000 individuals, of which 27,000 were contractors and 4,700 were government civilian employees. The 4,700 employees represent about 2.3 percent of the total, of which only 500 were non-DOD. So of the total number of deployed Americans, only 500 of 216,000 or .2 percent were non-DOD. It is difficult to conceive of how success will be achieved given that the problems in both of these countries include lack of democratic institutions, lack of infrastructure, religious and ethnic intolerance, lack of liberal education, unequal distribution of wealth, and poor economic prospects, in addition to the security situation.

While the security situation is the most immediate issue, the nonmilitary reforms will have longer-term implications for achieving the stated goals of these operations. Yet as the numbers indicate, few other departments are participating in these operations.

Reorganizing to Support a New National Security Strategy

The preceding discussion led to the conclusion that in order to respond to the emerging threats in the Information Age, the United States must conduct a comprehensive review of national security strategy, culminating with a new national security act. The result must also be a change in thinking and a reorganization of the government in some extremely significant ways.

First, we must develop "jointness" in the Interagency. To the military, "Joint" originally signified that the Services (Army, Navy, Air Force, Marines) could interoperate. As the DOD's thinking and capabilities have matured in this regard, Joint thinking has gone from interoperability to interdependence. The difference is subtle, but extremely important. Interoperable forces have the capability to operate together with cooperation and coordination; however, seams still exist. An interdependent force would mean that each Service would depend on the capabilities that the others provide. An example is fire support, where close air support provided by the Air Force is planned to be substituted for Army artillery.

This same concept applied to the Interagency implies that the elements of power would be fused into a focused, integrated superstructure designed to achieve stated national security goals. Given the construction of deployable sections from each of the relevant agencies for use in both day-to-day operations and crisis action, the expectation would be not only that the Foreign Service, intelligence organizations, and military could cooperate, but that elements from the Departments of Justice, Commerce, Education, and Health and Human Services, to name a few, would be molded into Interagency units. The practice of putting a team together on the fly would be replaced by using full-time, trained professionals. These units would work together so that each could learn the capabilities of the other elements of the team. As well, these units would train with the military on all phases of conflict, from deployment through major combat operations to reconstruction efforts. In the end, this is about the commitment of national power rather than the commitment of force.

Consider how this might work in a scenario that has led to conflict and the commitment of U.S. forces. Combat forces would conduct military missions as directed by the National Command Authorities. Embedded in the formations would be Army civil affairs units and Interagency teams. The civil affairs units would provide the immediate interface between the combat and security forces and the local populace while the Interagency units would interface initially with the civil affairs units until the security situation was stabilized. Together the civil affairs and Interagency units would call forward other national and coalition response elements to provide longer-term reconstruction assistance. The transition from combat operations to support and stability operations would begin as soon as the situation warranted it, rather than having to wait for a lengthy period of recruitment and training of Interagency personnel.

The manner in which the United States considers the commitment of forces should also be adjusted to account for the realities of the Information Age and the Interagency focus. Whether one is a believer in the Weinberger criteria discussed earlier or the Rumsfeld Test, which envisions smaller deployed forces with offshore reserves that can be deployed as necessary, a change to the commitment of forces is imperative. Clear revisions must include the following:

- Assessment of the ability to win quickly and decisively. Whether a small or overwhelming force should be employed or how the buildup should precede can be debated, but the need for a swift, decisive outcome is absolute. Time favors the enemy. The longer the conflict lasts, the more likely that the enemy's network can be energized and the public case made against coalition forces. This assessment cannot include just the combat phase, but must also extend the accomplishment of all stated objectives.

- Ensuring that the right preparations been have completed to ensure success. This includes the coordination of the Interagency units that will accompany the combat forces. All the elements of power must be coordinated to achieve the stated objectives. In this regard, we must develop the capability to pull the levers of national power in a coordinated manner rather than as stovepipes that do not fully cooperate.

- Application of a Darwinist approach to the use of force: There are some areas of the world and some situations that are beyond the scope of the United States to constructively influence with coercive means (Note: this is where a Red Team is essential). In these areas, perhaps only soft power is useful, or in the worst cases, perhaps no constructive interaction is possible. A further test must be an expansion of the interest question to assess whether the interaction is in the vital interest of the United states or is within the purview of the world's only superpower (or hyperpower) to solve.

We must clarify authorities, accountability, and responsibility as well. This clarification is in many ways at the heart of a new national security act. Just as the National Security Act of 1947 resulted in the reorganization of the U.S. government, which included the establishment of the CIA and the U.S. Air Force, so too should the new formulation of a national strategic concept. We must do an end-to-end evaluation of the requirements for national security and measure those requirements against existing capabilities. Where shortfalls exist, changes should be made to determine how resources should be shifted to fund necessary programs. Of course, risk is an essential component that must be considered; if the risk of not funding a particular program is only minimal, then perhaps some capabilities should not be funded.

For a new national security act, establishing clear accountability and authority is essential. Which organizations will be responsible for which aspects of national security? How will the various organizations and agencies interact? We must eliminate redundancies and unnecessary overlaps in capability. It goes without saying that it is not possible to hold someone responsible and accountable who lacks authority either through direct command relationships or through budgetary control. Therefore, aligning budgetary authority with mission and agency responsibilities is a must.

Within the DOD, a major reevaluation must be initiated with a keen eye toward true transformation to the Information Age. This transformation must also account for and describe the changes that will be required for DOD to appropriately interface with the other elements within our government. For examining these, the construct of "doctrine, organizations, training, material, leadership, personnel, and facilities" (DOTMLPF) should be incorporated to ensure that all aspects of the force have been addressed or at least considered.

Changes Required in the DOD: The Doctrine, Organizations, Training, Material, Leadership, Personnel, and Facilities Construct

In September 2004 an article appeared in the *Washington Post* that discussed deliberations at the Pentagon "considering a new, long-term strategy that shifts spending and resources away from large-scale warfare to build more agile, specialized forces for fighting guerrilla wars, confronting terrorism and handling less conventional threats."[5] The article went on to discuss the implications for defense spending of moving some funds "away from ships, tanks and planes and toward troops, elite Special Operations forces and intelligence gathering." Inherent in this article is the question of how to gain greater efficiency and effectiveness in the DOD while operating in a new networked Information Age environment.

The DOTMLPF construct has become the manner in which DOD and in particular the Joint Staff and military Services talk about building and assessing capabilities. My intent is not to enumerate the final, authoritative force structure, but rather to examine some key considerations for this future environment.

One necessary caveat is that there should be no expectation that all of these recommendations can be implemented today. Many will depend on technological and engineering enhancements that will emerge over a period of time. Some are on the near horizon while others will emerge in the next decade or so. Regardless of the time frame in which these advances will be able to be incorporated into the force, we must keep our eyes on these goals while continuing to maintain our current national security with currently available means.

A second important caveat concerns the title of this section. While many of the DOTMLPF recommendations relate to changes to the DOD, they also relate to recommendations for other departments and agencies. They are included in this section due to their strong linkages to the military element of power.

The idea here is that the way the military thinks, acts, and interacts across the DOTMLPF must be scrutinized to ensure progression toward developing and maximizing Information Age capabilities and enhancing cooperation with other agencies for articulating and executing a new national security strategy. Where found to be lacking, appropriate changes, and in some cases wholesale divestitures of programs and systems as well as changes in policies and procedures, must be undertaken.

As a preamble to this discussion, consider the following scenario:

> Based on growing tensions in a far corner of the globe, the President, through the Secretary of Defense, orders the deployment of an Interagency task force led by a four-star military commander to conduct combat operations to restore order, transition to peace operations, and finally assist in posthostility reconstruction. The task force has been organized with the necessary capabilities from across the Interagency to conduct successful postcombat operations.
>
> Instantaneously, the commander receives the warning order for the upcoming full-spectrum operation. Given the missions assigned and the operational situation, the expectation is that the force must be capable of peacekeeping, humanitarian operations, and major combat. The planning begins immediately upon receipt of the warning order with all elements of the Interagency force. All relevant agencies and organizations are brought into a 24-7 secure conference call at each of their respective home station locations. In all, over twenty stations are simultaneously brought into the constellation for real-time, collaborative planning. This capability is made possible through major investments in information technology and network capabilities. These capabilities

have evolved to the point that deployment of many analytical, management, and support headquarters is no longer required. The support requirements for the force are in turn greatly reduced as the in-theater force totals can be cut by over 30 percent due to these efficiencies. All assets, military and Interagency, required to be transported into the theater are identified and compete for Air Force and Navy lift.

Even before the President is briefed on the final plan, a national decision to maneuver the global information grid (GIG) is made.[6] Invisible to the rest of the grid users, an electronic cloud is maneuvered to provide optimum support for the upcoming operation. Information operations also begin immediately with probes into enemy networks. The operators of the network rapidly work to develop the complex, self-healing, adaptive network to ensure the timely flow of information throughout the operation. Their mission has expanded to include the Interagency data management requirements for the force. The networks have multiechelon security allowing classified and unclassified users to share the network, accessing information based on their level of authorization. Network tracking is provided to monitor the flow of digital traffic, ensure compliance with network standards and architecture, and provide security.

Throughout the deployment, the force continues collaborative planning using en route mission-planning capabilities. Commanders and Interagency leaders at all levels have a wide variety of high-capacity battle command (or command and control) systems to gain the much-needed information. Without having to select a transmission means, the commanders can call for the information and seconds later review the data—truly data on demand.

At each level of command and control, the benefits of operating in the Information Age are realized. Data are provided without having to be requested in a "push" system where relevant data is provided without having to initiate a formal request. Information such as "Blue Force Tracking which provides a real time lay down of all friendly forces," enemy situation, and commander's directives are piped directly to the subordinate commanders and Interagency operators.

The battle command network in the theater begins to be established early in the deployment cycle. However, even before the theater injection points are established, the "electronic cloud" that was unobtrusively maneuvered prior to the deployment is supporting the early entry forces and the theater buildup, providing connectivity and thus battle command capability through high capacity, omnidirectional radios that can be employed on the move. Through this capability, virtual command posts provide commanders and Interagency units moving with them with critical operational command information.

Even commanders at the lowest levels have access to actionable intelligence which gives a high degree of transparency to the battle space. Imagine the impact on the tactical fight if prior to assaulting an objective, the platoon leader does a 360-degree electronic survey of the area, gaining feeds from national technical means (refers to intelligence collection capabilities such as satellites, electronic eaves dropping, and imagery), in-theater surveillance including unmanned aerial and ground vehicles, and a real-time assessment of the enemy situation from the senior organization's intelligence staff.

On the front lines as well as in command posts, access to the latest situational data is available. Cultural questions can be researched in real-time or forwarded to higher headquarters for guidance and information. Coordination can be accomplished in real-time with the planning cycle reduced to seconds or minutes rather than days or weeks.

These new capabilities pervade all aspects of the battle space from direct combat to administrative and logistical support and from the military to the Interagency players. Even individual soldiers and Interagency operators throughout the battle space have real-time access and have been trained to maneuver through the network to gain information.

As military formations complete combat operations and reestablish security, the Interagency units begin to provide critical support to the local populations. Their needs are relayed back to fusion cells located outside the area of conflict that are tracking progress and making on-the-spot resource allocation decisions.

Doctrine For the military, doctrine is the glue that links strategy and policy to operations and tactics, providing "fundamental principles by which the military forces or elements thereof guide their actions in support of national objectives."[7] So it follows that if the national security strategy of the United States calls for having the ability to assist in the development of other nations or to intervene to alleviate instability, then the doctrine must support these requirements, and that since these are not purely military endeavors, other elements of power must have complementary doctrines to assist in these endeavors. We must therefore develop both combined military and Interagency doctrine that supports the full range of requirements embedded in our national strategy. This includes doctrine for national deployable capabilities including the military, Interagency members, and NGOs, the manner in which these organizations will cooperate, and the external support requirements.

The Information Age will necessitate being able to operate in a fully networked environment. Just as physical distances were shown to be a poor measure of the ability to interact in the globalization discussion, the same principle holds true for operations in the Information Age. For example, many support and management headquarters will be able to operate from sanctuary locations rather than deploying forward. The obvious benefit is to reduce the size of the total force (military and Interagency) that must be deployed and is therefore exposed to a hostile environment. With a smaller requirement for the in-theater force, the support footprint is also reduced. Said another way, the smaller force requires less support structure.

Examples of this concept will include organizations such as intelligence analysis units and logistics management headquarters that will be capable of providing support in a secure environment with systems they use on a daily basis rather than being required to move forward and establish life support systems in addition to doing their operational missions. Of course, this capability for long-distance support is only possible with assured communications and enhanced decision support capabilities. This same concept holds true for Interagency or NGO participants, which may be able to provide support and management from outside of theater, alleviating both security and support requirements.

Any Information Age doctrine to be considered must have the inherent capability to digitally enable all critical elements within the area of operation. This statement is deliberately vague as later it is argued that all military entities, including individual ground forces, must have a digital capability. While it is probably not necessary to have the same level of connectivity to individuals within each NGO, certainly there must be adequate linkage to the NGO.

New doctrine must also account for the changes resulting from the increased information and knowledge available to the force. If every system and soldier is digitally enabled, then an operation such as Iraq Freedom could have well over half a million entities that are being tracked, including all ships, aircraft, vehicles, containers, ground forces to the individual level, and major weapons systems. The capability to track all of these entities will be made possible by eliminating the discrete theater injection points for communications and information and replacing them with a digital "cloud" with a capability of linking all of the deployed pieces of the operation. Of course, the ability to track all of these disparate systems is one thing, while the ability to understand what is going on operationally and further to command and control these assets is quite another—the implications of data overload are addressed under the heading "Leadership."

This linking of systems will allow sensors and shooters to be paired to provide real-time targeting using a variety of means, including traditional killing systems, nonlethal information dominance capabilities, and soft power to attack the adversaries' will and persuade adversaries or potential adversaries.

Doctrine must change from sequential and linear to simultaneous and three-dimensional. An example of a system that will have considerably less relevance in the Information Age is the current military targeting system, which calls for a sequence of Observing, Detecting, Deciding, Delivering, and Assessing (ODDDA) for targeting. This is a very linear process in which targeting meetings are held on a cyclic basis and targets are nominated and developed within a predetermined timeline. In this system, targets are passed up hierarchical chains of command and assessed for their importance. The process is plodding and methodical, certainly not agile and flexible. Likewise, a related system to provide fixed-wing aircraft support calls for an Air Tasking Order (ATO) which is published every twenty-four hours. Both of these systems need to be examined to determine how they can be compressed to alter the Industrial Age paradigm.

Considering possible changes to the current military targeting system, it seems reasonable to decide on targeting priorities at the beginning of the sequence, so that as targets are detected, the desired effect can be delivered and assessed in real-time without needing any new decision. This implies essentially an automation of the process and a linking of the sensors and shooters as well as targets and effects.

The doctrine must also account for the capability to conduct seamless transitions between and within phases of the operation. In fact, one could argue that the use of the term phase comes from the Industrial Age and should be eliminated from the lexicon altogether. To conduct seamless transitions implies an ability to move along the spectrum of conflict rapidly and actually argues against overreliance on special-purpose forces. It also implies Interagency forces with a capability to rapidly transition to operations immediately following the termination of hostilities and when the local security situation permits. This discussion is presented in greater detail under "Organization."

It is quite clear that the future environment will not support nor can the U.S. allow a disjointed transition like the one that occurred after the fall of Baghdad in 2003 when a two-week gap occurred between major combat operations and the deployment of the Office of the High Representative (OHR) chief, Lieutenant General (Retired) Jay Garner, in Operation Iraqi Freedom. Transitions must occur in real-time and at the appropriate time. Failure to master the transitions will undoubtedly place mission success in jeopardy.

Planners at all levels must learn to think differently about the means available to engage targets. Most important information operations must be incorporated into all planning, training, and operations. We must have the capability to protect friendly information, attack enemy information, and establish public domain information dominance in the competition for ideas, hearts, and minds.

Organizations Organizations must also adapt to reflect the new Information Age doctrine. Major changes will be necessary as the structure of the force transitions from a distinct and hierarchical formation to a distributed and networked force. The way we think about organizations will also need to change. It is quite a commentary on the conduct of operations that the organizations have changed little since World War II. Certainly means have changed, but the basic conduct remains the same with phase lines, areas of operations, and objectives as means of controlling massed combat formations of divisions, air wings, and fleets.

Recent operations in both Iraq and Afghanistan provide insight into how the Information Age will change organizations and operations. The manner in which virtual units have been linked within the battle space is quite instructive. Consider that Army units engaged in a direct firefight are able to call on B-2 bombers flying out of Whiteman AFB in the United States to get critical fire support. The notion of systems from dispersed locations bringing their effects together at a critical point in the battle, enabled by Information Age technologies and communications, is powerful. The potential exists to have real-time linking of capabilities such that virtual controllers would have access to all sensors and shooters within the battle space and more specifically within the area in which they are operating. In this scenario, controllers could each have a screen depicting all enemy systems and capabilities within their areas on one side of the screen and a listing of all means for engaging the targets along the other. By simply assigning engagement means to the various targets, or pairing, targets could be engaged immediately with the appropriate means to achieve the desired effect. Could this imply that each major unit moving through the battle space will have a controller that provides oversight and target engagement capability? What would be the relationship between this controller and the commander on the ground?

The need to have Joint, Interagency, and Coalition-capable organizations has already been established and discussed in some detail. Suffice to say that this capability is essential to operating in a globalized environment in the Information Age and will be critical to mastering the transitions.

One essential attribute for developing future organizations will be to transition from single-purpose forces to multirole organizations. Many have looked at recent operations and concluded that more military police (MP) or civil affairs (CA) units are required to better maintain security or support local populations. This seems to be an Industrial Age solution. Perhaps it would be useful to examine, in the case of MPs, what they bring to the equation and work backward to find the answer. An MP force is primarily trained to interface with populations, crowd control, and law enforcement. Aside from the law enforcement aspect, the tasks are similar to those conducted by the infantry. The biggest difference is in the level of violence expected to be encountered during operations in their respective core competencies and their capabilities for use of force. The infantry tend to train and operate toward the higher end of the spectrum, while MPs tend to practice tasks and operate at the lower end of the spectrum. One major difference is that MPs are credentialed law enforcement officers. Perhaps a solution, then, is to build more infantry units and train them to operate across the full spectrum. To account for the legal distinction, it would be possible by training, say, three senior members of each platoon in law enforcement and providing them the same credentials as their MP counterparts to develop multirole infantry formations with greater full-spectrum capability and certainly a greater capacity for escalation control. This does not imply that infantry would supplant all MP units, but that rather than building additional MP units, a trained multirole infantry unit could perform many of these tasks while maintaining a greater capacity for escalation control.

The same concept could hold for civil affairs units. Perhaps "multirolling" engineer units to allow them to function more broadly in the area of civil support by infusing training and capabilities for conducting civil affairs tasks it would be possible to gain some efficiency as well. These same concepts should be incorporated to embed essential capabilities such as language and cultural immersion into general-purpose forces.

The key benefit of multirole organizations would be to eliminate the seams that result from using different organizations. Obviously training will be an issue, as requiring each unit to gain proficiency in a greater number and variety of tasks increases the training load, but Information Age training should be able to offset this somewhat. New training techniques are discussed further under "Training."

Opposing this concept of multiple roles for units is the development of separate forces for peace keeping operations or nation building. The concept of specialized forces has gained a following, but it is severely misguided, and certainly not in keeping with the development of multirole organizations. Specialized formations by design lack the flexibility to operate along the full spectrum of operations. For example, a specialized formations optimized for nation-building could be deployed and find itself involved in combat operations with little or no ability to respond or control the escalation of the conflict.

While the number of special operating forces must grow to provide a greater rotational capability for these types of specialized formations, there must also be a concerted effort to bring special operating force capabilities to general-purpose forces. Even if the number of special operating units were doubled, the number of these formations still would not be adequate: thus the proliferation of special capabilities in general-purpose forces would continue to be extremely beneficial and necessary. Military forces must also develop capabilities to perform or at least support some Interagency-type tasks, but this should not supplant a development of professional Interagency units with these capabilities.

Another significant initiative must be the elimination of redundant capabilities. Redundancy is not necessarily a bad trait because it may ensure a higher probability of success. However, if the redundancy results from a lack of coordination, then it must be examined for possible elimination. Earlier I discussed the interdependency that the Services are trying to achieve. The comparison of requirements to capability that must be conducted throughout the military should look to expand upon this concept as much as possible.

Information Age organizations must be capable of learning and adapting in real-time. The ability, as presented earlier, to "see first, understand first, act first, and finish decisively" will be imperative to operations in this new environment. Developing the ability to understand first combines several key components, including seeing, receiving, analyzing, and processing. Pattern recognition and discerning sequences are analytical capabilities that must be developed within organizations as well as by leaders and soldiers at all levels. The capability to progress from data collection to analysis to synthesis to understanding will be of paramount importance. Organizations must have embedded decision support systems that facilitate this rapid processing of information and thus allow for rapid and decisive action.

A case in point is the combating of Improvised Explosive Devices (IED) in Iraq. Using analytical techniques to understand the enemy's methods and capabilities, coalition forces have developed new tactics, techniques, and procedures (TTPs) to defeat over 90 percent of these devices and to reduce coalition injuries resulting from devices not found and disarmed. Pattern analysis, establishment of a database for cataloging incidents involving these IED, information dissemination, and the fielding of new equipment and new TTPs have greatly reduced casualties in the case of IED attacks.

The expansion of capabilities must include additional intelligence collection. However, an old-think concept is to add intelligence units. In the Information Age, it is not more that is better; it is better that is better. The addition of a variety of sensors, the concept that all participants in the operation are collectors, and additional human intelligence (HUMINT) will be essential to gaining a complete situational understanding in future conflict.

Training Our current military training system must be altered significantly to account for increased training requirements such as those discussed in the section on multirolling of units. While our Industrial Age training system has produced and even today produces the best-trained military in the world, information technology will provide the capability to gain greater efficiencies, train a broader range of tasks, and do so in less time than our current system.

To make the point, consider that a soldier from the World War II era would likely need little adjustment to fit into today's training environment. Most training is conducted in the same way as in his generation, with repetitive, hands-on training, long road marches, and considerable downtime between training events. Only in certain specialties such as aviation, special operating forces, and major weapons systems including tanks and Army infantry fighting vehicles have new techniques, including the use of simulations, been extensively employed.

Where Information Age techniques are introduced in training, the focus is on developing greater speed and proficiency in the Industrial Age processes. However, this is only half of the equation. We must also turn our attention to second- and third-order effects such as training and developing new doctrines and methods of combining systems and technologies in ways that have not been attempted before. The simple example is training each soldier to be an intelligence collector in the battle space. How will these new methodologies be trained? How much additional training time will be required? How will the increased complexity impact on the requirements for the quality of the force?

If, in the Information Age, forces will have greater access to information, a greater need for rapid decisions and transitions, and a larger area of operations (as a result of increased ability to acquire, engage, and impact at longer distances), then training must be adapted accordingly. Furthermore, the notion of tactical-level soldiers with the ability to have a strategic impact will become even more pronounced and mandates that training must be revised to account for this phenomenon as well.

The combination of training, education, and experience will be increasingly important in preparing for Information Age operations. Individual and unit training must be revised to maximize the experience, make use of Information Age technologies, and develop proficiency. Virtual technologies must be integrated into all aspects of training. The same holds true for integrating the training of typical Interagency tasks that military forces may participate in initially and for training Interagency personnel.

With a greater variety of operations expected to be conducted by individual units, education and experience will also become increasingly important. Education, in the words of General George Catlett Marshall, must be conducted to teach students how to think rather than what to think. This is an important distinction that leads to the essential notion that we must develop techniques to teach context down to the level of the individual soldier. Soldiers must understand the cultural sensitivities and environmental considerations of the situation and the implications of their actions for the overall operation. They must have a situational awareness that comes with both the best training and the best education. Interagency organizations must also be included in these training and educational opportunities. Again, virtual technologies can be incorporated to reinforce educational concepts.

Experience is perhaps even more difficult to provide. However, there is no substitute for experiential learning, and we must maximize the number of broad experiential opportunities. Today, many are calling for individual units to spend more time conducting repetitive training to achieve higher levels of proficiency. This seems to be in direct contrast to the development of the broader base of experience that will be essential to future national security operations. Rather, a more useful approach would be to ensure that soldiers and leaders alike be provided opportunities to experience other, nonmainstream military tasks and training. As an example, a tour at the State Department, NSC staff, Office of Secretary of Defense, or Joint Staff would provide key experiences that would almost certainly broaden an officer's horizons. One could argue that the officer who remained in units for a full twenty-year period might be the better war-fighter, but would in all likelihood not have the same full-spectrum ability as the officer who had a tour or two in these broadening assignments. In the Information Age, with the three-block war requirement to conduct full spectrum, interagency coordinated, nonlinear operations involving rapid transitions and decisions, the second officer undoubtedly would have the edge. Likewise, it would be useful to have Interagency personnel stationed with combat formations or at least periodically training with major units on a regular basis.

Training of analytical techniques down to the lowest levels is also a must—this recommendation is especially important considering that in the future each individual is expected to be a sensor. It is imperative to train all levels on how to shape data provided through sensors and other inputs into a coherent picture of the battle space and to develop the understanding of what it means to the immediate operation and within the broader context. Advanced analytical techniques augmented with virtual reality-enhanced scenarios will allow nearly continuous training in a wide variety of situations.

Material Most important, we must fundamentally change the way we think about systems. Today, we are largely overlaying Information Age networks on top of Industrial Age systems to provide surrogate Information Age capabilities. This methodology is important to the transition from the Industrial to the Information Age. However, at some point we must begin to develop revolutionary systems that are specifically designed with the Information Age in mind. Stated another way, today we are fielding evolutionary capabilities by simply embedding network capabilities. In the future, we must develop and field revolutionary capabilities for the Information Age.

New concepts such as trading mass for information will reduce the size and weight of the deployed force. The ability to see first, understand first, act first, and finish decisively, enables us to trade armor for information and allows lower system density within the battle space. Advanced techniques for avoiding detection will allow land forces to field more lightly armored systems that gain protection through advanced information systems rather than armored protection. Another example is the reduction in munitions stockpiles that must be deployed forward, given precision systems and highly accurate intelligence that will provide a higher probability of detection and a first-time hit on the target, whether using kinetic or other means of attack (e.g., an electromagnetic system that could disable an enemy system).

Every system must be digitally enabled. Even individuals must have the embedded capability to send and receive information that will lead to a 360-degree picture of the fight. Note that the development of systems and capabilities should be embedded, rather than applied. Today, many information technologies are attached after the fact (i.e., applied), but future systems should include information technology in the design. This digital capability would give U.S. forces significant advantages in the ability to understand the battle space, and would be like playing the game of Battleship—where opponents place ships on a game board and then must guess where the other's ships have been placed—with a complete view of the opponent's board and ship placement, certainly not a fair game.

Thinking differently about systems and capabilities is paramount for fielding an Information Age force. Proponents of the Comanche armed reconnaissance helicopter recently terminated by the Army, the Navy's Virginia Class attack submarine, or the F-22 advanced fighter aircraft argue that these systems use leap-ahead technologies that will provide significant enhancements over the systems they are (or were) intended to replace. However, these systems are really just better ways to perform Industrial Age maneuvers. They are evolutionary, not revolutionary, and many were initially designed in the late 1970s or early 1980s—clearly not the Information Age.

An example of a revolutionary capability would be the ability to employ unmanned air systems as a substitute for fighter aircraft to maintain air superiority within a theater. Perhaps it would be possible to take the same approach to protecting aircraft carriers and key U.S. cities where we are now flying combat air patrols for protection. Where requirements can be automated, digitized, or even performed using unmanned systems, every effort to do so should be made, to save critical manpower, gain greater efficiencies, and improve effectiveness. A key, then, is to identify and terminate systems that fail to demonstrate Information Age relevance.

Improvements in information technologies should provide the capability for the Services and Interagency to interact and cooperate as never before. We must determine how systems can complement each other to reduce redundancies and develop greater effectiveness. An example is the Army eliminating much of its artillery and relying on Navy and Air Force aircraft to provide fire support for front-line forces. Another example is the State Department providing intelligence information to the "All Source Analysis Center" located with Army forces.

All systems procured in the future should have the capability for embedded training. We must move away from separate trainers and systems to the maximum extent possible, and rely on training in the systems in which individuals fight.

We must also find a way to embed analysis capability and decision support in the systems that are being fielded. The goal must be to facilitate the development of context at the lowest level possible. The tank platoon leader with the capability for conducting at least some rudimentary analysis and with limited decision support that allows seeing first and understanding first will have a distinct advantage in the ability to act first and finish decisively.

The information technologies must provide both a package of relevant information and the ability for individuals to pull information from databases and

Web sites. To relieve individuals from having to request vital information, a standard set of information can be provided and updated as changes occur. This might include a series of maps linked to their positions as well as the capability to request other maps for areas where they expect to conduct future operations.

Leadership A full discussion of leadership could literally fill volumes and is certainly beyond the scope of this effort. Therefore, it is my intent to concentrate on what leadership capabilities will emerge as different or more critical in the Information Age.

As a backdrop to the discussion, the Office of Force Transformation within the Office of the Secretary of Defense uses a diagram with three interlocking circles, in which the intersection is referred to as network-centric warfare. The three domains are the physical, the cognitive, and information. The conclusion is that linking the ability to think (the cognitive) and act (the physical) with the ability to amass information, understand the situation, and gain knowledge leads to the higher-order capability to operate in a network-centric environment to achieve a higher degree of proficiency in operations. Clearly these physical, cognitive, and informational abilities will be essential to the military leader of the Information Age.

The leader of tomorrow must also have the values set and ethical makeup embodied throughout the Services today. In the Air Force, they talk about "integrity, service, and excellence." The Army promotes the seven values of "loyalty, duty, respect, selfless service, honor, integrity, and personal courage." The other Services expect similar traits of their members and especially their leaders. With the values-based foundation established, leaders must have the appropriate mix of training, education, and experiences to deal with the complex Information Age situations expected of tomorrow's leaders.

Major challenges Information Age leaders will need to cope with will be the increased amount of information available, compressed decision timelines, and the necessity to be able to develop the context for action. Several key facets of these challenges are discussed below.

The military (and Interagency counterparts) must develop leaders that are capable of something similar to three-dimensional chess. A high degree of mental agility will be required. We must also teach leaders to think strategically and operationally as well as tactically, and this must be done for junior leaders as well.

Leaders must also be taught to conduct something similar to simulations. Already, the military uses rock drills to walk through operations prior to execution and uses branches and sequels to look at other possible outcomes. This process must be expanded to look farther into the future and at nonmilitary outcomes as well. Some of the analysis of outcomes might even be counterintuitive, as it may become clear that a unit will need to suboptimize on combat operations to set the conditions for success in follow-up operations.

We must teach leaders to think Red, that is, to think like the enemy. This concept is more than simply asking, "What would the enemy do?" The more appropriate analysis begins with the statement, "I am the enemy. What am I going to do?" The difference is subtle, but important. To conduct this sort of analysis implies a significantly higher degree of understanding of the threat and the environment. To think like the enemy, one must ask questions such as these: What are my goals and objectives? How will I reach them? What must I do to defeat the Blue force?

The decision cycle and the ability of information operations to drive rapid and timely decisions has been discussed previously. It will be essential to operational success to master the decision cycle. The military must depart from the Military Decision-Making Process (MDMP), which is a very linear analytical tool for developing an operational or campaign plan. This decision process takes hours and days. Tools for the Information Age will need to operate in seconds and minutes.

In thinking about leadership, the military has a standard of looking "two levels down." What happens in the case of the network where the classic hierarchical system does not apply? How must leaders think differently in this networked force? Do we now look two levels out?

The ability to fight in the twenty-first-century battle space is related to hardware and software capabilities, but most directly linked to the human factors associated with battle command (also sometimes called command and control). Even small enhancements in battle command can translate to highly significant enhancements to the performance of the Joint Force. What allows the Joint Commander to "see first, understand first, act first, and finish decisively" is directly tied to battle command and Information Age warfare. The rest (i.e., the hardware and software) is really just the means.

The DOD must develop Joint Force Commanders that understand and believe the information that is coming through the network. At times this information is likely to seem incredible or even not plausible, but through maturing of network capabilities and advanced capabilities to ensure reliability, the commander can and must learn to exercise effective battle command.

Perhaps the most important aspect of the network will be the development of soldier information systems. The inclusion of the soldier as part of the network is the fundamental conceptual difference in the design. While the concept might appear foreign, 3,500 soldier "collectors" in an Army maneuver brigade combat team are likely to provide the most reliable "ground truth" for the commanders.

Associated with improving Information Age capabilities is the development of innovative solutions for improving battle command capabilities through information technology enhancements. Many of the airplanes, ships, tanks, and artillery systems of the Joint Force have been in the inventory for decades, yet have been improved, in some cases exponentially, through the incorporation of state-of-the-art network solutions. In some cases, DOD has designed its own capabilities to enhance battle command while in others DOD has looked externally to commercial solutions. This spirit of innovation must continue. We must make a continuous effort to reward innovation in the Joint Force, whether through creative hardware or software solutions or through changes in processes and procedures.

Personnel Perhaps nowhere will the Information Age have greater impact than on personnel. As a society, we have learned to think in a hierarchical fashion. Large corporations, the State Department and the military included, have all learned to operate in a linear, hierarchical manner. The inherent assumption in these types of systems is that people at the lowest levels have a set of information that is narrowly focused—they understand their lane, but may be clueless as to what is going on at the next workstation. But what if information technology provided the ability for these lower-level individuals, through seeing, analyzing, and understanding, to have a better picture of the circumstances than the boss or the boss's boss? This is entirely possible given the proliferation of information.

This sort of knowledge inversion will mandate dramatic cultural changes. While in the past information flowed up and down of discrete chains of command in stovepipe-style organizations, in the Information Age, the free flow of information will act like the elimination of trade barriers in the economy. Just as in a free trade zone goods and services flow unimpeded, in a networked force information will flow to anyone with a desire to examine it and with adequate access (through bandwidth and classification).

Operating in this emerging environment will require a different type of operator (i.e, Soldier, Sailor, Airman, Marine). At the individual level, intelligence and analytical capability will become more important than pure strength and endurance. The changes required will include the necessity to conduct complex analysis, avoid overspecialization, and develop cultural sensitivity. Mental agility and flexibility will be essential to operating in the Information Age, as well as the ability to rapidly transition to operations across the spectrum. The three-block war discussed previously will impact, not just organizations, but also individuals as they make rapid transitions in response to changes in the environment.

Obviously, major changes to the personnel system must be made to identify operators and leaders that have the capacity for rapid, independent, and nonlinear thought. The metrics used to recruit and retain will need to be adapted as well.

Facilities Information Age facilities must fully enable all aspects of support for the unit and the individual, including training, education, and developing critical experiences; preparing for a deployment; and support for the deployed force. Perhaps the most important aspect of this facilities development is to provide the identical capabilities during peacetime and training as for deployment and wartime. The same communications and decision support tools can easily support the full range of activities of individuals or units in garrison or within a deployed theater.

Major facilities should be Joint (representing two or more Services) and have Interagency units and liaisons elements residing on the post to allow for coordination, planning, and immediate transition to an operational footing. The combination of Joint and Interagency units coexisting at installations would facilitate the development of relationships and sharing of information that will be essential to Information Age operations.

Physically, facilities in the Information Age must have all of the tools and bandwidth to support full-spectrum operations and planning, including decision support tools and other analytical capabilities. Access to virtual libraries and databases must be ensured for all.

Implications for Resources

Certainly the move to the Information Age necessitates a change in spending priorities and programs for the United States. As a nation, in 2005 we spent over $460 billion on defense (including the supplemental for operations in Afghanistan and Iraq), almost $37 billion on homeland security (not including the portion contained in the DOD budget and spread across more than sixteen agencies), $10.3 billion for the State Department, and $5.1 billion for the FBI. These totals do not begin to address the totals for defense in other agencies such as the Department of Energy to ensure the viability of the nuclear stockpile.

Combined, the United States is spending well over half a trillion dollars on defense, yet it continues to have significant gaps in the capabilities required to prosecute the global war on terror, protect the homeland, and defend U.S. interests abroad. Stephen Flynn in *America the Vulnerable* described vulnerabilities in our critical infrastructure. We have shortfalls in defense such that Soldiers and Marines are deploying to Iraq and Afghanistan lacking all of the proper kit to protect themselves. The State Department is spending a total of $19.3 billion dollars on a variety of international assistance programs. But is that enough? And is the spending in the right areas? Given that the second echelon to be deployed against the United States in the globar war on terror is currently composed of young children and teenagers in poverty-stricken areas of the world where educational opportunities are poor, illiteracy is high, and prospects for economic growth is low, are we spending our resources appropriately?

Conceptually, a relationship seems to exist between spending and the means to secure national security. A dollar spent on defense yields a return of one dollar in national security capability, so if the resources are used for aircraft, ships, or tanks, the result is a one-for-one relationship. However, in areas where spending for security has been low or even nonexistent the payoff is likely to be much higher, say, one dollar of investment may yield a 20 to 30 percent higher return. The rationale is this: traditionally these programs have low levels of funding, especially when compared to resources allocated to defense. Thus even small enhancements, if used wisely, will have a greater impact.

This discussion in no way implies that defense or other traditional hard power funding should be cut. Rather, a realistic assessment process should be undertaken as part of the development of a new national security act. Additionally, to ensure that a reasonable balance is maintained over time, just as DOD conducts a Quadrennial Defense Review, the other departments should be required to submit a Quadrennial National Security Review (QNSR) or something similar, which describes their efforts toward national security.

For spending on the seams between organizations such as the Departments of Homeland Security, Defense, and Transportation, for example, to seal the gaps in port security, the payoffs in national security are likely to be even higher. Even within a department such as the DOD, the return on investment of the procurement of the latest piece of equipment is much smaller than the return on investment in a new capability. This is even more pronounced in the case of high-cost systems when the new capability trade-off is for a system that costs much less, such as a single fighter aircraft at a cost of a quarter billion dollars versus new flak vests for deployed Soldiers or Marines for the same amount. At $3,000 per vest, one fighter aircraft is the equivalent cost of over 83,000 vests, certainly a worthy consideration.

The issue of resources is really central to the discussion of national security, for without adequate resources, a strategy is really just a fantasy. As we examine resources for the national security strategy, key questions absolutely must include:

- Does the articulated strategy of the United States have adequate resources for success or do we have an *ends-ways-means-risk-environment* mismatch?
- Where should this nation choose to spend its next (or last) national security dollar? (Perhaps more specifically, is our national defense better served with an additional copy of the latest fighter aircraft or by spending those resources for the promotion of educational reforms in Arab communities overseas?)
- What increases in funding for soft power issues are appropriate? In what areas should investment be made to get the greatest return?

An example of a soft power program with long-term implications that is perhaps difficult to measure is a State Department initiative that brings a few dozen bright Muslim students to America for five weeks during the summer. The expressed purpose of the program is to expose the participants to the United States. During their trip, students attend classes on U.S. history, politics, and society. They are also exposed to a variety of cultural experiences including local soup kitchens, Fourth of July celebrations, and a visit to Ground Zero. The cost per student is $18,000, so the total cost per year is under $750,000.[8] A similar program is being funded at approximately $6 million per year. This initiative pays for 6,000 libraries for Arab classrooms to encourage students to do research and read books on topics that interest them. Of course, no program is without its limitations. In this case, the books have "no pigs and no women in swimsuits," in deference to cultural sensitivities. To create yet another program for enhancing liberal education, a participant from the Yale World Fellows Program recommended a global online university that would provide greater access to education.[9]

As a nation, we must look at security more broadly than just the Departments of Defense and Homeland Security, and perhaps be willing to make tough trade-offs. With an expanded program of interaction, we might be able to reach a future President of one of these nations. How much would it be worth to have a moderate Arab leader that had traveled in America and had a positive experience within the United States? How does this program contribute to the understanding and promotion of U.S. values, democracy, and respect for human rights?

As yet another example of the use of funds in nontraditional ways to enhance U.S. security, consider the goodwill that was generated following the 2004 tsunami in the Indian Ocean region. As of February 2005, the United States has pledged a minimum of $350 million for relief plus the deployment of military assets that were costing approximately $6 million per day.[10] The potential for a positive bounce from this assistance is quite significant, especially given that the hardest-hit country was Indonesia, the largest Muslim nation in the world. If there anything to be criticized, it is the slow pace at which the United States announced its initial contribution and offered support. While the long-term benefits will be difficult to measure, the potential certainly exists to generate great goodwill in the Muslim community. Of course, the ability to stay the course and the manner in which the aid is given will influence whether perceptions of the United States in the Muslim world will be positively or negatively affected.

What about infrastructure development? Simple initiatives such as building roads into remote areas to enhance transportation and communications throughout an impoverished country can be a powerful influence on long-term behavior. The military has a program in Latin America and the Caribbean called New Horizons, in which military units in coordination with the State Department and local authorities undertake development projects such as drilling wells or building schools. Funding for the program is quite modest. Can this program or one like it be expanded? Should it be run by a department other than the DOD?

We must also develop performance measures that assist in determining the effectiveness of resources being spent in support of national security strategies and policies. How can we measure the impact of our overall program? Do our policies and strategies translate into greater moderation in the Arab world, and perhaps greater security for the United States?

Another important aspect of a new strategy must be to encourage homegrown initiatives and internal development. For example, Al-Jazeera, the Arab television network, has demonstrated a lack of even-handedness and poor judgment in reporting with such events as the showing of the beheading of captives by terrorists in Iraq. At the same time, the fact that there is an Al-Jazeera is a positive sign, and we should do what we can to encourage and nurture the development of the network into a voice of moderation in the Arab world. While some called for taking Al-Jazeera off the air following the televising of the beheadings or the broadcasting of inflammatory bin Laden tapes, a more appropriate path was to criticize the behavior and work to gain more even treatment of events and reporting. While the path may not seem clear, eventually Al-Jazeera will become a mainstream network—the Information Age will see to that, or the network will not survive and Arabs will turn elsewhere for their information.

Some may interpret the above argument to mean that we need to dismantle the U.S. military and divert huge resources to soft power programs. This is certainly not the argument being advanced. Invariably, such a strategy would not serve U.S. interests well, as a variety of dangerous threats remain that could threaten our security conventionally, or, if you like, in an Industrial Age manner.

Rather, the argument being advanced is that we are a wealthy country with tremendous resources that has wisely invested in the traditional national security capabilities associated with being a superpower. But we can do more. U.S. interests are best served when all the elements of power are applied in a coordinated, integrated, and synchronized manner. But as we move to the Information Age, other nontraditional programs and policies will need more, if not equal, attention to ensure America's security. While I am not trying to be overly simplistic and flippant, even the rounding errors associated with some of the DOD big-dollar weapons programs would have a significant impact if applied to soft power programs.

To this end, a comprehensive dialogue should be initiated to examine how to best meet the national security needs of the United States in the Information Age. Outcomes would invariably include a need for changing historic roles and mission of government organizations, agencies, and departments. But this sort of dialogue is vital to America's long-term security—to do anything less puts the United States at great and unacceptable risk.

CONCLUSION

In MANY WAYS, this book has been a journey. As a career military officer in the U.S. Army, I have had many opportunities to travel the globe in support of U.S. national security strategy and implementation of national polices. Along the way, I have had occasions to fight for an increased share of the budget for my Service and to examine the manner in which our national treasure is spent.

Most recently, I have come to conclude that the national security strategy of the United States has a significant *ends-ways-means-risk-environment* mismatch that must be corrected. We are in the early stages of the Information Age and must recognize the challenges and opportunities that this will present to our nation, our grand strategy and policies, and throughout the globe.

Specifically, the United States has a national security strategy that is largely incongruent with the goals and objectives of our nation. We have developed organizations, policies, and processes in the Industrial Age to manage a very different world from that which we are encountering today or are likely to confront tomorrow as we move farther into the Information Age. Organizations such as the National Security Council or even processes such as the Quadrennial Defense Review are outdated and must be changed or perhaps even eliminated to adequately account for the changes in the security environment. Questions such as how the NSC and HSC fit together must be examined in considerable detail and with great clarity. In 1948, the Department of Defense and component parts held a session at Key West in which agreements were made concerning roles and missions. The same sort of dialogue is required across the U.S. government by all agencies with a role in the security and defense of our nation. Unfortunately, even with the agreements, it took until 1986 for the Goldwater-Nichols Defense Reform Act to delineate how the components of our defense would interact.

Unfortunately, we do not have another thirty-eight years like the period from 1948 to 1986 to get the roles, missions, and cooperation in place. We are in an emergent situation that will only compound the requirement for full-spectrum, agile, cross-governmental cooperation and responses for both policy formulation and execution of those policies.

In the introduction, the concept of delineating security as hard power and soft power applied externally (foreign) or internally (domestically) was introduced. The explanation that accompanied the construct was that we have historically focused our security initiatives using hard power against foreign targets. While this effort made great sense in the Industrial Age, its relevance in a globalized and highly intertwined world where nations, societies, and peoples are linked virtually must be reexamined.

Essentially, our security efforts throughout much of our nation's history have been confined to one-quarter of the potential area of consideration, which is hard power focused externally, leaving three-quarters largely uncovered. With the events of 9/11 and the ensuing self-examination, several changes have been made to redirect security focus to the homeland. Thus both hard and soft power have been focused domestically in response, although there are strong legal restrictions on the use of hard power in a domestic setting. The Department of Homeland Security has been established, a national alert system has been created, legislation such as the Patriot Act has been enacted (at least temporarily), and security in several key areas including airline security and infrastructure has seen some improvement as well.

But in critiquing the work to date, largely in response to the events of 9/11, one must observe that little emphasis has placed on focusing soft power on foreign audiences. One must also be concerned that changes made in the aftermath of 9/11 could potentially lead to seams that are easily exploitable by potential adversaries. Is there really a difference between defense and homeland security? Or is this an artificial barrier created inadvertently with the establishment of the Department of Homeland Security?

In my judgment, much work needs to be done to ensure the security of the United States, protect our citizens and property, and promote the sort of future global environment that is friendly to our nation and way of life. Taking small steps along multiple paths will undoubtedly put our nation at risk and fail to lead to the global future we seek—this is the current strategy we have selected as we are fighting a global war on terror, protecting the homeland, and moving into the Information Age along distinct paths.

The time is now to combine these efforts into a comprehensive national security and defense strategy with the requisite organizations, process, policies, and procedures to achieve the broad overarching goals and objectives of this new grand strategy. To this end, I make four specific recommendations for enhancing our national security and protecting U.S. interests and our people:

1. The world is moving into the Information Age at an alarming rate, and this trend will have a significant impact on the formulation and execution of U.S. national security strategy and policy. The Information Age and the accompanying globalization will dramatically increase the number and severity of threats facing the United States and our allies. We must understand and account for these changes in our new formulation of grand strategy.

2. The current definition and application of strategy, and national strategy in particular, are inadequate. They must be revised to more fully account for the changes brought on by the Information Age. Strategy has been defined as the linking of *ways* and *means* to achieve *ends* while mitigating *risk*. In the future, we must factor *environment* into any discussion of strategy.

3. The United States must rebalance its national strategy by rebalancing its ways and means. It is nearly impossible to have a discussion of national strategy without defaulting to military relationships, rather than addressing all major elements of national power (including political, military, economic, social, cultural, geographic, and informational) in a balanced manner. In the preconflict relationships between nations, states, and world actors, the nonmilitary ways and means can and should be preeminent. Our current national security strategy is highly weighted to the political-military, with little direct focus on the other elements of power. In the Information Age, the nonmilitary elements of power will dominate, with particular emphasis on information.

4. The U.S. government must be reorganized to more appropriately respond to the challenges of the Information Age. In addition, the DOD must undergo a holistic review and restructuring to develop the capabilities required in the Information Age. That will mean divesting of those capabilities that no longer fit into current strategy, operations, and tactics. The difficulty will be eliminating systems, procedures, and platforms that may have great capability, but are no longer effective within the defense system of the future.

The first and perhaps most important aspect will be to recognize that indeed a transition is underway and to understand the differences between the Industrial and Information Ages. Without this realization, the journey into this new age is likely to be filled with challenges and to result in many missed opportunities. One thing is perfectly clear: the adversaries of the future will not fail to take advantage of new information technologies to advance their interests. We must do the same. Furthermore, failure to respond adequately will both squander opportunities and endanger our nation.

Americans are often criticized for having cultural insensitivity or blind spots with regard to our policies. For this reason, if no other, our nation would do well to reconsider our approach to the formulation of grand strategy to account for the cultural aspects and political environment in addition to the more traditional formulation that accounts for *ends*, *ways*, *means*, and *risk*. This does not imply that we should allow our hands to be tied such that the global environment, international pressure, individual nations, or nonstate actors should control U.S. actions, but rather that the consideration of the *environment* can and should help to constructively shape how the United States operates within the international community of nations.

The key to U.S. interaction in future global affairs and ultimately in constructive engagement will be the degree to which our nation can synchronize the tools of state. Said another way, the ability to employ all of the elements of national power in a coordinated manner is essential. Promoting and if necessary assisting in building liberal democracies that operate within the norms of international behavior will help to ensure America's security. Undoubtedly, America must alter its capabilities to harness the full range of capabilities, and this will most certainly entail revising the organizations, structures, and processes of national security.

While a strong military with the ability to project forces and capabilities globally to protect U.S. interests, citizens, and property will remain a cornerstone of our national security strategy, the longer-term approach of incorporating soft power elements to reduce and perhaps even eliminate the need for employment of the military in some cases must take on a new sense of urgency. While the military can be useful in reestablishing security and terminating conflict on a short-term basis, most conflict is rooted in other than military causes and thus requires other than military responses.

Some may infer from the discussion of rebalancing of capabilities that the military budget should be cut to divert resources to nontraditional defense and security endeavors. This is not necessarily the case. In fact, there may be some areas where military spending should be increased in response to new or changing threats. Rather, the position being advanced is that a complete review of national security strategy must be conducted and appropriate changes made to provide the essential capabilities to ensure the security, prosperity, and survival of the United States. The result would be a new national security act that would both define and guide our new grand strategy.

Recently, there has been a great debate about the future of the American empire. Many wonder if America's best days are behind us. Will we fall prey to the failings of other empires such as the Roman, Byzantine, or Ottoman? These are important questions with very complex and perhaps even indefinable answers. However, for the sake of our nation, we must begin the process of examining these issues.

In large measure, I believe that the manner in which the United States responds and adapts to the Information Age and to the threats posed by the global war on terror will factor heavily into the answer.

APPENDIX A: INSTANCES OF USE OF UNITED STATES FORCES ABROAD, 1798–2001

1798–1800 *Undeclared naval war with France*. This contest included land actions, such as that in the Dominican Republic, city of Puerto Plata, where marines captured a French privateer under the guns of the forts. Congress authorized military action through a series of statutes.

1801–05 *Tripoli*. The First Barbary War included the U.S.S. *George Washington* and *Philadelphia* affairs and the Eaton expedition, during which a few marines landed with U.S. agent William Eaton to raise a force against Tripoli in an effort to free the crew of the *Philadelphia*. Tripoli declared war but not the United States, although Congress authorized U.S. military action by statute.

1806 *Mexico (Spanish territory)*. Capt. Z. M. Pike, with a platoon of troops, invaded Spanish territory at the headwaters of the Rio Grande on orders from Gen. James Wilkinson. He was made prisoner without resistance at a fort he constructed in present-day Colorado, taken to Mexico, and later released after seizure of his papers.

1806–10 *Gulf of Mexico*. American gunboats operated from New Orleans against Spanish and French privateers off the Mississippi Delta, chiefly under Capt. John Shaw and Master Commandant David Porter.

1810 *West Florida (Spanish territory)*. Gov. Claiborne of Louisiana, on orders of the president, occupied with troops territory in dispute east of Mississippi as far as the Pearl River, later the eastern boundary of Louisiana. He was authorized to seize as far east as the Perdido River.

1812 *Amelia Island and other parts of east Florida, then under Spain.* Temporary possession was authorized by President Madison and by Congress, to prevent occupation by any other power; but possession was obtained by Gen. George Matthews in so irregular a manner that his measures were disavowed by the president.

1812–15 *War of 1812.* On June 18, 1812, the United States declared war between the United States and the United Kingdom of Great Britain and Ireland. Among the issues leading to the war were British interception of neutral ships and blockades of the United States during British hostilities with France.

1813 *West Florida (Spanish territory).* On authority given by Congress, General Wilkinson seized Mobile Bay in April with 600 soldiers. A small Spanish garrison gave way. The United States advanced into disputed territory to the Perdido River, as projected in 1810. No fighting.

1813–14 *Marquesas Islands.* U.S. forces built a fort on the island of Nukahiva to protect three prize ships which had been captured from the British.

1814 *Spanish Florida.* Gen. Andrew Jackson took Pensacola and drove out the British, with whom the United States was at war.

1814–25 *Caribbean.* Engagements between pirates and American ships or squadrons took place repeatedly especially ashore and offshore about Cuba, Puerto Rico, Santo Domingo, and Yucatan. Three thousand pirate attacks on merchantmen were reported between 1815 and 1823. In 1822 Commodore James Biddle employed a squadron of two frigates, four sloops of war, two brigs, four schooners, and two gunboats in the West Indies.

1815 *Algiers.* The second Barbary War was declared against the United States by the Dey of Algiers of the Barbary states, an act not reciprocated by the United States. Congress did authorize a military expedition by statutes. A large fleet under Decatur attacked Algiers and obtained indemnities.

1815 *Tripoli.* After securing an agreement from Algiers, Decatur demonstrated with his squadron at Tunis and Tripoli, where he secured indemnities for offenses during the War of 1812.

1816 *Spanish Florida.* U.S. forces destroyed Nicholls Fort, called also Negro Fort, which harbored raiders making forays into U.S. territory.

1816–18 *Spanish Florida, First Seminole War.* The Seminole Indians, whose area was a haven for escaped slaves and border ruffians, were attacked by troops under Generals Jackson and Gaines and pursued into northern Florida. Spanish posts were attacked and occupied, British citizens executed. In 1819 the Floridas were ceded to the United States.

1817 *Amelia Island (Spanish territory off Florida).* Under orders of President Monroe, U.S. forces landed and expelled a group of smugglers, adventurers, and freebooters.

1818 *Oregon.* The U.S.S. *Ontario,* dispatched from Washington, landed at the Columbia River and in August took possession of Oregon territory.

Britain had conceded sovereignty but Russia and Spain asserted claims to the area.

1820–23 *Africa*. Naval units raided the slave traffic pursuant to the 1819 act of Congress.

1822 *Cuba*. U.S. naval forces suppressing piracy landed on the northwest coast of Cuba and burned a pirate station.

1823 *Cuba*. Brief landings in pursuit of pirates occurred April 8 near Escondido; April 16 near Cayo Blanco; July 11 at Siquapa Bay; July 21 at Cape Cruz; and October 23 at *Camrioca*.

1824 *Cuba*. In October the U.S.S. *Porpoise* landed bluejackets near Matanzas in pursuit of pirates. This was during the cruise authorized in 1822.

1824 *Puerto Rico (Spanish territory)*. Commodore David Porter with a landing party attacked the town of Fajardo which had sheltered pirates and insulted American naval officers. He landed with 200 men in November and forced an apology. Commodore Porter was later court-martialed for overstepping his powers.

1825 *Cuba*. In March cooperating American and British forces landed at Sagua La Grande to capture pirates.

1827 *Greece*. In October and November landing parties hunted pirates on the islands of Argenteire, Miconi, and Androse.

1831–32 *Falkland Islands*. Captain Duncan of the U.S.S. *Lexington* investigated the capture of three American sealing vessels and sought to protect American interests.

1832 *Sumatra*. February 6 to 9. A naval force landed and stormed a fort to punish natives of the town of Quallah Battoo for plundering the American ship *Friendship*.

1833 *Argentina*. October 31 to November 15. A force was sent ashore at Buenos Aires to protect the interests of the United States and other countries during an insurrection.

1835–36 *Peru*. December 10, 1835, to January 24, 1836, and August 31 to December 7, 1836. Marines protected American interests in Callao and Lima during an attempted revolution.

1836 *Mexico*. General Gaines occupied Nacogdoches (Tex.), disputed territory, from July to December during the Texan war for independence, under orders to cross the "imaginary boundary line" if an Indian outbreak threatened.

1838–39 *Sumatra*. December 24, 1838, to January 4, 1839. A naval force landed to punish natives of the towns of Quallah Battoo and Muckie (Mukki) for depredations on American shipping.

1840 *Fiji Islands*. July. Naval forces landed to punish natives for attacking American exploring and surveying parties.

1841 *Drummond Island, Kingsmill Group*. A naval party landed to avenge the murder of a seaman by the natives.

1841 *Samoa*. February 24. A naval party landed and burned towns after the murder of an American seaman on Upolu Island.

1842 *Mexico*. Commodore T.A.C. Jones, in command of a squadron long cruising off California, occupied Monterey, Calif., on October 19, believing war had come. He discovered peace, withdrew, and saluted. A similar incident occurred a week later at San Diego.

1843 *China*. Sailors and marines from the *St. Louis* were landed after a clash between Americans and Chinese at the trading post in Canton.

1843 *Africa*. November 29 to December 16. Four U.S. vessels demonstrated and landed various parties (one of 200 marines and sailors) to discourage piracy and the slave trade along the Ivory coast, and to punish attacks by the natives on American seamen and shipping.

1844 *Mexico*. President Tyler deployed U.S. forces to protect Texas against Mexico, pending Senate approval of a treaty of annexation. (Later rejected.) He defended his action against a Senate resolution of inquiry.

1846–48 *Mexican War*. On May 13, 1846, the United States recognized the existence of a state of war with Mexico. After the annexation of Texas in 1845, the United States and Mexico failed to resolve a boundary dispute and President Polk said that it was necessary to deploy forces in Mexico to meet a threatened invasion.

1849 *Smyrna*. In July a naval force gained release of an American seized by Austrian officials.

1851 *Turkey*. After a massacre of foreigners (including Americans) at Jaffa in January, a demonstration by the Mediterranean Squadron was ordered along the Turkish (Levant) coast.

1851 *Johanns Island (east of Africa)*. August. Forces from the U.S. sloop of war *Dale* exacted redress for the unlawful imprisonment of the captain of an American whaling brig.

1852–53 *Argentina*. February 3 to 12, 1852; September 17, 1852 to April 1853. Marines were landed and maintained in Buenos Aires to protect American interests during a revolution.

1853 *Nicaragua*. March 11 to 13. U.S. forces landed to protect American lives and interests during political disturbances.

1853–54 *Japan*. Commodore Perry and his naval expedition made a display of force leading to the "opening of Japan."

1853–54 *Ryukyu and Bonin Islands*. Commodore Perry on three visits before going to Japan and while waiting for a reply from Japan made a naval demonstration, landing marines twice, and secured a coaling concession from the ruler of Naha on Okinawa; he also demonstrated in the Bonin Islands with the purpose of securing facilities for commerce.

1854 *China*. April 4 to June 15 to 17. American and English ships landed forces to protect American interests in and near Shanghai during Chinese civil strife.

1854 *Nicaragua*. July 9 to 15. Naval forces bombarded and burned San Juan del Norte (Greytown) to avenge an insult to the American minister to Nicaragua.

1855 *China*. May 19 to 21. U.S. forces protected American interests in Shanghai and from August 3 to 5 fought pirates near Hong Kong.

1855 *Fiji Islands*. September 12 to November 4. An American naval force landed to seek reparations for depredations on American residents and seamen.

1855 *Uruguay*. November 25 to 29. U.S. and European naval forces landed to protect American interests during an attempted revolution in Montevideo.

1856 *Panama, Republic of New Grenada*. September 19 to 22. U.S. forces landed to protect American interests during an insurrection.

1856 *China*. October 22 to December 6. U.S. forces landed to protect American interests at Canton during hostilities between the British and the Chinese, and to avenge an assault upon an unarmed boat displaying the U.S. flag.

1857 *Nicaragua*. April to May, November to December. In May Commander C.H. Davis of the U.S. Navy, with some marines, received the surrender of William Walker, who had been attempting to get control of the country, and protected his men from the retaliation of native allies who had been fighting Walker. In November and December of the same year U.S. vessels *Saratoga*, *Wabash*, and *Fulton* opposed another attempt of William Walker on Nicaragua. Commodore Hiram Paulding's act of landing marines and compelling the removal of Walker to the United States was tacitly disavowed by Secretary of State Lewis Cass, and Paulding was forced into retirement.

1858 *Uruguay*. January 2 to 27. Forces from two U.S. warships landed to protect American property during a revolution in Montevideo.

1858 *Fiji Islands*. October 6 to 16. A marine expedition chastised natives for the murder of two American citizens at Waya.

1858–59 *Turkey*. The secretary of state requested a display of naval force along the Levant after a massacre of Americans at Jaffa and mistreatment elsewhere "to remind the authorities (of Turkey) of the power of the United States."

1859 *Paraguay*. Congress authorized a naval squadron to seek redress for an attack on a naval vessel in the Parana River during 1855. Apologies were made after a large display of force.

1859 *Mexico*. Two hundred U.S. soldiers crossed the Rio Grande in pursuit of the Mexican bandit Cortina.

1859 *China*. July 31 to August 2. A naval force landed to protect American interests in Shanghai.

1860 *Angola, Portuguese West Africa*. March 1. American residents at Kissembo called upon American and British ships to protect lives and property during problems with natives.

1860 *Colombia (Bay of Panama)*. September 27 to October 8. Naval forces landed to protect American interests during a revolution.

1863 *Japan*. July 16. The U.S.S. *Wyoming* retaliated against a firing on the American vessel *Pembroke* at Shimonoseki.

1864 *Japan*. July 14 to August 3. Naval forces protected the U.S. minister to Japan when he visited Yedo to negotiate concerning some American claims against Japan, and to make his negotiations easier by impressing the Japanese with American power.

1864 *Japan*. September 4 to 14. Naval forces of the United States, Great Britain, France, and the Netherlands compelled Japan and the Prince of Nagato in particular to permit the Straits of Shimonoseki to be used by foreign shipping in accordance with treaties already signed.

1865 *Panama*. March 9 and 10. U.S. forces protected the lives and property of American residents during a revolution.

1866 *China*. From June 20 to July 7, U.S. forces punished an assault on the American consul at Newchwang.

1866 *Mexico*. To protect American residents, General Sedgwick and 100 men in November obtained surrender of Matamoras. After three days he was ordered by the U.S. government to withdraw. His act was repudiated by the president.

1867 *Nicaragua*. Marines occupied Managua and Leon.

1867 *Formosa*. June 13. A naval force landed and burned a number of huts to punish the murder of the crew of a wrecked American vessel.

1868 *Japan (Osaka, Hiolo, Nagasaki, Yokohama, and Negata)*. February 4 to 8, April 4 to May 12, June 12 and 13. U.S. forces were landed to protect American interests during the civil war in Japan.

1868 *Uruguay*. February 7 and 8, 19 to 26. U.S. forces protected foreign residents and the customhouse during an insurrection at Montevideo.

1868 *Colombia*. April. U.S. forces protected passengers and treasure in transit at Aspinwall during the absence of local police or troops on the occasion of the death of the president of Colombia.

1870 *Mexico*. June 17 and 18. U.S. forces destroyed the pirate ship *Forward*, which had been run aground about 40 miles up the Rio Tecapan.

1870 *Hawaiian Islands*. September 21. U.S. forces placed the American flag at half mast upon the death of Queen Kalama, when the American consul at Honolulu would not assume responsibility for so doing.

1871 *Korea*. June 10 to 12. A U.S. naval force attacked and captured five forts to punish natives for depredations on Americans, particularly for murdering the crew of the *General Sherman* and burning the schooner, and for later firing on other American small boats taking soundings up the Salee River.

1873 *Colombia (Bay of Panama)*. May 7 to 22, September 23 to October 9. U.S. forces protected American interests during hostilities between local groups over control of the government of the State of Panama.

1873–96 *Mexico.* U.S. troops crossed the Mexican border repeatedly in pursuit of cattle thieves and other brigands. There were some reciprocal pursuits by Mexican troops into border territory. Mexico protested frequently. Notable cases were at Remolina in May 1873 and at Las Cuevas in 1875. Washington orders often supported these excursions. Agreements between Mexico and the United States, the first in 1882, finally legitimized such raids. They continued intermittently, with minor disputes, until 1896.

1874 *Hawaiian Islands.* February 12 to 20. Detachments from American vessels were landed to preserve order and protect American lives and interests during the coronation of a new king.

1876 *Mexico.* May 18. An American force was landed to police the town of Matamoras temporarily while it was without other government.

1882 *Egypt.* July 14 to 18. American forces landed to protect American interests during warfare between British and Egyptians and looting of the city of Alexandria by Arabs.

1885 *Panama (Colon).* January 18 and 19. U.S. forces were used to guard the valuables in transit over the Panama Railroad, and the safes and vaults of the company during revolutionary activity. In March, April, and May in the cities of Colon and Panama, the forces helped reestablish freedom of transit during revolutionary activity.

1888 *Korea.* June. A naval force was sent ashore to protect American residents in Seoul during unsettled political conditions, when an outbreak of the populace was expected.

1888 *Haiti.* December 20. A display of force persuaded the Haitian government to give up an American steamer which had been seized on the charge of breach of blockade.

1888–89 *Samoa.* November 14, 1888, to March 20, 1889. U.S. forces were landed to protect American citizens and the consulate during a native civil war.

1889 *Hawaiian Islands.* July 30 and 31. U.S. forces protected American interests at Honolulu during a revolution.

1890 *Argentina.* A naval party landed to protect U.S. consulate and legation in Buenos Aires.

1891 *Haiti.* U.S. forces sought to protect American lives and property on Navassa Island.

1891 *Bering Strait.* July 2 to October 5. Naval forces sought to stop seal poaching.

1891 *Chile.* August 28 to 30. U.S. forces protected the American consulate and the women and children who had taken refuge in it during a revolution in Valparaiso.

1893 *Hawaii.* January 16 to April 1. Marines were landed ostensibly to protect American lives and property, but many believed actually to promote a provisional government under Sanford B. Dole. This action was disavowed by the United States.

1894 *Brazil*. January. A display of naval force sought to protect American commerce and shipping at Rio de Janeiro during a Brazilian civil war.

1894 *Nicaragua*. July 6 to August 7. U.S. forces sought to protect American interests at Bluefields following a revolution.

1894–95 *China*. Marines were stationed at Tientsin and penetrated to Peking for protection purposes during the Sino-Japanese War.

1894–95 *China*. A naval vessel was beached and used as a fort at Newchwang for protection of American nationals.

1894–96 *Korea*. July 24, 1894, to April 3, 1896. A guard of marines was sent to protect the American legation and American lives and interests at Seoul during and following the Sino-Japanese War.

1895 *Colombia*. March 8 to 9. U.S. forces protected American interests during an attack on the town of Bocas del Toro by a bandit chieftain.

1896 *Nicaragua*. May 2 to 4. U.S. forces protected American interests in Corinto during political unrest.

1898 *Nicaragua*. February 7 and 8. U.S. forces protected American lives and property at San Juan del Sur.

1898 *The Spanish-American War*. On April 25, 1898, the United States declared war with Spain. The war followed a Cuban insurrection against Spanish rule and the sinking of the U.S.S. *Maine* in the harbor at Havana.

1898–99 *China*. November 5, 1898, to March 15, 1899. U.S. forces provided a guard for the legation at Peking and the consulate at Tientsin during contest between the Dowager Empress and her son.

1899 *Nicaragua*. American and British naval forces were landed to protect national interests at San Juan del Norte, February 22 to March 5, and at Bluefields a few weeks later in connection with the insurrection of Gen. Juan P. Reyes.

1899 *Samoa*. February to May 15. American and British naval forces were landed to protect national interests and to take part in a bloody contention over the succession to the throne.

1899–1901 *Philippine Islands*. U.S. forces protected American interests following the war with Spain and conquered the islands by defeating the Filipinos in their war for independence.

1900 *China*. May 24 to September 28. American troops participated in operations to protect foreign lives during the Boxer Uprising, particularly at Peking. For many years after this experience a permanent legation guard was maintained in Peking, and was strengthened at times as trouble threatened.

1901 *Colombia (State of Panama)*. November 20 to December 4. U.S. forces protected American property on the Isthmus and kept transit lines open during serious revolutionary disturbances.

1902 *Colombia*. April 16 to 23. U.S. forces protected American lives and property at Bocas del Toro during a civil war.

1902 *Colombia (State of Panama)*. September 17 to November 18. The United States placed armed guards on all trains crossing the Isthmus to keep the railroad line open, and stationed ships on both sides of Panama to prevent the landing of Colombian troops.

1903 *Honduras*. March 23 to 30 or 31. U.S. forces protected the American consulate and the steamship wharf at Puerto Cortez during a period of revolutionary activity.

1903 *Dominican Republic*. March 30 to April 21. A detachment of marines was landed to protect American interests in the city of Santo Domingo during a revolutionary outbreak.

1903 *Syria*. September 7 to 12. U.S. forces protected the American consulate in Beirut when a local Moslem uprising was feared.

1903–04 *Abyssinia*. Twenty-five marines were sent to Abyssinia to protect the U.S. consul general while he negotiated a treaty.

1903–14 *Panama*. U.S. forces sought to protect American interests and lives during and following the revolution for independence from Colombia over construction of the Isthmian Canal. With brief intermissions, U.S. Marines were stationed on the Isthmus from November 4, 1903, to January 21, 1914, to guard American interests.

1904 *Dominican Republic*. January 2 to February 11. American and British naval forces established an area in which no fighting would be allowed and protected American interests in Puerto Plata and Sosua and Santo Domingo City during revolutionary fighting.

1904 *Tangier, Morocco*. "We want either Perdicaris alive or Raisula dead." A squadron demonstrated to force release of a kidnapped American. Marines were landed to protect the consul general.

1904 *Panama*. November 17 to 24. U.S. forces protected American lives and property at Ancon at the time of a threatened insurrection.

1904–05 *Korea*. January 5, 1904, to November 11, 1905. A guard of marines was sent to protect the American legation in Seoul during the Russo-Japanese War.

1906–09 *Cuba*. September 1906 to January 23, 1909. U.S. forces sought to restore order, protect foreigners, and establish a stable government after serious revolutionary activity.

1907 *Honduras*. March 18 to June 8. To protect American interests during a war between Honduras and Nicaragua, troops were stationed in Trujillo, Ceiba, Puerto Cortez, San Pedro, Laguna and Choloma.

1910 *Nicaragua*. May 19 to September 4. U.S. forces protected American interests at Bluefields.

1911 *Honduras*. January 26. American naval detachments were landed to protect American lives and interests during a civil war in Honduras.

1911 *China*. As the nationalist revolution approached, in October an ensign and 10 men tried to enter Wuchang to rescue missionaries but retired on being warned away, and a small landing force guarded American private property and consulate at Hankow. Marines were deployed in November to guard the cable stations at Shanghai; landing forces were sent for protection in Nanking, Chinkiang, Taku and elsewhere.

1912 *Honduras*. A small force landed to prevent seizure by the government of an American-owned railroad at Puerto Cortez. The forces were withdrawn after the United States approved the action.

1912 *Panama*. Troops, on request of both political parties, supervised elections outside the Canal Zone.

1912 *Cuba*. June 5 to August 5. U.S. forces protected American interests in the Province of Oriente, and in Havana.

1912 *China*. August 24 to 26, on Kentucky Island, and August 26 to 30 at Camp Nicholson. U.S. forces protected Americans and American interests during revolutionary activity.

1912 *Turkey*. November 18 to December 3. U.S. forces guarded the American legation at Constantinople during a Balkan War.

1912–25 *Nicaragua*. August to November 1912. U.S. forces protected American interests during an attempted revolution. A small force, serving as a legation guard and seeking to promote peace and stability, remained until August 5, 1925.

1912–41 *China*. The disorders which began with the overthrow of the dynasty during the Kuomintang rebellion in 1912, which were redirected by the invasion of China by Japan, led to demonstrations and landing parties for the protection of U.S. interests in China continuously and at many points from 1912 on to 1941. The guard at Peking and along the route to the sea was maintained until 1941. In 1927, the United States had 5,670 troops ashore in China and 44 naval vessels in its waters. In 1933 the United States had 3,027 armed men ashore. The protective action was generally based on treaties with China concluded from 1858 to 1901.

1913 *Mexico*. September 5 to 7. A few marines landed at Ciaris Estero to aid in evacuating American citizens and others from the Yaqui Valley, made dangerous for foreigners by civil strife.

1914 *Haiti*. January 29 to February 9, February 20 to 21, October 19. Intermittently U.S. naval forces protected American nationals in a time of rioting and revolution.

1914 *Dominican Republic*. June and July. During a revolutionary movement, United States naval forces by gunfire stopped the bombardment of Puerto Plata, and by threat of force maintained Santo Domingo City as a neutral zone.

1914–17 *Mexico*. Undeclared Mexican-American hostilities followed the Dolphin affair and Villa's raids and included capture of Vera Cruz and later Pershing's expedition into northern Mexico.

1915–34 *Haiti.* July 28, 1915, to August 15, 1934. U.S. forces maintained order during a period of chronic political instability.

1916 *China.* American forces landed to quell a riot taking place on American property in Nanking.

1916–24 *Dominican Republic.* May 1916 to September 1924. American naval forces maintained order during a period of chronic and threatened insurrection.

1917 *China.* American troops were landed at Chungking to protect American lives during a political crisis.

1917–18 *World War I.* On April 6, 1917, the United States declared war with Germany and on December 7, 1917, with Austria-Hungary. Entrance of the United States into the war was precipitated by Germany's submarine warfare against neutral shipping.

1917–22 *Cuba.* U.S. forces protected American interests during an insurrection and subsequent unsettled conditions. Most of the United States armed forces left Cuba by August 1919, but two companies remained at Camaguey until February 1922.

1918–19 *Mexico.* After withdrawal of the Pershing expedition, U.S. troops entered Mexico in pursuit of bandits at least three times in 1918 and six times in 1919. In August 1918 American and Mexican troops fought at Nogales.

1918–20 *Panama.* U.S. forces were used for police duty according to treaty stipulations, at Chiriqui, during election disturbances and subsequent unrest.

1918–20 *Soviet Russia.* Marines were landed at and near Vladivostok in June and July to protect the American consulate and other points in the fighting between the Bolshevik troops and the Czech Army which had traversed Siberia from the western front. A joint proclamation of emergency government and neutrality was issued by the American, Japanese, British, French, and Czech commanders in July. In August 7,000 men were landed in Vladivostok and remained until January 1920, as part of an allied occupation force. In September 1918, 5,000 American troops joined the allied intervention force at Archangel and remained until June 1919. These operations were in response to the Bolshevik revolution in Russia and were partly supported by Czarist or Kerensky elements.

1919 *Dalmatia.* U.S. forces were landed at Trau at the request of Italian authorities to police order between the Italians and Serbs.

1919 *Turkey.* Marines from the U.S.S. *Arizona* were landed to guard the U.S. Consulate during the Greek occupation of Constantinople.

1919 *Honduras.* September 8 to 12. A landing force was sent ashore to maintain order in a neutral zone during an attempted revolution.

1920 *China.* March 14. A landing force was sent ashore for a few hours to protect lives during a disturbance at Kiukiang.

1920 *Guatemala.* April 9 to 27. U.S. forces protected the American legation and other American interests, such as the cable station, during a period of fighting between Unionists and the government of Guatemala.

1920–22 *Russia (Siberia).* February 16, 1920, to November 19, 1922. A Marine guard was sent to protect the U.S. radio station and property on Russian Island, Bay of Vladivostok.

1921 *Panama-Costa Rica.* American naval squadrons demonstrated in April on both sides of the Isthmus to prevent war between the two countries over a boundary dispute.

1922 *Turkey.* September and October. A landing force was sent ashore with consent of both Greek and Turkish authorities, to protect American lives and property when the Turkish Nationalists entered Smyrna.

1922–23 *China.* Between April 1922 and November 1923 marines were landed five times to protect Americans during periods of unrest.

1924 *Honduras.* February 28 to March 31, September 10 to 15. U.S. forces protected American lives and interests during election hostilities.

1924 *China.* September. Marines were landed to protect Americans and other foreigners in Shanghai during Chinese factional hostilities.

1925 *China.* January 15 to August 29. Fighting of Chinese factions accompanied by riots and demonstrations in Shanghai brought the landing of American forces to protect lives and property in the International Settlement.

1925 *Honduras.* April 19 to 21. U.S. forces protected foreigners at La Ceiba during a political upheaval.

1925 *Panama.* October 12 to 23. Strikes and rent riots led to the landing of about 600 American troops to keep order and protect American interests.

1926–33 *Nicaragua.* May 7 to June 5, 1926; August 27, 1926, to January 3, 1933. The coup d'etat of General Chamorro aroused revolutionary activities leading to the landing of American marines to protect the interests of the United States. U.S. forces came and went intermittently until January 3, 1933.

1926 *China.* August and September. The Nationalist attack on Hankow brought the landing of American naval forces to protect American citizens. A small guard was maintained at the consulate general even after September 16, when the rest of the forces were withdrawn. Likewise, when Nationalist forces captured Kiukiang, naval forces were landed for the protection of foreigners November 4 to 6.

1927 *China.* February. Fighting at Shanghai caused American naval forces and marines to be increased. In March a naval guard was stationed at the American consulate at Nanking after Nationalist forces captured the city. American and British destroyers later used shell fire to protect Americans and other foreigners. Subsequently additional forces of marines and naval vessels were stationed in the vicinity of Shanghai and Tientsin.

1932 *China.* American forces were landed to protect American interests during the Japanese occupation of Shanghai.

1933 *Cuba.* During a revolution against President Gerardo Machado naval forces demonstrated but no landing was made.

1934 *China.* Marines landed at Foochow to protect the American Consulate.

1940 *Newfoundland, Bermuda, St. Lucia, Bahamas, Jamaica, Antigua, Trinidad, and British Guiana.* Troops were sent to guard air and naval bases obtained by negotiation with Great Britain. These were sometimes called lend-lease bases.

1941 *Greenland.* Greenland was taken under protection of the United States in April.

1941 *Netherlands (Dutch Guiana).* In November the president ordered American troops to occupy Dutch Guiana, but by agreement with the Netherlands government in exile, Brazil cooperated to protect aluminum ore supply from the bauxite mines in Surinam.

1941 *Iceland.* Iceland was taken under the protection of the United States, with consent of its government, for strategic reasons.

1941 *Germany.* Sometime in the spring the president ordered the navy to patrol ship lanes to Europe. By July U.S. warships were convoying and by September were attacking German submarines. In November, the Neutrality Act was partly repealed to protect U.S. military aid to Britain.

1941–45 *World War II.* On December 8, 1941, the United States declared war with Japan, on December 11 with Germany and Italy, and on June 5, 1942, with Bulgaria, Hungary and Rumania. The United States declared war against Japan after the surprise bombing of Pearl Harbor, and against Germany and Italy after those nations, under the dictators Hitler and Mussolini, declared war against the United States. The U.S. declared war against Bulgaria, Hungary and Rumania in response to the declarations of war by those nations against the United States.

1945 *China.* In October 50,000 U.S. Marines were sent to North China to assist Chinese Nationalist authorities in disarming and repatriating the Japanese in China and in controlling ports, railroads, and airfields. This was in addition to approximately 60,000 U.S. forces remaining in China at the end of World War II.

1946 *Trieste.* President Truman ordered the augmentation of U.S. troops along the zonal occupation line and the reinforcement of air forces in northern Italy after Yugoslav forces shot down an unarmed U.S. Army transport plane flying over Venezia Giulia. Earlier U.S. naval units had been dispatched to the scene.

1948 *Palestine.* A marine consular guard was sent to Jerusalem to protect the U.S. consul general.

1948 *Berlin.* After the Soviet Union established a land blockade of the U.S., British, and French sectors of Berlin on June 24, 1948, the United States and its allies airlifted supplies to Berlin until after the blockade was lifted in May 1949.

1948–49 *China*. Marines were dispatched to Nanking to protect the American embassy when the city fell to Communist troops, and to Shanghai to aid in the protection and evacuation of Americans.

1950–53 *Korean War*. The United States responded to North Korean invasion of South Korea by going to its assistance, pursuant to United Nations Security Council resolutions. U.S. forces deployed in Korea exceeded 300,000 during the last year of the conflict. Over 36,600 U.S. military were killed in action.

1950–55 *Formosa (Taiwan)*. In June 1950 at the beginning of the Korean War, President Truman ordered the U.S. Seventh Fleet to prevent Chinese Communist attacks upon Formosa and Chinese Nationalist operations against mainland China.

1954–55 *China*. Naval units evacuated U.S. civilians and military personnel from the Tachen Islands.

1956 *Egypt*. A marine battalion evacuated U.S. nationals and other persons from Alexandria during the Suez crisis.

1958 *Lebanon*. Marines were landed in Lebanon at the invitation of its government to help protect against threatened insurrection supported from the outside. The president's action was supported by a Congressional resolution passed in 1957 that authorized such actions in that area of the world.

1959–60 *The Caribbean*. 2d Marine Ground Task Force was deployed to protect U.S. nationals during the Cuban crisis.

1962 *Thailand*. The 3d Marine Expeditionary Unit landed on May 17, 1962, to support that country during the threat of Communist pressure from outside; by July 30 the 5,000 marines had been withdrawn.

1962 *Cuba*. On October 22, President Kennedy instituted a "quarantine" on the shipment of offensive missiles to Cuba from the Soviet Union. He also warned the Soviet Union that the launching of any missile from Cuba against any nation in the Western Hemisphere would bring about U.S. nuclear retaliation on the Soviet Union. A negotiated settlement was achieved in a few days.

1962–75 *Laos*. From October 1962 until 1975, the United States played an important role in military support of anti-Communist forces in Laos.

1964 *Congo*. The United States sent four transport planes to provide airlift for Congolese troops during a rebellion and to transport Belgian paratroopers to rescue foreigners. This and subsequent mentions of presidential reports or notifications refer to reports the president has submitted to Congress related to the War Powers Resolution (Public Law 91–148, November 7, 1973). For a discussion of the War Powers Resolution and various types of reports required under it, see The War Powers Resolution: Presidential Compliance, CARS Issue Brief IB81050.

1964–73 *Vietnam War*. U.S. military advisers had been in South Vietnam for a decade, and their numbers had been increased as the military position of the

Saigon government became weaker. After citing what he termed were attacks on U.S. destroyers in the Tonkin Gulf, President Johnson asked in August 1964 for a resolution expressing U.S. determination to support freedom and protect peace in Southeast Asia. Congress responded with the Tonkin Gulf Resolution, expressing support for "all necessary measures" the president might take to repel armed attack against U.S. forces and prevent further aggression. Following this resolution, and following a Communist attack on a U.S. installation in central Vietnam, the United States escalated its participation in the war to a peak of 543,000 by April 1969.

1965 *Dominican Republic.* The United States intervened to protect lives and property during a Dominican revolt and sent more troops as fears grew that the revolutionary forces were coming increasingly under Communist control.

1967 *Congo.* The United States sent three military transport aircraft with crews to provide the Congo central government with logistical support during a revolt.

1970 *Cambodia.* U.S. troops were ordered into Cambodia to clean out Communist sanctuaries from which Viet Cong and North Vietnamese attacked U.S. and South Vietnamese forces in Vietnam. The object of this attack, which lasted from April 30 to June 30, was to ensure the continuing safe withdrawal of American forces from South Vietnam and to assist the program of Vietnamization.

1974 *Evacuation from Cyprus.* U.S. naval forces evacuated U.S. civilians during hostilities between Turkish and Greek Cypriot forces.

1975 *Evacuation from Vietnam.* On April 3, 1975, President Ford reported U.S. naval vessels, helicopters, and marines had been sent to assist in evacuation of refugees and U.S. nationals from Vietnam.

1975 *Evacuation from Cambodia.* On April 12, 1975, President Ford reported that he had ordered U.S. military forces to proceed with the planned evacuation of U.S. citizens from Cambodia.

1975 *South Vietnam.* On April 30, 1975, President Ford reported that a force of 70 evacuation helicopters and 865 marines had evacuated about 1,400 U.S. citizens and 5,500 third country nationals and South Vietnamese from landing zones near the U.S. embassy in Saigon and the Tan Son Naut Airfield.

1975 *Mayaguez incident.* On May 15, 1975, President Ford reported he had ordered military forces to retake the SS *Mayaguez*, a merchant vessel en route from Hong Kong to Thailand with a U.S. citizen crew which was seized by Cambodian naval patrol boats in international waters and forced to proceed to a nearby island.

1976 *Lebanon.* On July 22 and 23, 1974, helicopters from five U.S. naval vessels evacuated approximately 250 Americans and Europeans from Lebanon during fighting between Lebanese factions after an overland convoy evacuation had been blocked by hostilities.

1976 *Korea*. Additional forces were sent to Korea after two American soldiers were killed by North Korean soldiers in the demilitarized zone between North and South Korea while cutting down a tree.

1978 *Zaire*. From May 19 through June 1978, the United States utilized military transport aircraft to provide logistical support to Belgian and French rescue operations in Zaire.

1980 *Iran*. On April 26, 1980, President Carter reported the use of six U.S. transport planes and eight helicopters in an unsuccessful attempt to rescue American hostages being held in Iran.

1981 *El Salvador*. After a guerilla offensive against the government of El Salvador, additional U.S. military advisers were sent to El Salvador, bringing the total to approximately 55, to assist in training government forces in counterinsurgency.

1981 *Libya*. On August 19, 1981, U.S. planes based on the carrier U.S.S. *Nimitz* shot down two Libyan jets over the Gulf of Sidra after one of the Libyan jets had fired a heat-seeking missile. The United States periodically held freedom of navigation exercises in the Gulf of Sidra, claimed by Libya as territorial waters but considered international waters by the United States.

1982 *Sinai*. On March 19, 1982, President Reagan reported the deployment of military personnel and equipment to participate in the Multinational Force and Observers in the Sinai. Participation had been authorized by the Multinational Force and Observers Resolution, Public Law 97–132.

1982 *Lebanon*. On August 21, 1982, President Reagan reported the dispatch of 80 marines to serve in the multinational force to assist in the withdrawal of members of the Palestine Liberation force from Beirut. The marines left Sept. 20, 1982.

1982–1983 *Lebanon*. On September 29, 1982, President Reagan reported the deployment of 1,200 marines to serve in a temporary multinational force to facilitate the restoration of Lebanese government sovereignty. On Sept. 29, 1983, Congress passed the Multinational Force in Lebanon Resolution (P.L. 98–119) authorizing the continued participation for eighteen months.

1983 *Egypt*. After a Libyan plane bombed a city in Sudan on March 18, 1983, and Sudan and Egypt appealed for assistance, the United States dispatched an AWACS electronic surveillance plane to Egypt.

1983–89 *Honduras*. In July 1983 the United States undertook a series of exercises in Honduras that some believed might lead to conflict with Nicaragua. On March 25, 1986, unarmed U.S. military helicopters and crewmen ferried Honduran troops to the Nicaraguan border to repel Nicaraguan troops.

1983 *Chad*. On August 8, 1983, President Reagan reported the deployment of two AWACS electronic surveillance planes and eight F-15 fighter planes and ground logistical support forces to assist Chad against Libyan and rebel forces.

1983 *Grenada*. On October 25, 1983, President Reagan reported a landing on Grenada by marines and army airborne troops to protect lives and assist in the restoration of law and order and at the request of five members of the Organization of Eastern Caribbean States.

1984 *Persian Gulf*. On June 5, 1984, Saudi Arabian jet fighter planes, aided by intelligence from a U.S. AWACS electronic surveillance aircraft and fueled by a U.S. KC-10 tanker, shot down two Iranian fighter planes over an area of the Persian Gulf proclaimed as a protected zone for shipping.

1985 *Italy*. On October 10, 1985, U.S. Navy pilots intercepted an Egyptian airliner and forced it to land in Sicily. The airliner was carrying the hijackers of the Italian cruise ship *Achille Lauro* who had killed an American citizen during the hijacking.

1986 *Libya*. On March 26, 1986, President Reagan reported to Congress that, on March 24 and 25, U.S. forces, while engaged in freedom of navigation exercises around the Gulf of Sidra, had been attacked by Libyan missiles and the United States had responded with missiles.

1986 *Libya*. On April 16, 1986, President Reagan reported that U.S. air and naval forces had conducted bombing strikes on terrorist facilities and military installations in Libya.

1986 *Bolivia*. U.S. Army personnel and aircraft assisted Bolivia in antidrug operations.

1987–88 *Persian Gulf*. After the Iran-Iraq War resulted in several military incidents in the Persian Gulf, the United States increased U.S. joint military forces operations in the Persian Gulf and adopted a policy of reflagging and escorting Kuwaiti oil tankers through the Gulf. President Reagan reported that U.S. Navy ships had been fired upon or struck mines or taken other military action on September 23, October 10, and October 20, 1987, and April 19, July 4, and July 14, 1988. The United States gradually reduced its forces after a cease-fire between Iran and Iraq on August 20, 1988.

1988 *Panama*. In mid-March and April 1988, during a period of instability in Panama and as pressure grew for Panamanian military leader General Manuel Noriega to resign, the United States sent 1,000 troops to Panama, to "further safeguard the canal, U.S. lives, property and interests in the area." The forces supplemented 10,000 U.S. military personnel already in Panama.

1989 *Libya*. On January 4, 1989, two U.S. Navy F-14 aircraft based on the U.S.S. *John F. Kennedy* shot down two Libyan jet fighters over the Mediterranean Sea about 70 miles north of Libya. The U.S. pilots said the Libyan planes had demonstrated hostile intentions.

1989 *Panama*. On May 11, 1989, in response to General Noriega's disregard of the results of the Panamanian election, President Bush ordered a brigade-sized force of approximately 1,900 troops to augment the estimated 11,000 U.S. forces already in the area.

1989 *Andean Initiative in War on Drugs.* On September 15, 1989, President Bush announced that military and law enforcement assistance would be sent to help the Andean nations of Colombia, Bolivia, and Peru combat illicit drug producers and traffickers. By mid-September there were 50–100 U.S. military advisers in Colombia in connection with transport and training in the use of military equipment, plus seven Special Forces teams of 2–12 persons to train troops in the three countries.

1989 *Philippines.* On December 2, 1989, President Bush reported that on December 1 U.S. fighter planes from Clark Air Base in the Philippines had assisted the Aquino government to repel a coup attempt. In addition, 100 marines were sent from the U.S. Navy base at Subic Bay to protect the U.S. embassy in Manila.

1989–90 *Panama.* On December 21, 1989, President Bush reported that he had ordered U.S. military forces to Panama to protect the lives of American citizens and bring General Noriega to justice. By February 13, 1990, all the invasion forces had been withdrawn.

1990 *Liberia.* On August 6, 1990, President Bush reported that a reinforced rifle company had been sent to provide additional security to the U.S. embassy in Monrovia, and that helicopter teams had evacuated U.S. citizens from Liberia.

1990 *Saudi Arabia.* On August 9, 1990, President Bush reported that he had ordered the forward deployment of substantial elements of the U.S. armed forces into the Persian Gulf region to help defend Saudi Arabia after the August 2 invasion of Kuwait by Iraq. On November 16, 1990, he reported the continued buildup of the forces to ensure an adequate offensive military option.

1991 *Iraq.* On January 18, 1991, President Bush reported that he had directed U.S. armed forces to commence combat operations on January 16 against Iraqi forces and military targets in Iraq and Kuwait, in conjunction with a coalition of allies and U.N. Security Council resolutions. On January 12 Congress had passed the Authorization for Use of Military Force against Iraq Resolution (P.L. 102–1). Combat operations were suspended on February 28, 1991.

1991 *Iraq.* On May 17, 1991, President Bush stated in a status report to Congress that the Iraqi repression of the Kurdish people had necessitated a limited introduction of U.S. forces into northern Iraq for emergency relief purposes.

1991 *Zaire.* On September 25–27, 1991, after widespread looting and rioting broke out in Kinshasa, U.S. Air Force C-141s transported 100 Belgian troops and equipment into Kinshasa. U.S. planes also carried 300 French troops into the Central African Republic and hauled back American citizens and third country nationals from locations outside Zaire.

1992 *Sierra Leone*. On May 3, 1992, U.S. military planes evacuated Americans from Sierra Leone, where military leaders had overthrown the government.

1992 *Kuwait*. On August 3, 1992, the United States began a series of military exercises in Kuwait, following Iraqi refusal to recognize a new border drawn up by the United Nations and refusal to cooperate with U.N. inspection teams.

1992 *Iraq*. On September 16, 1992, President Bush stated in a status report to Congress that he had ordered U.S. participation in the enforcement of a prohibition against Iraqi flights in a specified zone in southern Iraq, and aerial reconnaissance to monitor Iraqi compliance with the ceasefire resolution.

1992 *Somalia*. On December 10, 1992, President Bush reported that he had deployed U.S. armed forces to Somalia in response to a humanitarian crisis and a U.N. Security Council Resolution determining that the situation constituted a threat to international peace. This operation, called Operation Restore Hope, was part of a U.S.-led United Nations Unified Task Force (UNITAF) and came to an end on May 4, 1993. U.S. forces continued to participate in the successor United Nations Operation in Somalia (UN-OSOM II), which the U.N. Security Council authorized to assist Somalia in political reconciliation and restoration of peace.

1993 *Iraq*. On January 19, 1993, President Bush said in a status report that on December 27, 1992, U.S. aircraft had shot down an Iraqi aircraft in the prohibited zone; on January 13 aircraft from the United States and coalition partners had attacked missile bases in southern Iraq; and further military actions had occurred on January 17 and 18. Administration officials said the United States was deploying a battalion task force to Kuwait to underline the continuing U.S. commitment to Kuwaiti independence.

1993 *Iraq*. On January 21, 1993, shortly after his inauguration, President Clinton said the United States would continue the Bush policy on Iraq, and U.S. aircraft fired at targets in Iraq after pilots sensed Iraqi radar or antiaircraft fire directed at them.

1993 *Bosnia*. On February 28, 1993, the United States began an airdrop of relief supplies aimed at Muslims surrounded by Serbian forces in Bosnia.

1993 *Bosnia*. On April 13, 1993, President Clinton reported U.S. forces were participating in a NATO air action to enforce a U.N. ban on all unauthorized military flights over Bosnia-Herzegovina.

1993 *Iraq*. In a status report on Iraq of May 24, President Clinton said that on April 9 and April 18 U.S. planes had bombed or fired missiles at Iraqi antiaircraft sites that had tracked U.S. aircraft.

1993 *Somalia*. On June 10, 1993, President Clinton reported that in response to attacks against U.N. forces in Somalia by a factional leader, the U.S. Quick Reaction Force in the area had participated in military action to quell the violence. On July 1 President Clinton reported further air and ground military operations on June 12 and June 17 aimed at neutralizing military capabilities that had impeded U.N. efforts to deliver humanitarian relief and promote national reconstruction, and additional instances occurred in the following months.

1993 *Iraq*. On June 28, 1993, President Clinton reported that on June 26 U.S. naval forces had launched missiles against the Iraqi Intelligence Service's headquarters in Baghdad in response to an unsuccessful attempt to assassinate former President Bush in Kuwait in April 1993.

1993 *Iraq*. In a status report of July 22, 1993, President Clinton said on June 19 a U.S. aircraft had fired a missile at an Iraqi antiaircraft site displaying hostile intent. U.S. planes also bombed an Iraqi missile battery on August 19, 1993.

1993 *Macedonia*. On July 9, 1993, President Clinton reported the deployment of 350 U.S. soldiers to the former Yugoslav Republic of Macedonia to participate in the U.N. Protection Force to help maintain stability in the area of former Yugoslavia.

1993 *Haiti*. On October 20, 1993, President Clinton reported that U.S. ships had begun to enforce a U.N. embargo against Haiti.

1994 *Bosnia*. On February 17, 1994, President Clinton reported that the United States had expanded its participation in United Nations and NATO efforts to reach a peaceful solution to the conflict in former Yugoslavia and that 60 U.S. aircraft were available for participation in the authorized NATO missions.

1994 *Bosnia*. On March 1, 1994, President Clinton reported that on February 28 U.S. planes patrolling the "no-fly zone" in former Yugoslavia under the North Atlantic Treaty Organization (NATO) shot down four Serbian Galeb planes.

1994 *Bosnia*. On April 12, 1994, President Clinton reported that on April 10 and 11, U.S. warplanes under NATO command had fired against Bosnian Serb forces shelling the "safe" city of Gorazde.

1994 *Rwanda*. On April 12, 1994, President Clinton reported that combat-equipped U.S. military forces had been deployed to Burundi to conduct possible noncombatant evacuation operations of U.S. citizens and other third-country nationals from Rwanda, where widespread fighting had broken out. By September 30, 1994, all U.S. troops had departed from Rwanda and surrounding nations. In the Defense Appropriations Act for FY1995 (P.L. 103–335, signed September 30, 1994), Congress barred use of funds for U.S. military participation in or around Rwanda after October 7, 1994, except for any action necessary to protect U.S. citizens.

1994 *Macedonia*. On April 19, 1994, President Clinton reported that the U.S. contingent in the former Yugoslav Republic of Macedonia had been augmented by a reinforced company of 200 personnel.

1994 *Haiti*. On April 20, 1994, President Clinton reported that U.S. naval forces had continued enforcement of the U.N. embargo in the waters around Haiti and that 712 vessels had been boarded since October 20, 1993.

1994 *Bosnia.* On August 22, 1994, President Clinton reported the use on August
5 of U.S. aircraft under NATO to attack Bosnian Serb heavy weapons in the
Sarajevo heavy weapons exclusion zone upon request of the U.N. Protection
Forces.

1994 *Haiti.* On September 21, 1994, President Clinton reported the deployment
of 1,500 troops to Haiti to restore democracy in Haiti. The troop level was
subsequently increased to 20,000.

1994 *Bosnia.* On November 22, 1994, President Clinton reported the use of U.S.
combat aircraft on November 21, 1994, under NATO, to attack bases used
by Serbs to attack the town of Bihac in Bosnia.

1994 *Macedonia.* On December 22, 1994, President Clinton reported that the
U.S. Army contingent in the former Yugoslav Republic of Macedonia continued its peacekeeping mission and that the current contingent would soon
be replaced by about 500 soldiers from the 3rd Battalion, 5th Cavalry
Regiment, 1st Armored Division from Kirchgons, Germany.

1995 *Somalia.* On March 1, 1995, President Clinton reported that on February 27,
1995, 1,800 combat-equipped U.S. armed forces personnel began deployment into Mogadishu, Somalia, to assist in the withdrawal of U.N. forces
assigned there to the United Nations Operation in Somalia (UNOSOM II).
This mission was completed on March 3, 1995.

1995 *Haiti.* On March 21, 1995, President Clinton reported that U.S. military
forces in Haiti as part of a U.N. Multinational Force had been reduced to just
under 5,300 personnel. He noted that as of March 31, 1995, approximately
2,500 U.S. personnel would remain in Haiti as part of the U.N. Mission in
Haiti (UNMIH).

1995 *Bosnia.* On May 24, 1995, President Clinton reported that U.S. combat-
equipped fighter aircraft and other aircraft continued to contribute to NATO's
enforcement of the no-fly zone in airspace over Bosnia-Herzegovina. U.S.
aircraft, he noted, were also available for close air support of U.N. forces in
Croatia. Roughly 500 U.S. soldiers continued to be deployed in the former
Yugoslav Republic of Macedonia as part of the U.N. Preventive Deployment
Force (UNPREDEP). U.S. forces continued to support U.N. refugee and
embargo operations in this region.

1995 *Bosnia.* On September 1, 1995, President Clinton reported that "U.S.
combat and support aircraft" had been used beginning on August 29, 1995,
in a series of NATO air strikes against Bosnian Serb Army (BSA) forces in
Bosnia-Herzegovina that were threatening the U.N.-declared safe areas of
Sarajevo, Tuzla, and Gorazde. He noted that during the first day of operations, "some 300 sorties were flown against 23 targets in the vicinity of
Sarajevo, Tuzla, Gorazde and Mostar."

1995 *Haiti.* On September 21, 1995, President Clinton reported that currently the
United States had 2,400 military personnel in Haiti as participants in the

U.N. Mission in Haiti (UNMIH). In addition, 260 U.S. military personnel were assigned to the U.S. Support Group Haiti.

1995 *Bosnia*. On December 6, 1995, President Clinton reported to Congress that he had "ordered the deployment of approximately 1,500 U.S. military personnel to Bosnia and Herzegovina and Croatia as part of a NATO 'enabling force' to lay the groundwork for the prompt and safe deployment of the NATO-led Implementation Force (IFOR)," which would be used to implement the Bosnian peace agreement after its signing. The president also noted that he had authorized deployment of roughly 3,000 other U.S. military personnel to Hungary, Italy, and Croatia to establish infrastructure for the enabling force and the IFOR.

1995 *Bosnia*. On December 21, 1995, President Clinton reported to Congress that he had ordered the deployment of approximately 20,000 U.S. military personnel to participate in the NATO-led Implementation Force (IFOR) in the Republic of Bosnia-Herzegovina, and approximately 5,000 U.S. military personnel would be deployed in other former Yugoslav states, primarily in Croatia. In addition, about 7,000 U.S. support forces would be deployed to Hungary, Italy and Croatia and other regional states in support of IFOR's mission.

1996 *Haiti*. On March 21, 1996, President Clinton reported to Congress that beginning in January 1996 there had been a "phased reduction" in the number of U.S. personnel assigned to the United Nations Mission in Haiti (UNMIH). As of March 21, 309 U.S. personnel remained a part of UNMIH. These U.S. forces were "equipped for combat."

1996 *Liberia*. On April 11, 1996, President Clinton reported to Congress that on April 9, 1996, due to the "deterioration of the security situation and the resulting threat to American citizens" in Liberia he had ordered U.S. military forces to evacuate from that country "private U.S. citizens and certain third-country nationals who had taken refuge in the U.S. Embassy compound."

1996 *Liberia*. On May 20, 1996, President Clinton reported to Congress the continued deployment of U.S. military forces in Liberia to evacuate both American citizens and other foreign personnel, and to respond to various isolated "attacks on the American Embassy complex" in Liberia. The president noted that the deployment of U.S. forces would continue until there was no longer any need for enhanced security at the embassy and a requirement to maintain an evacuation capability in the country.

1996 *Central African Republic*. On May 23, 1996, President Clinton reported to Congress the deployment of U.S. military personnel to Bangui, Central African Republic, to conduct the evacuation from that country of "private U.S. citizens and certain U.S. Government employees," and to provide "enhanced security for the American Embassy in Bangui."

1996 *Bosnia*. On June 21, 1996, President Clinton reported to Congress that U.S. forces totaling about 17,000 remained deployed in Bosnia "under NATO operational command and control" as part of the NATO Implementation Force (IFOR). In addition, about 5,500 U.S. military personnel were deployed in Hungary, Italy and Croatia, and other regional states to provide "logistical and other support to IFOR." The president noted that it was the intention that IFOR would complete the withdrawal of all troops in the weeks after December 20, 1996, on a schedule "set by NATO commanders consistent with the safety of troops and the logistical requirements for an orderly withdrawal." He also noted that a U.S. Army contingent (of about 500 U.S. soldiers) remained in the former Yugoslav Republic of Macedonia as part of the United Nations Preventive Deployment Force (UNPREDEP).

1996 *Rwanda and Zaire.* On December 2, 1996, President Clinton reported to Congress that to support the humanitarian efforts of the United Nations regarding refugees in Rwanda and the Great Lakes Region of Eastern Zaire, he had authorized the use of U.S. personnel and aircraft, including AC-130U planes to help in surveying the region in support of humanitarian operations, although fighting still was occurring in the area, and U.S. aircraft had been subject to fire when on flight duty.

1996 *Bosnia.* On December 20, 1996, President Clinton reported to Congress that he had authorized U.S. participation in an IFOR follow-on force in Bosnia, known as SFOR (Stabilization Force), under NATO command. The president said the U.S. forces contribution to SFOR was to be "about 8,500" personnel whose primary mission was to deter or prevent a resumption of hostilities or new threats to peace in Bosnia. SFOR's duration in Bosnia was expected to be 18 months, with progressive reductions and eventual withdrawal.

1997 *Albania.* On March 15, 1997, President Clinton reported to Congress that on March 13, 1997, he had utilized U.S. military forces to evacuate certain U.S. government employees and private U.S. citizens from Tirana, Albania, and to enhance security for the U.S. embassy in that city.

1997 *Congo and Gabon.* On March 27, 1997, President Clinton reported to Congress that on March 25, 1997, a standby evacuation force of U.S. military personnel had been deployed to Congo and Gabon to provide enhanced security for American private citizens, government employees, and selected third-country nationals in Zaire, and to be available for any necessary evacuation operation.

1997 *Sierra Leone.* On May 30, 1997, President Clinton reported to Congress that on May 29 and May 30, 1997, U.S. military personnel were deployed to Freetown, Sierra Leone, to prepare for and undertake the evacuation of certain U.S. government employees and private U.S. citizens.

1997 *Bosnia.* On June 20, 1997, President Clinton reported to Congress that U.S. armed forces continued to support peacekeeping operations in Bosnia and other states in the region in support of the NATO-led Stabilization Force (SFOR). He reported that currently most U.S. military personnel involved in

SFOR were in Bosnia, near Tuzla, and about 2,800 U.S. troops were deployed in Hungary, Croatia, Italy, and other regional states to provide logistics and other support to SFOR. A U.S. Army contingent of about 500 also remained in the ormer Yugoslav Republic of Macedonia as part of the U.N. Preventive Deployment Force (UNPREDEP).

1997 *Cambodia*. On July 11, 1997, President Clinton reported to Congress that in an effort to ensure the security of American citizens in Cambodia during a period of domestic conflict there, he had deployed a task force of about 550 U.S. military personnel to Utapao Air Base in Thailand. These personnel were to be available for possible emergency evacuation operations in Cambodia as deemed necessary.

1997 *Bosnia*. On December 19, 1997, President Clinton reported to Congress that he intended "in principle" to have the United States participate in a security presence in Bosnia when the NATO SFOR contingent withdrew in the summer of 1998.

1998 *Guinea-Bissau*. On June 12, 1998, President Clinton reported to Congress that, on June 10, 1998, in response to an army mutiny in Guinea-Bissau endangering the U.S. embassy, U.S. government employees and citizens in that country, he had deployed a standby evacuation force of U.S. military personnel to Dakar, Senegal, to remove such individuals, as well as selected third-country nationals, from the city of Bissau. The deployment continued until the necessary evacuations were completed.

1998 *Bosnia*. On June 19, 1998, President Clinton reported to Congress regarding activities in the last six months of combat-equipped U.S. forces in support of NATO's SFOR in Bosnia and surrounding areas of former Yugoslavia.

1998 *Kenya and Tanzania*. On August 10, 1998, President Clinton reported to Congress that he had deployed, on August 7, 1998, a Joint Task Force of U.S. military personnel to Nairobi, Kenya, to coordinate the medical and disaster assistance related to the bombings of the U.S. embassies in Kenya and Tanzania. He also reported that teams of 50–100 security personnel had arrived in Nairobi, Kenya, and Dar es Salaam, Tanzania, to enhance the security of the U.S. embassies and citizens there.

1998 *Albania*. On August 18, 1998, President Clinton reported to Congress that he had, on August 16, 1998, deployed 200 U.S. Marines and 10 Navy SEALS to the U.S. embassy compound in Tirana, Albania, to enhance security against reported threats against U.S. personnel.

1998 *Afghanistan and Sudan*. On August 21, 1998, by letter, President Clinton reported to Congress that he had authorized airstrikes on August 20 against camps and installations in Afghanistan and Sudan used by the Osama bin Laden terrorist organization. The president did so based on what he viewed as convincing information that the bin Laden organization was responsible for the bombings, on August 7, 1998, of the U.S. embassies in Kenya and Tanzania.

1998 *Liberia*. On September 29, 1998, President Clinton reported to Congress that on September 27, 1998, he had, due to political instability and civil disorder in Liberia, deployed a standby response and evacuation force of 30 U.S. military personnel to augment the security force at the U.S. embassy in Monrovia, and to provide for a rapid evacuation capability, as needed, to remove U.S. citizens and government personnel from the country.

1998 *Iraq*. During the period from December 16–23, 1998, the United States, together with the United Kingdom, conducted a bombing campaign, termed Operation Desert Fox, against Iraqi industrial facilities deemed capable of producing weapons of mass destruction, and against other Iraqi military and security targets.

1998–99 *Iraq*. Beginning in late December 1998, and continuing during 1999, the United States, together with forces of the coalition enforcing the "no-fly" zones over Iraq, conducted military operations against the Iraqi air defense system on numerous occasions in response to actual or potential threats against aircraft enforcing the "no-fly" zones in northern and southern Iraq.

1999 *Bosnia*. On January 19, 1999, President Clinton reported to Congress that he was continuing to authorize the use of combat-equipped U.S. armed forces in Bosnia and other states in the region as participants in and supporters of the NATO-led Stabilization Force (SFOR). He noted that the U.S. SFOR military personnel totaled about 6,900, with about 2,300 U.S. military personnel deployed to Hungary, Croatia, Italy and other regional states. Also some 350 U.S. military personnel remained deployed in the Former Yugoslav Republic of Macedonia (FYROM) as part of the UN Preventative Deployment Force (UNPREDEP).

1999 *Kenya*. On February 25, 1999, President Clinton reported to Congress that he was continuing to deploy U.S. military personnel in that country to assist in providing security for the U.S. embassy and American citizens in Nairobi, pending completion of renovations of the American embassy facility in Nairobi, subject of a terrorist bombing in August 1998.

1999 *Yugoslavia*. On March 26, 1999, President Clinton reported to Congress that, on March 24, 1999, U.S. military forces, at his direction, and in coalition with NATO allies, had commenced air strikes against Yugoslavia in response to the Yugoslav government's campaign of violence and repression against the ethnic Albanian population in Kosovo.

1999 *Yugoslavia/Albania*. On April 7, 1999, President Clinton reported to Congress that he had ordered additional U.S. military forces to Albania, including rotary wing aircraft, artillery, and tactical missile systems to enhance NATO's ability to conduct effective air operations in Yugoslavia. About 2,500 soldiers and aviators were deployed as part of this task force. The president also reported the deployment of U.S. military forces to Albania and Macedonia to support humanitarian disaster relief operations for Kosovar refugees.

1999 *Yugoslavia/Albania*. On May 25, 1999, President Clinton reported to Congress, "consistent with the war Powers Resolution" that he had directed "deployment of additional aircraft and forces to support NATO's ongoing efforts [against Yugoslavia], including several thousand additional U.S. Armed Forces personnel to Albania in support of the deep strike force located there." He also directed that additional U.S. forces be deployed to the region to assist in "humanitarian operations."

1999 *Yugoslavia/Kosovo*. On June 12, 1999, President Clinton reported to Congress "consistent with the War Powers Resolution" that he had directed the deployment of about "7,000 U.S. military personnel as the U.S. contribution to the approximately 50,000-member, NATO-led security force (KFOR)" currently being assembled in Kosovo. He also noted that about "1,500 U.S. military personnel, under separate U.S. command and control, will deploy to other countries in the region, as our national support element, in support of KFOR."

1999 *Bosnia*. On July 19, 1999, President Clinton reported to Congress "consistent with the War Powers Resolution" that about 6,200 U.S. military personnel were continuing to participate in the NATO-led Stabilization Force (SFOR) in Bosnia, and that another 2,200 personnel were supporting SFOR operations from Hungary, Croatia, and Italy. He also noted that U.S. military personnel remain in the former Yugoslav Republic of Macedonia to support the international security presence in Kosovo (KFOR).

1999 *East Timor*. On October 8, 1999, President Clinton reported to Congress "consistent with the War Powers Resolution" that he had directed the deployment of a limited number of U.S. military forces to East Timor to support the U.N. multinational force (INTERFET) aimed at restoring peace to East Timor. U.S. support has been limited initially to "communications, logistics, planning assistance and transportation." The president further noted that he had authorized deployment of the amphibious ship USS *Belleau Wood*, together with its helicopters and her complement of personnel from the 31st Marine Expeditionary Unit (Special Operations Capable) (MEU SOC) to the East Timor region, to provide helicopter airlift and search and rescue support to the multinational operation. U.S. participation was anticipated to continue until the transition to a U.N. peacekeeping operation was complete.

1999 *Yugoslavia/Kosovo*. On December 15, 1999, President Clinton reported to Congress "consistent with the War Powers Resolution" that U.S. combat-equipped military personnel continued to serve as part of the NATO-led security force in Kosovo (KFOR). He noted that the American contribution to KFOR in Kosovo was "approximately 8,500 U.S. military personnel." U.S. forces were deployed in a sector centered around "Urosevac in the eastern portion of Kosovo." For U.S. KFOR forces, "maintaining public security is a key task." Other U.S. military personnel are deployed to other countries in the region to serve in administrative and logistics support roles for U.S. forces in KFOR. Of these forces, about 1,500 U.S. military personnel are in Macedonia and Greece, and occasionally in Albania.

1999–2000 *Iraq.* At various times during 1999 and continuing throughout 2000 the United States, together with forces of the coalition enforcing the "no-fly" zones over Iraq, conducted military operations against the Iraqi air defense system on numerous occasions in response to actual or potential threats against aircraft enforcing the "no-fly" zones in northern and southern Iraq.

2000 *Bosnia.* On January 25, 2000, President Clinton reported to Congress "consistent with the War Powers Resolution" that the U.S. continued to provide combat-equipped U.S. armed forces to Bosnia and Herzegovina and other states in the region as part of the NATO-led Stabilization Force (SFOR). The president noted that the U.S. force contribution was being reduced from "approximately 6,200 to 4,600 personnel," with the U.S. forces assigned to Multinational Division, North, centered around the city of Tuzla. He added that approximately 1,500 U.S. military personnel were deployed to Hungary, Croatia, and Italy to provide "logistical and other support to SFOR," and that U.S. forces continue to support SFOR in "efforts to apprehend persons indicted for war crimes."

2000 *East Timor.* On February 25, 2000, President Clinton reported to Congress "consistent with the War Powers Resolution" that he had authorized the participation of a small number of U.S. military personnel in support of the United Nations Transitional Administration in East Timor (UNTAET), which has a mandate to maintain law and order throughout East Timor, and to facilitate establishment of an effective administration there, delivery of humanitarian assistance and support the building of self-government. The president reported that the U.S. contingent was small: three military observers, and one judge advocate. To facilitate and coordinate U.S. military activities in East Timor, the president also authorized the deployment of a support group (USGET), consisting of 30 U.S. personnel. U.S. personnel would be temporarily deployed to East Timor, on a rotational basis, and through periodic ship visits, during which U.S. forces would conduct "humanitarian and assistance activities throughout East Timor." Rotational activities were expected to continue through the summer of 2000.

2000 *Sierra Leone.* On May 12, 2000, President Clinton, "consistent with the War Powers Resolution" reported to Congress that he had ordered a U.S. Navy patrol craft to deploy to Sierra Leone to be ready to support evacuation operations from that country if needed. He also authorized a U.S. C-17 aircraft to deliver "ammunition, and other supplies and equipment" to Sierra Leone in support of United Nations peacekeeping operations there.

2000 *Yugoslavia/Kosovo.* On June 16, 2000, President Clinton reported to Congress, "consistent with the War Powers Resolution," that the U.S. was continuing to provide military personnel to the NATO-led KFOR security force in Kosovo. U.S. forces were numbered at 7,500, but were scheduled to be reduced to 6,000 when ongoing troop rotations were completed. U.S. forces in Kosovo were assigned to a sector centered near Gnjilane in eastern Kosovo. Other U.S. military personnel were deployed to other countries serving in administrative and logistics support roles, with approximately 1,000 U.S. personnel in Macedonia, Albania and Greece.

2000 *Bosnia.* On July 25, 2000, President Clinton reported to Congress, "consistent with the War Powers Resolution," that combat-equipped U.S. military personnel continued to participate in the NATO-led Stabilization Force (SFOR) in Bosnia and Herzegovina, being deployed to Bosnia, and other states in the region in support of peacekeeping efforts in former Yugoslavia. U.S. military personnel levels have been reduced from 6,200 to 4,600. Apart from the forces in Bosnia, approximately 1,000 U.S. personnel continue to be deployed in support roles in Hungary, Croatia, and Italy.

2000 *East Timor.* On August 25, 2000, President Clinton reported to Congress, "consistent with the War Powers Resolution," that the United States was currently contributing three military observers to the United Nations Transitional Administration in East Timor (UNTAET) that was charged by the UN with restoring and maintaining peace and security there. He also noted that the U.S. was maintaining a military presence in East Timor separate from UNTAET, comprised of about 30 U.S. personnel who facilitate and coordinate U.S. military activities in East Timor and rotational operations of U.S. forces there. U.S. forces currently conduct humanitarian and civic assistance activities for East Timor's citizens. U.S. rotational presence operations in East Timor are presently expected, the president said, to continue through December 2000.

2000 *Yemen.* On October 14, 2000, President Clinton reported to Congress, "consistent with the War Powers Resolution," that on October 12, 2000, in the wake of an attack on the USS *Cole* in the port of Aden, Yemen, he had authorized deployment of about 45 military personnel from U.S. Naval Forces Central Command to Aden to provide "medical, security, and disaster response assistance." The president further reported that on October 13, 2000, about 50 U.S. military security personnel arrived in Aden, and that additional "security elements" may be deployed to the area, to enhance the ability of the U.S. to ensure the security of the USS *Cole* and the personnel responding to the incident. In addition, two U.S. Navy surface combatant vessels are operating in or near Yemeni territorial waters to provide communications and other support, as required.

2000 *Yugoslavia/Kosovo.* On December 18, 2000, President Clinton reported to Congress, "consistent with the War Powers Resolution," that the United States was continuing to provide approximately 5,600 U.S. military personnel in support of peacekeeping efforts in Kosovo as part of the NATO-led international security force in Kosovo (KFOR). An additional 500 U.S.

military personnel were deployed as the National Support Element in Macedonia, with an occasional presence in Albania and Greece. U.S. forces were assigned to a sector centered around Gnjilane in the eastern portion of Kosovo. The president noted that the mission for these U.S. military forces was maintaining a safe and secure environment through conducting "security patrols in urban areas and in the countryside throughout their sector."

2001 *East Timor.* On March 2, 2001, President George W. Bush reported to Congress, "consistent with the War Powers Resolution," that U.S. armed forces were continuing to support the United Nations peacekeeping effort in East Timor aimed at providing security and maintaining law and order in East Timor, coordinating delivery of humanitarian assistance, and helping establish the basis for self-government in East Timor. The United States currently has three military observers attached to the United Nations Transitional Administration in East Timor (UNTAET). The United States also has a separate military presence, the U.S. Support Group East Timor (USGET), of approximately 12 U.S. personnel, including a security detachment, which "facilitates and coordinates" U.S. military activities in East Timor.

2001 *Yugoslavia/Kosovo.* On May 18, 2001, President George W. Bush reported to Congress, "consistent with the War Powers Resolution," that the United States was continuing to provide approximately 6,000 U.S. military personnel in support of peacekeeping efforts in Kosovo as part of the NATO-led international security force in Kosovo (KFOR). An additional 500 U.S. military personnel were deployed as the National Support Element in Macedonia, with an occasional presence in Greece and Albania. U.S. forces in Kosovo were assigned to a sector centered around Gnjilane in the eastern portion. President Bush noted that the mission for these U.S. military forces was maintaining a safe and secure environment through conducting security patrols in urban areas and in the countryside through their sector.

2001 *Bosnia.* On July 25, 2001, President George W. Bush reported to Congress, "consistent with the War Powers Resolution," about 3,800 combat-equipped U.S. armed forces continued to be deployed in Bosnia and Herzegovina, and other regional states as part of the NATO-led Stabilization Force (SFOR). Most were based at Tuzla in Bosnia. About 500 others were based in Hungary, Croatia, and Italy, providing logistical and other support.

2001 *Iraq.* At various times throughout 2001, the United States, together with forces of the coalition enforcing the "no-fly" zones over Iraq, conducted military operations against the Iraqi air defense system on numerous occasions in response to actual or potential threats against aircraft enforcing the "no-fly" zones in northern and southern Iraq.

2001 *East Timor.* On August 31, 2001, President George W. Bush reported to Congress, "consistent with the War Powers Resolution," that U.S. armed forces were continuing to support the United Nations peacekeeping effort in East Timor aimed at providing security and maintaining law and order in

East Timor, coordinating delivery of humanitarian assistance, and helping establish the basis for self-government in East Timor. The United States had three military observers attached to the United Nations Transitional Administration in East Timor (UNTAET). The United States also had a separate military presence, the U.S. Support Group East Timor (USGET), of approximately 20 U.S. personnel, including a security detachment, which "facilitates and coordinates" U.S. military activities in East Timor, as well as a rotational presence of U.S. forces through temporary deployments to East Timor. The president stated that U.S. forces would continue a presence through December 2001, while options for a U.S. presence in 2002 were being reviewed, with the president's objective being redeployment of USGET personnel, as circumstances permit.

2001 *Terrorism threat.* On September 24, 2001, President George W. Bush reported to Congress, "consistent with the War Powers Resolution," and "Senate Joint Resolution 23" that in response to terrorist attacks on the World Trade Center and the Pentagon he had ordered the "deployment of various combat-equipped and combat support forces to a number of foreign nations in the Central and Pacific Command areas of operations." The president noted that in efforts to "prevent and deter terrorism" he might find it necessary to order additional forces into these and other areas of the world...." He stated that he could not now predict "the scope and duration of these deployments," nor the "actions necessary to counter the terrorist threat to the United States."

2001 *Afghanistan.* On October 9, 2001, President George W. Bush reported to Congress, "consistent with the War Powers Resolution," and "Senate Joint Resolution 23" that on October 7, 2001, U.S. armed forces "began combat action in Afghanistan against Al Qaida terrorists and their Talban supporters." The president stated that he had directed this military action in response to the September 11, 2001, attacks on U.S. "territory, our citizens, and our way of life, and to the continuing threat of terrorist acts against the United States and our friends and allies." This military action was "part of our campaign against terrorism" and was "designed to disrupt the use of Afghanistan as a terrorist base of operations."

2001 *Yugoslavia/Kosovo.* On November 19, 2001, President George W. Bush reported to Congress, "consistent with the War Powers Resolution," that the United States was continuing to provide approximately 5,500 U.S. military personnel in support of peacekeeping efforts in Kosovo as part of the NATO-led international security force in Kosovo (KFOR). An additional 500 U.S. military personnel were deployed as the National Support Element in Macedonia, with an occasional presence in Greece and Albania. U.S. forces in Kosovo were assigned to a sector centered around Gnjilane in the eastern portion. President Bush noted that the mission for these U.S. military forces was maintaining a safe and secure environment through conducting security patrols in urban areas and in the countryside through their sector.

APPENDIX B: RECOMMENDATIONS FROM THE COMMISSION ON NATIONAL SECURITY/21ST CENTURY

SECURING THE NATIONAL HOMELAND

1. The president should develop a comprehensive strategy to heighten America's ability to prevent and protect against all forms of attack on the homeland, and to respond to such attacks if prevention and protection fail.

2. The president should propose, and Congress should agree to create, a National Homeland Security Agency (NHSA) with responsibility for planning, coordinating, and integrating various U.S. government activities involved in homeland security. The Federal Emergency Management Agency (FEMA) should be a key building block in this effort.

3. The president should propose to Congress the transfer of the Customs Service, the Border Patrol, and Coast Guard to the National Homeland Security Agency, while preserving them as distinct entities.

4. The president should ensure that the National Intelligence Council: include homeland security and asymmetric threats as an area of analysis; assign that portfolio to a National Intelligence Officer; and produce National Intelligence Estimates on these threats.

5. The president should propose to Congress the establishment of an assistant secretary of defense for homeland security within the Office of the Secretary of Defense, reporting directly to the secretary.

6. The secretary of defense, at the president's direction, should make homeland security a primary mission of the National Guard, and the Guard should be

organized, properly trained, and adequately equipped to undertake that mission.

7. Congress should establish a special body to deal with homeland security issues, as has been done with intelligence oversight. Members should be chosen for their expertise in foreign policy, defense, intelligence, law enforcement, and appropriations. This body should also include members of all relevant Congressional committees as well as ex officio members from the leadership of both houses of Congress.

RECAPITALIZING AMERICA'S STRENGTHS IN SCIENCE AND EDUCATION

8. The president should propose, and the Congress should support, doubling the U.S. government's investment in science and technology R&D by 2010.

9. The president should empower his science advisor to establish nonmilitary R&D objectives that meet changing national needs, and to be responsible for coordinating budget development within the relevant departments and agencies.

10. The president should propose, and the Congress should fund, the reorganization of the national laboratories, providing individual laboratories with new mission goals that minimize overlap.

11. The president should propose, and Congress should pass, a National Security Science and Technology Education Act (NSSTEA) with four sections: reduced-interest loans and scholarships for students to pursue degrees in science, mathematics, and engineering; loan forgiveness and scholarships for those in these fields entering government or military service; a National Security Teaching Program to foster science and math teaching at the K-12 level; and increased funding for professional development for science and math teachers.

12. The president should direct the Department of Education to work with the states to devise a comprehensive plan to avert a looming shortage of quality teachers. This plan should emphasize raising teacher compensation, improving infrastructure support, reforming the certification process, and expanding existing programs targeted at districts with especially acute problems.

13. The president and Congress should devise a targeted program to strengthen the historically black colleges and universities in our country, and should particularly support those that emphasize science, mathematics, and engineering.

INSTITUTIONAL REDESIGN

14. The president should personally guide a top-down strategic planning process and delegate authority to the national security advisor to coordinate that process.

15. The president should prepare and present to the Congress an overall national security budget to serve the critical goals that emerge from the NSC strategic planning process. Separately, the president should continue to submit budgets for individual national security departments and agencies for Congressional review and appropriation.

16. The National Security Council (NSC) should be responsible for advising the president and for coordinating the multiplicity of national security activities, broadly defined to include economic and domestic law enforcement activities as well as the traditional national security agenda. The NSC advisor and staff should resist the temptation to assume a central policymaking and operational role.

17. The president should propose to the Congress that the secretary of the treasury be made a statutory member of the National Security Council.

18. The president should abolish the National Economic Council, distributing its domestic economic policy responsibilities to the Domestic Policy Council and its international economic responsibilities to the National Security Council.

19. The president should propose to the Congress a plan to reorganize the State Department, creating five undersecretaries, with responsibility for overseeing the regions of Africa, Asia, Europe, Inter-America, and Near East/South Asia, and redefining the responsibilities of the undersecretary for global affairs. These new undersecretaries would operate in conjunction with the existing undersecretary for management.

20. The president should propose to the Congress that the U.S. Agency for International Development be consolidated into the State Department.

21. The secretary of state should give greater emphasis to strategic planning in the State Department and link it directly to the allocation of resources through the establishment of a Strategic Planning, Assistance, and Budget Office.

22. The president should ask Congress to appropriate funds to the State Department in a single integrated foreign operations budget, which would include all foreign assistance programs and activities as well as all expenses for personnel and operations.

23. The president should ensure that ambassadors have the requisite area knowledge as well as leadership and management skills to function effectively.

He should therefore appoint an independent, bipartisan advisory panel to the Secretary of State to vet ambassadorial appointees, career and noncareer alike.

24. The secretary of defense should propose to Congress a restructuring plan for the Office of the Under Secretary of Defense for Policy that would abolish the Office of the Assistant Secretary for Special Operations and Low-Intensity Conflict (SOLIC), and create a new office of an assistant secretary dedicated to strategy and planning (S/P).

25. Based on a review of the core roles and responsibilities of the staffs of the Office of the Secretary of Defense, the Joint Staff, the military services, and the CINCs, the secretary of defense should reorganize and reduce those staffs by 10 to 15 percent.

26. The secretary of defense should establish a ten-year goal of reducing infrastructure costs by 20 to 25 percent through outsourcing and privatizing as many DOD support agencies as possible.

27. The Congress and the secretary of defense should move the quadrennial defense review to the second year of a presidential term.

28. The secretary of defense should introduce a new process that would require the services and defense agencies to compete for the allocation of some resources within the overall defense budget.

29. The secretary of defense should establish and employ a two-track acquisition system, one for major acquisitions and a second, "fast track" for a limited number of potential breakthrough systems, especially those in the area of command and control.

30. The secretary of defense should foster innovation by directing a return to the pattern of increased prototyping and testing of selected weapons and support systems.

31. Congress should implement two-year defense budgeting *solely* for the modernization element of the DOD budget (R&D/procurement) because of its long-term character, and it should expand the use of multiyear procurement.

32. Congress should modernize Defense Department auditing and oversight requirements by rewriting relevant sections of U.S. Code, Title 10, and the Federal Acquisition Regulations.

33. The secretary of defense should direct the DOD to shift from the threat-based 2MTW force sizing process to one which measures requirements against recent operational activity trends, actual intelligence estimates of potential adversaries' capabilities, and national security objectives once formulated in the new administration's national security strategy.

34. The Defense Department should devote its highest priority to improving and furthering expeditionary capabilities.

35. The president should establish an Interagency Working Group on Space (IWGS) at the National Security Council to coordinate all aspects of the nation's space policy, and place on the NSC staff those with the necessary expertise in this area.

36. The president should order the setting of national intelligence priorities through National Security Council guidance to the Director of Central Intelligence.

37. The Director of Central Intelligence should emphasize the recruitment of human intelligence sources on terrorism as one of the intelligence community's highest priorities, and ensure that operational guidelines are balanced between security needs and respect for American values and principles.

38. The intelligence community should place new emphasis on collection and analysis of economic and science/technology security concerns, and incorporate more open-source intelligence into analytical products. Congress should support this new emphasis by increasing significantly the National Foreign Intelligence Program (NFIP) budget for collection and analysis.

THE HUMAN REQUIREMENTS FOR NATIONAL SECURITY

39. Congress should significantly expand the National Security Education Act (NSEA) to include broad support for social sciences, humanities, and foreign languages in exchange for military and civilian service to the nation.

40. The executive and legislative branches should cooperate to revise the current presidential appointee process by reducing the impediments that have made high-level public service undesirable to many distinguished Americans. Specifically, they should reduce the number of Senate confirmed and non-career Senior Executive Service (SES) positions by 25 percent; shorten the appointment process; and revise draconian ethics regulations.

41. The president should order the overhauling of the Foreign Service system by revamping the examination process, dramatically improving the level of ongoing professional education, and making leadership a core value of the State Department.

42. The president should order the elimination of recruitment hurdles for the Civil Service, ensure a faster and easier hiring process, and see to it that strengthened professional education and retention programs are worthy of full funding by Congress.

43. The executive branch should establish a National Security Service Corps (NSSC) to enhance civilian career paths, and to provide a corps of policy experts with broad-based experience throughout the executive branch.

44. Congress should significantly enhance the Montgomery GI Bill, as well as strengthen recently passed and pending legislation supporting benefits—including transition, medical, and home ownership—for qualified veterans.

45. Congress and the Defense Department should cooperate to decentralize military personnel legislation dictating the terms of enlistment/commissioning, career management, retirement, and compensation.

THE ROLE OF CONGRESS

46. The Congressional leadership should conduct a thorough bicameral, bipartisan review of the legislative branch relationship to national security and foreign policy.

47. Congressional and executive branch leaders must build programs to encourage individual members to acquire knowledge and experience in both national security and foreign policy.

48. Congress should rationalize its current committee structure so that it best serves U.S. national security objectives; specifically, it should merge the current authorizing committees with the relevant appropriations subcommittees.

49. The executive ranch must ensure a sustained focus on foreign policy and national security consultation with Congress and devote resources to it. For its part, Congress must make consultation a higher priority and form a permanent consultative group of Congressional leaders as part of this effort.

50. The president should create an implementing mechanism to ensure that the major recommendations of this commission result in the critical reforms necessary to ensure American national security and global leadership over the next quarter century.

APPENDIX C: RECOMMENDATIONS FROM THE 9/11 COMMISSION AND COMMISSION ON NATIONAL SECURITY/21ST CENTURY

Recommendations from the 9/11 Commission

	Focus		Element of Power										
	Foreign	Domestic	Political	Defense/Military	Homeland Defense	Intelligence	Legal	Economic	Science and Technology	Cultural	Human Rights/Liberties	Education	Informational
Recommendation: The U.S. government must identify and prioritize actual or potential terrorist sanctuaries. For each, it should have a realistic strategy to keep possible terrorists insecure and on the run, using all elements of national power. We should reach out, listen to, and work with other countries that can help.	1	1	1	1	1	1	1	1		1	1	1	1
Recommendation: If Musharraf stands for enlightened moderation in a fight for his life and for the life of his country, the United States should be willing to make hard choices too, and make the difficult long-term commitment to the future of Pakistan. Sustaining the current scale of aid to Pakistan, the United States should support Pakistan's government in its struggle against extremists with a comprehensive effort that extends from military aid to support for better education, so long as Pakistan's leaders remain willing to make difficult choices of their own.	1		1	1				1			1	1	1

Recommendation: The President and the Congress deserve praise for their efforts in Afghanistan so far. Now the United States and the international community should make a long-term commitment to a secure and stable Afghanistan, in order to give the government a reasonable opportunity to improve the life of the Afghan people. Afghanistan must not again become a sanctuary for international crime and terrorism. The United States and the international community should help the Afghan government extend its authority over the country, with a strategy and nation-by-nation commitments to achieve their objectives.

Recommendation: The problems in the U.S.-Saudi relationship must be confronted, openly. The United States and Saudi Arabia must determine if they can build a relationship that political leaders on both sides are prepared to publicly defend—a relationship about more than oil. It should include a shared commitment to political and economic reform, as Saudis make common cause with the outside world. It should include a shared interest in greater tolerance and cultural respect, translating into a commitment to fight the violent extremists who foment hatred.

Recommendation: The U.S. government must define what the message is, what it stands for. We should offer an example of moral leadership in the world, committed to treat people humanely, abide by the rule of law, and be generous and caring to our neighbors. America and Muslim friends can agree on respect for human dignity and opportunity. To Muslim parents, terrorists like Bin Ladin have nothing to offer their children but visions of violence and death. America and its friends have a crucial advantage—we can offer these parents a vision that might give their children a better future. If we heed the views of thoughtful leaders in the Arab and Muslim world, a moderate consensus can be found.

Appendix C (*continued*)

Recommendation	Foreign	Domestic	Political	Defense/Military	Homeland Defense	Intelligence	Legal	Economic	Science and Technology	Cultural	Human Rights/Liberties	Education	Informational
Recommendation: Where Muslim governments, even those who are friends, do not respect these principles, the United States must stand for a better future. One of the lessons of the long Cold War was that short-term gains in cooperating with the most repressive and brutal governments were too often outweighed by long-term setbacks for America's stature and interests.	1		1	1		1	1	1	1	1	1		1
Recommendation: Just as we did in the Cold War, we need to defend our ideals abroad vigorously. America does stand up for its values. The United States defended, and still defends, Muslims against tyrants and criminals in Somalia, Bosnia, Kosovo, Afghanistan, and Iraq. If the United States does not act aggressively to define itself in the Islamic world, the extremists will gladly do the job for us.	1		1						1	1			1

Table header group labels: **Focus** (Foreign, Domestic, Political), **Element of Power** (Defense/Military, Homeland Defense, Intelligence, Legal, Economic, Science and Technology, Cultural, Human Rights/Liberties, Education, Informational)

Recommendation: The U.S. government should offer to join with other nations in generously supporting a new International Youth Opportunity Fund. Funds will be spent directly for building and operating primary and secondary schools in those Muslim states that commit to sensibly investing their own money in public education.

Recommendation: A comprehensive U.S. strategy to counter terrorism should include economic policies that encourage development, more open societies, and opportunities for people to improve the lives of their families and to enhance prospects for their children's future.

Recommendation: The United States should engage other nations in developing a comprehensive coalition strategy against Islamist terrorism. There are several multilateral institutions in which such issues should be addressed. But the most important policies should be discussed and coordinated in a flexible contact group of leading coalition governments. This is a good place, for example, to develop joint strategies for targeting terrorist travel, or for hammering out a common strategy for the places where terrorists may be finding sanctuary.

Recommendation: The United States should engage its friends to develop a common coalition approach toward the detention and humane treatment of captured terrorists. New principles might draw upon Article 3 of the Geneva Conventions on the law of armed conflict. That article was specifically designed for those cases in which the usual laws of war did not apply. Its minimum standards are generally accepted throughout the world as customary international law.

Appendix C (*continued*)

Recommendation	Focus		Element of Power										
	Foreign	Domestic	Political	Defense/Military	Homeland Defense	Intelligence	Legal	Economic	Science and Technology	Cultural	Human Rights/Liberties	Education	Informational
Recommendation: Our report shows that al Qaeda has tried to acquire or make weapons of mass destruction for at least ten years. There is no doubt the United States would be a prime target. Preventing the proliferation of these weapons warrants a maximum effort—by strengthening counterproliferation efforts, expanding the Proliferation Security Initiative, and supporting the Cooperative Threat Reduction program.	1		1	1	1	1	1						
Recommendation: Vigorous efforts to track terrorist financing must remain front and center in U.S. counterterrorism efforts. The government has recognized that information about terrorist money helps us to understand their networks, search them out, and disrupt their operations. Intelligence and law enforcement have targeted the relatively small number of financial facilitators—individuals al Qaeda relied on for their ability to raise and deliver money—at the core of al Qaeda's revenue stream. These efforts have worked. The death or capture of several important facilitators has decreased the amount of money available to al Qaeda and has increased its costs and difficulty in raising and moving that money. Captures have additionally provided a windfall of intelligence that can be used to continue the cycle of disruption.	1		1	1	1		1						

Recommendation: Targeting travel is at least as powerful a weapon against terrorists as targeting their money. The United States should combine terrorist travel intelligence, operations, and law enforcement in a strategy to intercept terrorists, find terrorist travel facilitators, and constrain terrorist mobility.

Recommendation: The U.S. border security system should be integrated into a larger network of screening points that includes our transportation system and access to vital facilities, such as nuclear reactors. The President should direct the Department of Homeland Security to lead the effort to design a comprehensive screening system, addressing common problems and setting common standards with systemwide goals in mind. Extending those standards among other governments could dramatically strengthen America and the world's collective ability to intercept individuals who pose catastrophic threats.

Recommendation: The Department of Homeland Security, properly supported by the Congress, should complete, as quickly as possible, a biometric entry-exit screening system, including a single system for speeding qualified travelers. It should be integrated with the system that provides benefits to foreigners seeking to stay in the United States. Linking biometric passports to good data systems and decisionmaking is a fundamental goal. No one can hide his or her debt by acquiring a credit card with a slightly different name. Yet today, a terrorist can defeat the link to electronic records by tossing away an old passport and slightly altering the name in the new one.

Appendix C (*continued*)

Recommendation	Informational	Education	Human Rights/Liberties	Cultural	Science and Technology	Economic	Legal	Intelligence	Homeland Defense	Defense/Military	Political	Domestic	Foreign
Recommendation: The U.S. government cannot meet its own obligations to the American people to prevent the entry of terrorists without a major effort to collaborate with other governments. We should do more to exchange terrorist information with trusted allies, and raise U.S. and global border security standards for travel and border crossing over the medium and long term through extensive international cooperation.							1		1	1			1
Recommendation: Secure identification should begin in the United States. The federal government should set standards for the issuance of birth certificates and sources of identification, such as drivers licenses. Fraud in identification documents is no longer just a problem of theft. At many entry points to vulnerable facilities, including gates for boarding aircraft, sources of identification are the last opportunity to ensure that people are who they say they are and to check whether they are terrorists.							1		1			1	

Column group headers: **Focus** (Domestic, Foreign); **Element of Power** (Informational, Education, Human Rights/Liberties, Cultural, Science and Technology, Economic, Legal, Intelligence, Homeland Defense, Defense/Military, Political)

Recommendation: Hard choices must be made in allocating limited resources. The U.S. government should identify and evaluate the transportation assets that need to be protected, set risk-based priorities for defending them, select the most practical and cost-effective ways of doing so, and then develop a plan, budget, and funding to implement the effort. The plan should assign roles and missions to the relevant authorities (federal, state, regional, and local) and to private stakeholders. In measuring effectiveness, perfection is unattainable. But terrorists should perceive that potential targets are defended. They may be deterred by a significant chance of failure.

Recommendation: Improved use of "no-fly" and "automatic selectee" lists should not be delayed while the argument about a successor to CAPPS continues. This screening function should be performed by the TSA, and it should utilize the larger set of watchlists maintained by the federal government. Air carriers should be required to supply the information needed to test and implement this new system.

Recommendation: The TSA and the Congress must give priority attention to improving the ability of screening checkpoints to detect explosives on passengers. As a start, each individual selected for special screening should be screened for explosives. Further, the TSA should conduct a human factors study, a method often used in the private sector, to understand problems in screener performance and set attainable objectives for individual screeners and for the checkpoints where screening takes place.

Appendix C (*continued*)

	Focus		Element of Power										
Recommendation	Foreign	Domestic	Political	Defense/Military	Homeland Defense	Intelligence	Legal	Economic	Science and Technology	Cultural	Human Rights/Liberties	Education	Informational
Recommendation: As the President determines the guidelines for information sharing among government agencies and by those agencies with the private sector, he should safeguard the privacy of individuals about whom information is shared.		1		1	1	1							
Recommendation: The burden of proof for retaining a particular governmental power should be on the executive, to explain (a) that the power actually materially enhances security and (b) that there is adequate supervision of the executive's use of the powers to ensure protection of civil liberties. If the power is granted, there must be adequate guidelines and oversight to properly confine its use.		1					1			1			
Recommendation: At this time of increased and consolidated government authority, there should be a board within the executive branch to oversee adherence to the guidelines we recommend and the commitment the government makes to defend our civil liberties.		1					1			1			

Recommendation: Homeland security assistance should be based strictly on an assessment of risks and vulnerabilities. Now, in 2004, Washington, D.C., and New York City are certainly at the top of any such list. We understand the contention that every state and city needs to have some minimum infrastructure for emergency response. But federal homeland security assistance should not remain a program for general revenue sharing. It should supplement state and local resources based on the risks or vulnerabilities that merit additional support. Congress should not use this money as a pork barrel.

Recommendation: Emergency response agencies nationwide should adopt the Incident Command System (ICS). When multiple agencies or multiple jurisdictions are involved, they should adopt a unified command. Both are proven frameworks for emergency response. We strongly support the decision that federal homeland security funding will be contingent, as of October 1, 2004, upon the adoption and regular use of ICS and unified command procedures. In the future, the Department of Homeland Security should consider making funding contingent on aggressive and realistic training in accordance with ICS and unified command procedures.

Recommendation: Congress should support pending legislation which provides for the expedited and increased assignment of radio spectrum for public safety purposes. Furthermore, high-risk urban areas such as New York City and Washington, D.C., should establish signal corps units to ensure communications connectivity between and among civilian authorities, local first responders, and the National Guard. Federal funding of such units should be given high priority by Congress.

Appendix C (*continued*)

Recommendation	Focus			Element of Power									
	Foreign	Domestic	Political	Defense/Military	Homeland Defense	Intelligence	Legal	Economic	Science and Technology	Cultural	Human Rights/Liberties	Education	Informational
Recommendation: We endorse the American National Standards Institute's recommended standard for private preparedness. We were encouraged by Secretary Tom Ridge's praise of the standard, and urge the Department of Homeland Security to promote its adoption. We also encourage the insurance and credit-rating industries to look closely at a company's compliance with the ANSI standard in assessing its insurability and creditworthiness. We believe that compliance with the standard should define the standard of care owed by a company to its employees and the public for legal purposes. Private-sector preparedness is not a luxury; it is a cost of doing business in the post-9/11 world. It is ignored at a tremendous potential cost in lives, money, and national security.	1			1			1	1					

Recommendation: We recommend the establishment of a National Counterterrorism Center (NCTC), built on the foundation of the existing Terrorist Threat Integration Center (TTIC). Breaking the older mold of national government organization, this NCTC should be a center for joint operational planning and joint intelligence, staffed by personnel from the various agencies. The head of the NCTC should have authority to evaluate the performance of the people assigned to the Center.

Recommendation: The current position of Director of Central Intelligence should be replaced by a National Intelligence Director with two main areas of responsibility: (1) to oversee national intelligence centers on specific subjects of interest across the U.S. government and (2) to manage the national intelligence program and oversee the agencies that contribute to it.

Recommendation: The CIA Director should emphasize (a) rebuilding the CIA's analytic capabilities; (b) transforming the clandestine service by building its human intelligence capabilities; (c) developing a stronger language program, with high standards and sufficient financial incentives; (d) renewing emphasis on recruiting diversity among operations officers so they can blend more easily in foreign cities; (e) ensuring a seamless relationship between human source collection and signals collection at the operational level; and (f) stressing a better balance between unilateral and liaison operations.

Appendix C (*continued*)

Recommendation	Foreign	Domestic	Political	Defense/Military	Homeland Defense	Intelligence	Legal	Economic	Science and Technology	Cultural	Human Rights/Liberties	Education	Informational
Recommendation: Lead responsibility for directing and executing paramilitary operations, whether clandestine or covert, should shift to the Defense Department. There it should be consolidated with the capabilities for training, direction, and execution of such operations already being developed in the Special Operations Command.	1			1		1	1						
Recommendation: Finally, to combat the secrecy and complexity we have described, the overall amounts of money being appropriated for national intelligence and to its component agencies should no longer be kept secret. Congress should pass a separate appropriations act for intelligence, defending the broad allocation of how these tens of billions of dollars have been assigned among the varieties of intelligence work.		1			1								
Recommendation: Information procedures should provide incentives for sharing, to restore a better balance between security and shared knowledge.	1				1								

Focus — Foreign, Domestic
Element of Power — Political, Defense/Military, Homeland Defense, Intelligence, Legal, Economic, Science and Technology, Cultural, Human Rights/Liberties, Education, Informational

Recommendation: The president should lead the government-wide effort to bring the major national security institutions into the information revolution. He should coordinate the resolution of the legal, policy, and technical issues across agencies to create a "trusted information network."

Recommendation: Congressional oversight for intelligence—and counterterrorism—is now dysfunctional. Congress should address this problem. We have considered various alternatives: A joint committee on the old model of the Joint Committee on Atomic Energy is one. A single committee in each house of Congress, combining authorizing and appropriating authorities, is another.

Recommendation: Congress should create a single, principal point of oversight and review for homeland security. Congressional leaders are best able to judge what committee should have jurisdiction over this department and its duties. But we believe that Congress does have the obligation to choose one in the House and one in the Senate, and that this committee should be a permanent standing committee with a nonpartisan staff.

Recommendation: Since a catastrophic attack could occur with little or no notice, we should minimize as much as possible the disruption of national security policymaking during the change of administrations by accelerating the process for national security appointments. We think the process could be improved significantly so transitions can work more effectively and allow new officials to assume their new responsibilities as quickly as possible.

Appendix C (*continued*)

	Focus		Element of Power										
	Foreign	Domestic	Political	Defense/Military	Homeland Defense	Intelligence	Legal	Economic	Science and Technology	Cultural	Human Rights/Liberties	Education	Informational
Recommendation: A specialized and integrated national security workforce should be established at the FBI consisting of agents, analysts, linguists, and surveillance specialists who are recruited, trained, rewarded, and retained to ensure the development of an institutional culture imbued with a deep expertise in intelligence and national security.		1		1	1	1	1						
Recommendation: The Department of Defense and its oversight committees should regularly assess the adequacy of Northern Command's strategies and planning to defend the United States against military threats to the homeland.		1		1	1	1							
Recommendation: The Department of Homeland Security and its oversight committees should regularly assess the types of threats the country faces to determine (a) the adequacy of the government's plans—and the progress against those plans—to protect America's critical infrastructure and (b) the readiness of the government to respond to the threats that the United States might face.		1		1									
	15	28	11	17	24	30	25	7	0	8	9	8	

APPENDIX D: THE NORTH ATLANTIC TREATY

WASHINGTON D.C.—4 April 1949. The Parties to this Treaty reaffirm their faith in the purposes and principles of the Charter of the United Nations and their desire to live in peace with all peoples and all governments. They are determined to safeguard the freedom, common heritage and civilisation of their peoples, founded on the principles of democracy, individual liberty and the rule of law. They seek to promote stability and well-being in the North Atlantic area. They are resolved to unite their efforts for collective defence and for the preservation of peace and security. They therefore agree to this North Atlantic Treaty:

ARTICLE 1

The Parties undertake, as set forth in the chart of the United Nations, to settle any international dispute in which they may be involved by peaceful means in such a manner that international peace and security and justice are not endangered, and to refrain in their international relations from the threat or use of force in any manner inconsistent with the purposes of the United Nations.

ARTICLE 2

The Parties will contribute toward the further development of peaceful and friendly international relations by strengthening their free institutions, by bringing about a better understanding of the principles upon which these institutions are founded, and by promoting conditions of stability and well-being. They will seek to eliminate conflict in their international economic policies and will encourage economic collaboration between any or all of them.

ARTICLE 3

In order more effectively to achieve the objectives of this Treaty, the Parties, separately and jointly, by means of continuous and effective self-help and mutual aid, will maintain and develop their individual and collective capacity to resist armed attack.

ARTICLE 4

The Parties will consult together whenever, in the opinion of any of them, the territorial integrity, political independence or security of any of the Parties is threatened.

ARTICLE 5

The Parties agree that an armed attack against one or more of them in Europe or North America shall be considered an attack against them all and consequently they agree that, if such an armed attack occurs, each of them, in exercise of the right of individual or collective self-defence recognised by Article 51 of the Charter of the United Nations, will assist the Party or Parties so attacked by taking forthwith, individually and in concert with the other Parties, such action as it deems necessary, including the use of armed force, to restore and maintain the security of the North Atlantic area.

Any such armed attack and all measures taken as a result thereof shall immediately be reported to the Security Council. Such measures shall be terminated when the Security Council has taken the measures necessary to restore and maintain international peace and security.

ARTICLE 6[1]

For the purpose of Article 5, an armed attack on one or more of the Parties is deemed to include an armed attack:

- on the territory of any of the Parties in Europe or North America, on the Algerian Departments of France,[2] on the territory of or on the Islands under the jurisdiction of any of the Parties in the North Atlantic area north of the Tropic of Cancer;

- on the forces, vessels, or aircraft of any of the Parties, when in or over these territories or any other area in Europe in which occupation forces of any of the Parties were stationed on the date when the Treaty entered into force or the Mediterranean Sea or the North Atlantic area north of the Tropic of Cancer.

ARTICLE 7

This Treaty does not affect, and shall not be interpreted as affecting in any way the rights and obligations under the Charter of the Parties which are members of the United Nations, or the primary responsibility of the Security Council for the maintenance of international peace and security.

ARTICLE 8

Each Party declares that none of the international engagements now in force between it and any other of the Parties or any third State is in conflict with the provisions of this Treaty, and undertakes not to enter into any international engagement in conflict with this Treaty.

ARTICLE 9

The Parties hereby establish a Council, on which each of them shall be represented, to consider matters concerning the implementation of this Treaty. The Council shall be so organised as to be able to meet promptly at any time. The Council shall set up such subsidiary bodies as may be necessary; in particular it shall establish immediately a defence committee which shall recommend measures for the implementation of Articles 3 and 5.

ARTICLE 10

The Parties may, by unanimous agreement, invite any other European State in a position to further the principles of this Treaty and to contribute to the security of the North Atlantic area to accede to this Treaty. Any State so invited may become a Party to the Treaty by depositing its instrument of accession with the Government of the United States of America. The Government of the United States of America will inform each of the Parties of the deposit of each such instrument of accession.

ARTICLE 11

This Treaty shall be ratified and its provisions carried out by the Parties in accordance with their respective constitutional processes. The instruments of ratification shall be deposited as soon as possible with the Government of the United States of America, which will notify all the other signatories of each deposit. The Treaty shall enter into force between the States which have ratified it as soon as the ratifications of the majority of the signatories, including the ratifications of Belgium, Canada, France, Luxembourg, the Netherlands, the United Kingdom and the United States, have been deposited and shall come into effect with respect to other States on the date of the deposit of their ratifications.[3]

ARTICLE 12

After the Treaty has been in force for ten years, or at any time thereafter, the Parties shall, if any of them so requests, consult together for the purpose of reviewing the Treaty, having regard for the factors then affecting peace and security in the North Atlantic area, including the development of universal as well as regional arrangements under the Charter of the United Nations for the maintenance of international peace and security.

ARTICLE 13

After the Treaty has been in force for twenty years, any Party may cease to be a Party one year after its notice of denunciation has been given to the Government of the United States of America, which will inform the Governments of the other Parties of the deposit of each notice of denunciation.

ARTICLE 14

This Treaty, of which the English and French texts are equally authentic, shall be deposited in the archives of the Government of the United States of America. Duly certified copies will be transmitted by that Government to the Governments of other signatories.

NOTES

Introduction

1. *Hard power* refers to the use of political, military, and intelligence elements primarily, while *soft power* refers to the collection of the other elements of power, including economic, social, cultural, and informational, to name a few. While this is the grouping of hard and soft power that is incorporated into this book, there is no universally accepted delineation of which elements fit into which category. For example, some place economics in the hard power category, while I have chosen to incorporate it into the soft power category for reasons that are articulated later.

Chapter 1

1. *The National Security Strategy of the United States of America*, The White House, Washington, DC, September 2002, p. iii.

2. *The 9/11 Commission Report: Final Report of the National Commission on Terrorist Attacks Upon the United States* (New York: W.W. Norton), 411.

3. This is significant as it requires all the Services to agree to the same definitions of the term.

4. *The American Heritage Dictionary of the English Language*, 4th ed.; s.v. "Strategy," "National Strategy," and "Military Strategy."

5. With the publishing of the National Strategy for Homeland Security (NSHS) by the White House in July 2002, there are now two security strategies (i.e., the NSS and the NSHS) that must be considered.

Chapter 2

1. Carl Shapiro and Hal R. Varian, *Information Rules* (Cambridge, MA: Harvard Business School Press, 1998).

2. Shapiro and Varian, p. 13.

3. *Encarta Dictionary*. CD-ROM. Microsoft Corporation. Encarta Encyclopedia (Online Version), May 6, 2005, http://encarta.msn.com/encyclopedia_1741588397/Globalization.html.

4. Data are from the online version of Microsoft's Annual Report from 2004, January 14, 2005. It accounts for gross revenue. Available at: http://www.microsoft.com/msft/ar.mspx.

5. Using Central Intelligence Agency (CIA) data from the *CIA Factbook* online, December 16, 2004. Available at: http://www.cia.gov/cia/publications/factbook.

6. *The National Security Strategy of the United States of America*, p. 21.

7. Susan E. Rice, *The New National Security Strategy: Focus on Failed States*, Policy Brief #116 (Washington, DC: The Brookings Institution, February 2003), 2.

8. Regional Indicators: European Union (EU). January 19, 2005. Available at: http://www.eia.doe.gov/emeu/cabs/euro.html.

9. Samuel P. Huntington, "The Clash of Civilizations," *Foreign Affairs* (Summer 1993): 22.

10. Max Boot, unpublished manuscript, Council on Foreign Relations. Sources cited include Trevor N. Dupuy, *The Evolution of Weapons and Warfare* (Cambridge, MA: Da Capo Press, 1990), 310. All figures on lethality and dispersion up to 1973 are also from Dupuy, *Weapons and Warfare*, 312. The figure on dispersion and lethality for the Gulf War comes from *The Precision Revolution: GPS and the Future of Aerial Warfare* (Annapolis, MD: Naval Institute Press, 2002), 126.

11. David C. Gompert, *Right Makes Might: Freedom and Power in the Information Age* (Washington, DC: Institute for National and Strategic Studies, National Defense University), 29.

12. Carl von Clausewitz, *On War*. Index Edition Edited and Translated by Michael Howard and Peter Paret (Princeton, NJ: Princeton University Press, 1976), 87.

13. "Iran Jails More Journalists and Blocks Web Sites," *New York Times*, November 7, 2004.

14. Examining the armies of the world, most have some sort of armored capability. However, for most nations possessing these systems, the numbers are small and the systems are for troop carrying rather than offensive armored operations, such as operations employing heavily armored tanks. The proliferation of inexpensive, small arms and machine guns has been extensive and helps to fuel conflict around the world. The most numerous of these systems is the AK-47 assault rifle, previously the mainstay of the nations of the Warsaw Pact and now proliferated in virtually every country worldwide and used by armies, citizens, and terrorists. Other classes of weapons that have been widely proliferated are small-caliber rockets or missiles—this proliferation has been extensive and reflects a major threat around the globe.

15. Anthony H. Cordesman, *Trends in Arms Exports Since the Cold War* (Washington, DC: Center for Strategic and International Studies, January 2001).

16. Sun Tzu, *The Art of War*, James Clavell ed. (New York: Delacorte Press, 1983), 2.

17. Keay Davidson, *San Francisco Chronicle*, San Francisco, CA, October 4, 2004, A-1.

18. Stephen Flynn, *America the Vulnerable* (New York: Harper Collins Book, 2004), book jacket.

19. Ivo H. Daalder and James M. Lindsay, *America Unbound: The Bush Revolution in Foreign Policy* (Washington, DC: Brookings Institution Press, 2003), 81.

20. *Information Operations*, U.S. Army Manual (Washington, DC: Department of the Army, August 27, 1996).

21. Clinton NSS. *The National Security Strategy of the United States of America, A National Strategy of Engagement and Enlargement*, The White House, Washington, DC, February 1996, p. 3.

22. Bush NSS. *The National Security Strategy of the United States of America*, The White House, Washington, DC, September 2002, p. 17.

23. Note that in Afghanistan, the early phases of the operation were almost a unilateral action, in October 2001, relying on other nations for overflight and basing. However, by the end of 2004, the reconstruction of this country was being led by a NATO coalition.

24. Data are from a DOD online briefing, "Welcome to the Department of Defense" from the official DOD Web site. The Department of Defense Official Websites, http://www.dod.mil/pubs/dod101/, About DOD Brief as of May 5, 2005. The 2.6 million includes all services and the active and reserve components.

25. The calculation is based on the population data contained in the *CIA World Factbook* online, which lists the population of the United States and Israel as 293 million and 6.2 million, respectively. The casualty data were provided by the International Policy Institute for Counter-Terrorism, "Breakdown of Fatalities: 27 September 2000 through 1 May 2004," January 18, 2005. Available at: http://www.ict.org.il/. Of note is that during this same period the Palestinians lost 2,806 people.

Chapter 3

1. On June 12, 1812, the United States declared war on Britain to settle a long-standing set of issues, including the impressment of American soldiers by the British, territorial disputes concerning the Northwest Territory and the border with Canada, and a naval blockade by France that angered the United States. In what was to be the culmination of the conflict, the Americans and British largely fought to a stalemate, with the British unable to capture the ports of Baltimore and New Orleans, the United States unable to acquire any additional territory in Canada, and the U.S. fleet demonstrating superiority over the British fleet.

2. Timber, coal, and iron ore were plentiful and allowed for independent development. There were few resources that the United States did not have within its own borders, certainly those needed for success in the Industrial Age. Geography and resources, coupled with values and national psyche, were also key ingredients in the early success of the United States. The pioneer spirit and can-do attitude instilled a high degree of self-reliance.

3. With the end of the Napoleonic Wars in 1815 and the breakup of the Spanish empire in the New World, our hemisphere began to decolonize. Between 1815 and 1822, Jose de San Martin led Argentina to independence, while Bernardo O'Higgins in Chile and Simón Bolívar in Venezuela guided their countries out of colonialism. The new republics sought—and expected—recognition by the United States, and many Americans endorsed that idea. However, President James Monroe and his secretary of state, John Quincy Adams, were not willing to risk war for nations they did not know would survive. From their point of view, as long as the other European powers did not intervene, the government of the United States was content to allow Spain and her colonies fight it out. Other powers also expressed interest in the Western Hemisphere. Great Britain was torn between monarchical principle and a desire for new markets; South America as a whole constituted, at the time, a much larger market for English goods than the United States. When Russia and France proposed that England join in helping Spain regain her New World colonies, Great Britain vetoed the idea. The United States was also negotiating with Spain to purchase the Floridas—once that treaty was ratified, the Monroe administration began to extend recognition to the new Latin American republics—Argentina, Chile, Peru, Colombia, and Mexico were all recognized in 1822. In 1823, France and Spain considered going to war with the new republics with the backing of the Holy Alliance (Russia, Prussia, and Austria). Not unexpectedly, this news appalled the British government as it threatened the work done by British statesmen to get and keep France out of the New World. In response, George Canning, the British foreign minister, proposed that the United States and Great Britain join to warn off France and Spain from intervention. Both Jefferson and Madison urged Monroe to accept the offer, but John Quincy Adams was more suspicious. Adams also was quite concerned about Russia's efforts to extend its influence down the Pacific coast from Alaska south to California, then owned by Mexico. Adams argued and finally won over the Cabinet to an independent policy for the Western Hemisphere.

4. J. D. Richardson, ed., *Compilation of the Messages and Papers of the Presidents*, Vol. 2 (1907), 287. Reprint by IndyPublish.com (July 31, 2004).

5. Congressional Research Service. *Instances of the Use of United States Armed Forces Abroad, 1798–2001* (Washington, DC: Author CRS, 2002), 8.

6. Blue-water navy refers to the ability of the navy to travel long distances from the United States into international waters and operate independently for lengthy periods of time.

7. Russell Weigley, *The History of the United States* (New York: Macmillan Co, 1967), 296.

8. Ibid.

9. Henry L. Stimson and George McBundy, *On Active Service* (New York: Harper & Brothers, 1948), 506.

10. Alfred Thayer Mahan, *The Influence of Sea Power Upon History, 1660–1793*, 2nd Ed (Revised). [Boston, MA: Little, Brown & Co, 1940 (ca 1890, 1918)], 138.

11. Alfred Thayer Mahan, *Lessons of the War with Spain and Other Articles* (Boston: Little Brown & Co, 1918), 106.

12. Congressional Research Service, *Instances of the Use of United States Armed Forces Abroad*, 2.

13. "The Causes of World War One," FirstworldWar.com, March 27, 2004, p. 3. Available at: http://firstworldwar.com/origins/index.htm.

14. For example, the European alliances originated in 1866 when Bismarck, the first prime minister of Prussia and chancellor of the German Empire, began organizing international relationships to ensure his vision of a greater Germany. The list of alliances that Bismarck pursued is lengthy, including the Three Emperors League in 1873, which allied Germany, Austria-Hungary, and Russia; the Triple Alliance in 1881, which allied Germany, Austria-Hungary, and Italy; and the Reinsurance Treaty in 1887, which Germany signed with Russia. With some concern about Germany's alliances, France, Russia, Italy, and Britain set about ensuring their security with treaties of their own, including a secret Franco-Italian treaty, Franco-Russian agreements in 1892, and the Entente Cordial between Britain, France, and Russia in 1904.

15. Larry H. Addington, *The Patterns of War Since the Eighteenth Century* (Bloomington, IN: Bloomington University Press, 1984), 122–23.

16. Ibid., 146.

17. Ibid., 147.

18. Britannica Student Encyclopedia. "League of Nations." Retrieved September 9, 2004, from Encyclopedia Britannica Online.

19. *The Columbia Encyclopedia*, 6th ed., "The League of Nations." 2001. Articles 1 through 7 concerned organization, providing for an assembly, composed of all member nations; a council, composed of the great powers (originally Great Britain, France, Italy, and Japan, and later Germany and the Soviet Union) and four other, nonpermanent members; and a secretariat. Both the assembly and the council were empowered to discuss "any matter within the sphere of action of the League or affecting the peace of the world." In both the assembly and the council, unanimous decisions were required. Articles 8 and 9 recognized the need for disarmament and set up military commissions. Article 10 was an attempt to guarantee the territorial integrity and political independence of member states against aggression. Articles 11 through 17 provided for the establishment of the Permanent Court of International Justice for arbitration and conciliation, and for sanctions against aggressors. The remainder of the articles dealt with treaties, colonial mandates, international cooperation in humanitarian enterprises, and amendments to the covenant.

20. Ibid. Noteworthy successes included "settling the Swedish-Finnish dispute over the Aland Islands (1920–21), guaranteeing the security of Albania (1921), rescuing Austria from economic disaster, settling the division of Upper Silesia (1922), and preventing the outbreak of war in the Balkans between Greece and Bulgaria (1925). In addition, the League extended considerable aid to refugees; it helped to suppress white slave and opium traffic; it did pioneering work in surveys of health; it extended financial aid to needy states; and it furthered international cooperation in labor relations and many other fields."

21. Other treaties included the Nine-Power Treaty, which reaffirmed international support for a China open-door policy; the Four-Power Treaty, which called for the United States, Britain, France, and Japan to respect each other's interests in the Pacific and Far East; the Five-Power Treaty, which imposed limits on the world's five most powerful navies; the Washington Naval Treaty, which placed limits on naval weaponry; and the London Naval Conference, in which Britain, Japan, and the United States agreed to limit fleet sizes in their respective navies.

22. Weigley, *The American Way of War* (Bloomington: Indiana University Press, 1973), 313–14.

23. MSN Encarta Online, "Aircraft Production during World War II," September 13, 2004. Available at: http://encarta.msn.com/media_701500594/Aircraft_Production_During_World_War_II.html.

24. MSN Encarta Online, "Tank Production during World War II," September 13, 2004. Available at: http://encarta.msn.com/media_701500593/Tank_Production_During_World_War_II.html, May 5, 2005. The tank production for six of the major combatants was: United States (60,973), Soviet Union (54,500), UK (23,202), Germany (19,926), Italy (4,600), and Japan (2,464).

25. Weigley, *The American Way of War*, 281.

26. National Security Act of 1947, Act of July 26, 1947 (As Amended), [50 U.S.C. 401], Section 2.

27. "The History of the National Security Council," The White House, available at: http://www.whitehouse.gov/nsc/history.html.

28. Ibid.

29. S. Nelson Drew, ed., *NSC-68: Forcing the Strategy of Containment* (Washington, DC: Institute for National Strategic Studies, National Defense University, 1994), 1.

30. Ibid., 8.

31. Mr. X, "The Strategy of Containment," *Foreign Affairs* (July 1946). "X," "The Sources of Soviet Conduct," *Foreign Affairs*, XXV (July 1947), 575.

32. Drew, *NSC-68*, 14.

33. Ibid., 9.

34. See Appendix D for NATO charter.

35. Despite the strength of the alliance, the history of NATO has not been without some controversy. The question of alliance leadership was raised in 1966. French President De Gaulle began to express serious concerns about the direction NATO was heading, in particular about the preeminent U.S. leadership role. France was not alone, as several allies were concerned about the alliance policy of massive retaliation that called for the U.S. nuclear umbrella to be used only in response to an initial attack by the Soviets, rather than in a preemptive manner, as some argued. Shortly thereafter, France withdrew from the integrated military command structure. This turn of events made France somewhat of an outcast within NATO and has contributed at times to anti-France feelings within the United States but also had the benefit of causing the Soviet Union and Warsaw Pact to have a nuclear wildcard in dealing with NATO nations. France remained in the alliance but pulled its forces out from under alliance command and control. Also significantly, the NATO headquarters was forced to move from Paris based on the French withdrawal. In response to concerns from alliance members, NATO's Defense Planning Committee did decide to replace the strategic concept of massive retaliation with a new strategy, flexible response, which was based on developing a set of graduated and balanced responses involving the use of conventional as well as nuclear weapons. This strategic concept prevailed throughout the remainder of the Cold War period.

36. United Nations Charter. May 7, 2005. Available at: http://www.un.org/aboutun/charter/index.html, from the Preamble Section.

37. The first IMF and World Bank meeting was held in July 1944 in Bretton Woods, New Hampshire. This meeting served as the economic component associated with the establishment of the United Nations. The UN came into existence in October 1945, and the Articles of Agreement were signed in December 1945. The bylaws were adopted at a

meeting in Savannah, Georgia, in March 1946. The Bretton Woods agreement established stable yet adjustable exchange rates for the various currencies of the signatory nations. The value of the various national currencies was set to the US dollar as the standard. Of course, the agreement also required the signatory nations to give up a degree of sovereignty with regard to setting national monetary policies. In the 1960s, pressures developed that culminated in the collapse of the Bretton Woods system in 1971. The system was reluctantly replaced with a regime of floating exchange rates. The IMF was established as an international organization to promote international monetary cooperation, exchange stability, and orderly exchange arrangements; to foster economic growth and high levels of employment; and to provide temporary financial assistance to countries to help ease balance of payments adjustments. Since the IMF was established, its purposes have remained unchanged but its operations–which involve surveillance, technical assistance, and financial assistance–have developed to meet the changing needs of its member countries in an evolving world economy. The IMF began in 1945 with less than 50 member nations and has grown to 184 members today.

38. From data set in Richard F. Grimmett, *Instances of Use of United States Armed Forces Abroad, 1798–1999*, CRS Report for Congress RL30172 (Congressional Research Service, May 17, 1999; updated February 5, 2002).

39. Stefan T. Possony, Jerry E. Pournelle, and Francis X. Kane, *The Strategy of Technology* (Cambridge, MA: Harvard University Press, 1970), 5.

40. The Strategic Arms Limitations Talks (SALT) I, or SALT talks as they were named, called for freezing at existing levels the number of ICBM sites, while allowing for additional SLBMs. In addition, several older systems were to be dismantled. The discussion lasted from 1969 to 1972 with the result being the Anti-Ballistic Missile treaty and the interim agreement on strategic offensive arms. The Anti-Ballistic Missile or ABM treaty was designed to reduce the threat of a first strike. It was signed in 1972 and ratified by the Senate in 1973. Provisions included limitations to two ABM sites such that a national missile defense shield could not be created to allow for the penetration of retaliatory "second strike" forces and limitations on ABM technology development. This agreement was key to the system of strategic deterrence described previously. The SALT II treaty was intended to replace the interim agreement on strategic offensive arms. The intent of the agreement was to limit offensive nuclear capability. The treaty was signed, but never ratified due to the Soviet invasion of Afghanistan. Essentially, both sides agreed to abide by the treaty despite the fact that it was not ratified by the Senate. The Intermediate Nuclear Force (INF) Treaty was the first nuclear arms control treaty to eliminate a class of weapons. The treaty called for the destruction of a nuclear ground-based ballistic and cruise missile with ranges between 500 and 5,500 kilometers. It spurred the establishment of the On-Site Inspection Agency for the verification of treaty compliance. The agreement was signed by Presidents Reagan and Gorbachev in 1987 and entered into force in June 1988.

41. The Nuclear Non-Proliferation Treaty was signed by the United States, Soviet Union, and sixty other nations. The provisions of this treaty prohibited the nuclear countries from transferring nuclear systems, the means of producing nuclear weapons systems, or the technology. This treaty entered into force in 1970 and the number of participants has continued to expand. It remains in force today. Confidence and Security Building Measures in Europe established a system of confidence-building measures in Europe that put limits on military activities such as the size and frequency of exercises and provided a system of

early warning indicators. The negotiation of this treaty occurred over a lengthy period involving a number of key meetings, including the Helsinki Final Act (1975), the Madrid Follow-Up meeting (1980-83), and the Conference on Confidence and Security Building Measures in Europe (1984-86). The Conventional Forces in Europe Treaty placed limits on the national holdings of NATO and Warsaw Pact conventional weapons. Although this treaty was not concluded until 1990, much of the negotiations were held during the period under consideration. Also, the unsuccessful precursor to the CFE negotiations, the Mutual and Balanced Force Reduction talks, were conducted from 1973 to 1989.

42. Peter M. Leenhouts, *The Roots of Military Reform: The Development of the Goldwater-Nichols Defense Reorganization Act of 1986* (Washington, DC: National War College, December 5, 1997), 4.

43. "Message from the President of the United States of America Transmitting His Views on the Future Structure and Organization of Our Defense Establishment and the Legislative Steps That Should Be taken to Implement Defense Reforms" (Washington, DC, 1986), 1.

44. The objectives were, first, to maintain the security of our nation and our allies. The United States, in cooperation with its allies, must seek to deter any aggression that could threaten that security and, should deterrence fail, must be prepared to repel or defeat any military attack and end the conflict on terms favorable to the United States, its interests, and its allies. Second, to respond to the challenges of the global economy. Our national security and economic strength are indivisible. As the global economy evolves in increasingly interdependent ways, we must be aware of the economic factors that may affect our national security, now or in the future. Since our dependence on foreign sources of supply has grown in many critical areas, the potential vulnerability of our supply lines is a matter of concern. Additionally, the threat of a global spiral of protectionism must be combated, and the problem of debt in the developing world is a burden on international prosperity. Third, to defend and advance the cause of democracy, freedom, and human rights throughout the world. To ignore the fate of millions around the world who seek freedom betrays our national heritage and over time would endanger our own freedom and that of our allies. Fourth, to resolve peacefully disputes that affect U.S. interests in troubled regions of the world. Regional conflicts that involve allies or friends of the United States may threaten U.S. interests and frequently pose the risk of escalation to wider conflagration. Conflicts or attempts to subvert friendly governments, which are instigated or supported by the Soviets and their client states, represent a particularly serious threat to the international system and thereby to U.S. interests. Fifth, to build effective and friendly relationships with all nations with whom there is a basis of shared concern. The world today includes over 150 nations. Not one of them is the equal of the United States in total power or wealth, but each is sovereign and most, if not all, touch U.S. interests directly or indirectly.

45. Percentage was calculated using the U.S. Census Bureau, *Statistical Abstract of the United States: 2004–2005*, p. 327, looking at the years 1975 and 1990 as the year prior and the year after the period in question in constant (2000) dollars.

46. John L. Romjue, "The Evolution of the AirLand Battle Concept," *Air University Review*, 1981, p. 5.

47. In one account, the economic strangulation of the Soviet Union is described as follows: In May 1981, at Notre Dame University, the recently inaugurated Reagan

predicted that the years ahead would be great ones for the cause of freedom and that Communism was "a sad, bizarre chapter in human history whose last pages are even now being written." At the time, few took his words as more than a morale-boosting exhortation, but in fact the Soviet economy and polity were under terrific stress in the last Brezhnev years, though the Soviets did their best to hide the fact. They were running hidden budget deficits of 7 or 8 percent of GNP, suffering from extreme inflation that took the form (because of price controls) of chronic shortages of consumer goods, and falling farther behind the West in computers and other technologies vital to civilian and military performance. The Reagan administration recognized and sought to exploit this Soviet economic vulnerability. Secretary of Defense Caspar Weinberger and his aide Richard Perle tightened controls on the export of strategic technologies to the Soviet bloc. CIA Director William Casey persuaded Saudi Arabia to drive down the price of oil, thereby denying the Soviet Union billions of dollars it expected to glean from its own petroleum exports. The United States also pressured its European allies to cancel or delay a massive pipeline project for the importation of natural gas from Siberia, thereby denying the Soviets another large source of hard currency. Such economic warfare, waged at a time when the Soviet budget was already strained by the Afghan war and a renewed strategic arms race, pushed the Soviet economy to the brink of collapse. Demoralization took the form of a growing black market, widespread alcoholism, the highest abortion rate in the world, and a declining life span. In an open society such symptoms might have provoked protests and reforms, leadership changes, possibly even revolution. The totalitarian state, however, thoroughly suppressed civil society, while even the Communist party, stifled by its jealous and fearful *nomenklatura* (official hierarchy), was incapable of adjusting. In sum, the Stalinist methods of terror, propaganda, and mass exploitation of labor and resources had served well enough to force an industrial revolution in Russia, but they were inadequate to the needs of the postindustrial world.

Chapter 4

1. As defined in *Encarta Encyclopedia*, "the emergence of a global society in which economic, political, environmental, and cultural events in one part of the world quickly come to have significance for people in other parts of the world. Globalization is the result of advances in communication, transportation, and information technologies."

2. Data are from International Monetary Fund, *World Development Report 2003* (World Bank, 2003).

3. Colin Powell with Joseph E. Persico, *My American Journey* (New York: Random House, 1995), 576.

4. Nunn-Lugar Facts, from U.S. Senate information. Senators Sam Nunn [D-GA] and Richard Lugar [R-IN] began in 1991 work on a piece of US legislation entitled "The Soviet Nuclear Threat Reduction Act of 1991" (Public Law 102-228, 12/12/91, Title II Soviet Weapons Destruction). This legislation became the basis of the cooperative threat reduction programs for the United States.

5. David Isenberg, *The Quadrennial Defense Review Reiterating the Tired Status Quo* (Washington, DC: Dyn Meridian, 1998), 2.

6. Franklin C. Spinney, "Porkbarrels and Budgeteers: What Went Wrong with the Quadrennial Defense Review," *Strategic Review*, Fall 1997, 1–2.

7. Office of Force Transformation, Department of Defense Website, May 7, 2005. Available at: http://www.oft.osd.mil/what_is_transformation.cfm.

8. Office of Force Transformation, Department of Defense Website, May 7, 2005. Available at: http://www.oft.osd.mil/initiatives/ncw/.

9. U.S. Army Draft White Paper, *An Army At War–A Campaign Quality Army with Joint and Expeditionary Mindset.* Headquarters, Department of the Army, Washington, DC, U.S. Army White Paper, March 21, 2004, p. 5.

10. U.S. Census Bureau, *Statistical Abstract of the United States: 2004–2005,* p. 807.

11. Kenneth Juster and Simon Lazarus, *An Assessment of the National Economic Council* (Washington, DC: Brookings Institution Press, 1997).

12. U.S. Commission on National Security/21st Century Web site. Available at: http://www.nssg.gov/Reports/reports.htm, September 21, 2004, p. 1.

13. Homeland Security Act of 2002, H.R. 5005, Section 101: Executive Department: Mission, November 2002. Available at: http://www.pfir.org/2002-hr5005.

14. National Strategy for Homeland Security, The White House, Washington, DC, 2002, p. 5.

15. CRS Report to Congress, *The Patriot Act: A Sketch* (Washington, DC: CRS, April 18, 2002), 1. In describing the legal changes as a result of the Patriot Act, a CRS report also states the following: "Congress passed the USA PATRIOT Act (the Act) in response to the terrorists' attacks of September 11, 2001. The Act gives federal officials greater authority to track and intercept communications, both for law enforcement and foreign intelligence gathering purposes. It vests the Secretary of the Treasury with regulatory powers to combat corruption of U.S. financial institutions for foreign money laundering purposes. It seeks to further close our borders to foreign terrorists and to detain and remove those within our borders. It creates new crimes, new penalties, and new procedural efficiencies for use against domestic and international terrorists." The Patriot Act, H. R. 3162, Washington, DC, November 2001. Instances of Use of United States Armed Forces Abroad, 1798–2001, Congressional Research Service, The Library of Congress (Washington, DC: Richard F. Grimmett, 2002).

Chapter 5

1. Daalder and Lindsay, *America Unbound*, 123.

2. From a briefing from the Office of the Secretary of Defense from the Joint Defense Capability Study, Washington DC, September 12, 2003.

3. Third Presidential Debate, October 13, 2004, question from moderator.

4. Only includes the fifty states and District of Columbia.

5. Thomas E. Ricks, "Shift from Traditional War Seen at Pentagon," *Washington Post*, September 3, 2004, p. 1.

6. The global information grid refers to a military network system that provides information technology capabilities for voice, data, and video across the world.

7. Department of Defense, *Dictionary of Military Terms.* November 30, 2004. Available at: http://ww.dtic.mil./doctrine/jel/doddict/.

8. Eric L. Wee, "Worlds Apart," *The Washington Post Magazine*, Washington, DC, November 7, 2004, 16–22, 32–33.

9. This is a program designed to bring approximately twenty students to the United States to study at Yale for approximately six months. The participants are specially selected based on their demonstrated leadership skills and potential for continued and increasing levels of responsibility in their respective countries.

10. Thom Shanker and James Brook, "Tsunami Tests U.S. Forces' Logistics, but Gives Pentagon a Chance to Show a Human Face," *New York Times*, January 9, 2005.

Appendix D

1. The definition of the territories to which Article 5 applies was revised by Article 2 of the Protocol to the North Atlantic Treaty on the accession of Greece and Turkey, signed on October 22, 1951.

2. On January 16, 1963, the North Atlantic Council noted that insofar as the former Algerian Departments of France were concerned, the relevant clauses of this treaty had become inapplicable as from July 3, 1962.

3. The treaty came into force on August 24, 1949, after the deposition of the ratifications of all signatory states.

INDEX

ABOUT THE AUTHOR

DANIEL M. GERSTEIN is a Military Fellow at the Council on Foreign Relations. A Gulf War veteran, he holds degrees from West Point, the Command and General Staff College, and the National War College.

www.ingramcontent.com/pod-product-compliance
Lightning Source LLC
LaVergne TN
LVHW011941060326
832903LV00045B/114